THE CONSTITUTION OF MEXICO

This book provides an overview of Mexico's political evolution since it became independent from Spain in 1821, and its current constitutional arrangements, principles and structures. The aim is to explain this evolution as the result of struggles between the interests and ideologies of different groups within Mexican society, each with a different political vision of how the state should be organised. Chapter 1 reviews Mexico's constitutional trajectory, and explains why democracy, republicanism, federalism, separation of state and Church, protection of fundamental rights and the Nation's ownership of mineral resources first became constitutional principles. Chapters 2, 3, 4 and 5 deal respectively with democracy and the electoral system, and the legislative, executive and judicial branches of federal government. Chapter 6 introduces the institutional structure of Mexico's federal system, while Chapter 7 discusses the rules, principles and institutions for the protection of human rights. Chapter 8 examines the constitutional regime of Mexico's economy. The conclusion explains how a series of factors has combined to produce a gap between the formal Constitution and what can be seen as the living constitution; bridging that gap presents Mexican politics and society with one of its great contemporary challenges.

Constitutional Systems of the World
General Editors: Peter Leyland and Andrew Harding
Associate Editors: Benjamin L Berger and Grégoire Webber

In the era of globalisation, issues of constitutional law and good governance are being seen increasingly as vital issues in all types of society. Since the end of the Cold War, there have been dramatic developments in democratic and legal reform, and post-conflict societies are also in the throes of reconstructing their governance systems. Even societies already firmly based on constitutional governance and the rule of law have undergone constitutional change and experimentation with new forms of governance; and their constitutional systems are increasingly subjected to comparative analysis and transplantation. Constitutional texts for practically every country in the world are now easily available on the internet. However, texts which enable one to understand the true context, purposes, interpretation and incidents of a constitutional system are much harder to locate, and are often extremely detailed and descriptive. This series seeks to provide scholars and students with accessible introductions to the constitutional systems of the world, supplying both a road map for the novice and, at the same time, a deeper understanding of the key historical, political and legal events which have shaped the constitutional landscape of each country. Each book in this series deals with a single country, or a group of countries with a common constitutional history, and each author is an expert in their field.

Published volumes

The Constitution of the United Kingdom; The Constitution of the United States; The Constitution of Vietnam; The Constitution of South Africa; The Constitution of Japan; The Constitution of Germany; The Constitution of Finland; The Constitution of Australia; The Constitution of the Republic of Austria; The Constitution of the Russian Federation; The Constitutional System of Thailand; The Constitution of Malaysia; The Constitution of China; The Constitution of Indonesia; The Constitution of France; The Constitution of Spain

Link to series website
http://www.hartpub.co.uk/series/csw

The Constitution of Mexico

A Contextual Analysis

José María Serna de la Garza

·HART·

OXFORD · LONDON · NEW YORK · NEW DELHI · SYDNEY

HART PUBLISHING

Bloomsbury Publishing Plc

Kemp House, Chawley Park, Cumnor Hill, Oxford, OX2 9PH, UK

1385 Broadway, New York, NY 10018, USA

29 Earlsfort Terrace, Dublin 2, Ireland

HART PUBLISHING, the Hart/Stag logo, BLOOMSBURY and the Diana logo are
trademarks of Bloomsbury Publishing Plc

First published in Great Britain 2013

A catalogue record for this book is available from the British Library.

ISBN: 978-1-84946-288-4

Typeset by Hope Services Ltd, Abingdon

To find out more about our authors and books visit www.hartpublishing.co.uk.
Here you will find extracts, author information, details of forthcoming events
and the option to sign up for our newsletters.

In memory of Jorge Carpizo (1944–2012)

Acknowledgements

This book would not have been possible without the support of many people. First and foremost, I would like to thank Andrew Harding, Peter Leyland and Gregoire Webber for their guidance and advice as editors of Hart's *Constitutional Systems of the World* series. Their contribution has been of fundamental importance in the completion of this work. Besides, I would like to thank Héctor Fix Fierro, Director of the Institute of Legal Research of the National University of Mexico, for supporting and encouraging my work in this project. Also, I would like to express my sincere gratitude to Armin von Bogdandy, Director of the Institute Max Planck for Comparative Public Law and International Law (Heidelberg, Germany), for his support and for providing me with a good environment and facilities to work on this book during my research internship at that Institute during the summer of 2011.

I would also like to gratefully acknowledge the support of the *Coordinación de Humanidades* of Mexico's National University and its coordinator, Estela Morales Campos, which gave me the opportunity to work during the Spring of 2012 at the University of Texas at Austin. Thanks to this support I had access to the Nettie Lee Benson Latin American Collection of the Teresa Lozano Long Institute of Latin American Studies and to the Library of the School of Law of that university. The materials I found in both collections were fundamental for the completion of this book. I am grateful to all the UT people who guided and advised me during this internship, including Charles R Hale, David Block and Jonathan Pratter.

Finally, a loving mention goes to my wife Anita Veitl and my daughters Ana Sofía and Lorena for their understanding and support of me in completing this work.

Contents

Table of Cases

Mexico

Inter-American Court of Human Rights

Inter-American Commission of Human Rights

Table of Legislation

1

Mexico's Constitutional Trajectory

Introduction – Democracy – Republicanism – Federalism –
Separation of State and Church – Fundamental Rights – The
Nation's Ownership of Mineral Resources – Conclusion

I. INTRODUCTION

MEXICO'S CURRENT CONSTITUTION, in force since 1917, is the result of a long and sometimes disturbed historical evolution that dates back to the country's independence from Spain in 1821. The formation of a newly independent state entailed the adoption of a constitution and a process that deeply divided Mexican society, particularly during the nineteenth century. Eventually, after adopting several constitutional documents, and after two foreign invasions, the Constitution of 1857 acquired some measure of stability and started to rule Mexico's political processes in 1867.

In the last third of the nineteenth century, there were scant conditions for constitutional government to flourish in Mexico. In 1877, a prominent general, Porfirio Díaz, a hero in the war against the French invasion, became president of the Republic. He stayed in power for more than 30 years, until he was forced out of office in 1911 by the movement known as the Mexican revolution. The Constitution of 1917, currently in force, emerged from this movement.

In this opening chapter, I explore this historical process and identify the forces and reasons that explain the main features of Mexico's constitutional system. I proceed thematically rather than chronologically, with the goal of providing a framework that will serve as a guide for the topics and issues examined and discussed in the rest of the book.

Our starting point in this analysis is article 40 of the Mexican Constitution, which describes Mexico's form of government as being:

- Federal: the Mexican state is 'composed of "free and sovereign States in all that concerns their internal government", but united in a Federation established according to the principles of this fundamental law'.
- Democratic: the designation of the people who form the legislative and executive powers requires free, authentic and periodic elections.
- Representative: the power to create statute laws to organise the social life of the polity is, mostly, in the hands of federal and State legislatures.[1]
- Republican: the head of state is elected for a six-year term, and cannot be re-elected (the same happens with the governors of the States and the Chief of Government of the Federal District).
- Laic: there shall be no official religion of the Republic, which shall be neutral in its relations with all religious creeds.

In addition to these principles, the Constitution includes a catalogue of fundamental rights (in its first 29 articles) and establishes the principle of separation of powers (article 49). Mexico's formal constitution is close to the tradition, values and institutional designs that characterise many Western liberal democracies. Mexico's living constitution tells a somewhat more complicated tale.

With this distinction between the formal and living constitutions, I want to address the lack of real efficacy of constitutional rules to moderate and control political power in Mexico. This has happened under different forms throughout the country's history. For instance, from independence up to the last part of the nineteenth century, the efficacy of constitutional rules was impeded by the constant interruption of successive constitutional orders. As we shall see, this was a manifestation of the intense struggle in which Mexican political groups were involved in order to define the country's constitutional shape and identity as an independent nation-state.

[1] Just recently, a constitutional amendment published on 9 August 2012 introduced the possibility of having 'citizens' legislative initiative' and 'popular consultations' at the federal level. Moreover, many States have started to introduce into their constitutions institutions such as referendum, plebiscite and popular legislative initiative. For details see L Córdova Vianello, 'La Reforma Electoral y el Cambio Político en México' in D Zovatto and J Orozco (eds), *Reforma Política y Electoral en América Latina 1978–2007* (Mexico, UNAM and IDEA, 2008) 689–90.

Furthermore, and in spite of the fact that the Constitution of 1857 was never officially derogated from during the dictatorship of General Porfirio Díaz (1877–1911), in actual practice it was constantly infringed and put aside. Finally, with the regime that emerged after the Mexican revolution, the Constitution of 1917 was conditioned in actual practice by the hegemonic party system that existed until 2000.[2] In this way: federalism was weakened by the centralising logic of a political regime characterised by a very strong federal Executive; democracy was subservient to the regime's ability to control electoral results; political representation was restricted by a president who was recognised as the true leader of the 'official' party, which in turn controlled the vast majority of positions in the federal and State legislatures; and republicanism was qualified by the president's ability to determine who would run for governor in the States and to significantly influence the designation of his own successor.

In this book, I will explain how diverse political forces pushed for a series of constitutional and legal reforms that eventually led to the collapse of the hegemonic party system. In turn, I will discuss the challenges, debates and tensions that can be found in Mexico's attempt to consolidate its incipient democratic regime.

Before doing so, I explain why the principles of democracy, republicanism, federalism, fundamental rights, and others like the separation of the state and the Church and the nation's ownership of mineral resources, form part of the constitutional text. My claim is that we have to examine the historical process in which different political forces confronted each other in order to define the shape and structures of the new state that was created after independence from Spain.

II. DEMOCRACY

New Spain (the name of the Spanish colony of what today is Mexico) was a fragmented society, with differentiated groups divided along ethnic,

---

[2] By hegemonic party system I mean one in which in spite of the existence of several political parties, one of them is clearly predominant and political-electoral competition is unequal and unfair, which in turn prevents the possibility of rotation in government. Under this kind of party system rotation cannot happen. See G Sartori, *Parties and Party Systems – A Framework for Analysis* vol I (Cambridge, Cambridge University Press, 1976).

social and cultural lines. Spaniards, who were the most privileged stratum in the colonial society, controlled the most important political, ecclesiastical and economic positions, to the exclusion of all other sectors. For its part, the creole elite, of Spanish origin but born in the New Spain, was well educated, but had little access to the top political and social positions. Furthermore, there was an indigenous population (which by the 1820s formed around 40 per cent of the population), living in isolated communities, which were a matter of interest for the colonial power in two principal ways: as cheap labour force and as subjects for conversion to Catholicism. Finally, there was the *mestizo* sector of the population, a mixture of Spaniards and Indians and the different *castas* formed of diverse combinations of European, Indians and Africans that also formed part of the colony's population.

The creoles, who belonged to a middle class of low-ranking soldiers, priests, officials of the colonial administration, lawyers, and merchants, provided the initial leadership for independence. Appealing to the impoverished sectors of Indians, peasants and mine-workers, they formed the groups and armies that fought for independence as of 15 September 1810.

The political forces that originally envisioned and fought for Mexico's independence from Spain articulated their discourse around the democratic principle. For example, in the context of the debates arising as a consequence of the abdication of the Spanish King in favour of Napoleon in 1808, Primo de Verdad (a prominent creole member of Mexico City council) argued that sovereignty passed to the people of New Spain through its representatives. Moreover, he argued that in the absence of the legitimate King, the viceroy should continue governing the country but with a different status (as an official 'in charge' of the realm), and should call a congress formed of representatives of the cities, the villages and all other parts of the realm, which would be in charge of the latter's affairs.[3]

Different documents produced by the original movement of independence invoked the democratic principle as a precondition for the formation of a new and independent state. That was true of the so-called *Elementos Constitucionales* of 30 April 1812, drafted by the insurgent leader Ignacio López Rayón, as well as of the *Sentimientos de la*

[3] For this audacious argument, Primo de Verdad ended up in prison, where he met his death.

Nación,[4] produced by the military leader José María Morelos. In addition, we can also recall the Constitution of Apatzingán of 1814 (a document drafted by the insurgent forces which was never actually in force, but which expressed the ideology, goals and political project of the revolutionary forces).[5] Independence from Spain was achieved in 1821, and the democratic principle was established in Mexico's first constitution (1824). However, in the course of the nineteenth century, the conservative forces, noting that they could not just erase the demand for democratic government, tried to resist it and to establish limits on it to the extent possible. One example of this can be found in what has been labelled a case of 'oligarchic constitutionalism', a regime established by the so-called Seven Constitutional Laws (*Siete Leyes*) of 1836. These laws established a façade of democratic government: there would be regular elections to designate the people who would govern, but both the right to vote and to be elected to the most important public offices was limited to persons who had a certain level of income per year. Moreover, the Second Constitutional Law of 1836 created the so-called 'Supreme Conservation Power' which was a sort of power-above-the-other-powers, formed of five members elected in an indirect way through a procedure that included the proposals of departmental *Juntas*,[6] the formation of a list of three candidates by the Chamber of Deputies, and the final decision of the Senate by majority vote. This entity had the power, among others, to declare the nullity of a statute or a decree for being contrary to the Constitution, after a petition by the Executive, the High Court of Justice or no less than 18 members of the Legislature; the power to declare the nullity of decisions of the Supreme Court of Justice, after a petition by either of the two other powers, and 'only in case of usurpation of powers'; and the power to declare, upon the request of Congress 'what

---

[4] Proclaimed on 14 September 1813 as the guiding document of the movement. Article 1 declared independence from Spain; while article 5 stated the principle of popular sovereignty.

[5] Article 5 of this constitutional text established the principle of popular sovereignty, which would be exercised by a national representation formed of deputies elected by citizens.

[6] The Laws of 1836 abolished federalism and, therefore, States and their governments. Instead, there would be departments and departmental governments, called *Juntas*, led by a governor who would be appointed by the president of the Republic after the proposal of a list of three candidates from the respective *Junta*.

is the will of the nation', in extraordinary cases in which it might be convenient.[7]

Furthermore, article 17 of this Second Constitutional Law established that this supreme power would be responsible only to God and public opinion, and that its members in no circumstances would be judged or reprimanded under law for their opinions. As it is possible to see, the Seven Constitutional Laws of 1836 (being the result of a compromise between the Catholic Church, its allies and the military), established a centralised system of government, concentrating power in a group of five persons who were answerable to nobody, and with no mechanisms of accountability and political or legal control.

The Seven Constitutional Laws of 1836 failed to take root, and in the end the same groups that promoted them called upon General Santa Anna in 1853 to govern the country through dictatorship. This, in turn, provoked a reaction of Mexico's democratic forces, which eventually sacked the dictator after a three-year civil war (1853–56). This process led to the Constitution of 1857, which definitively implanted democracy as a basic principle of Mexico's formal constitution.

However, democracy failed to take root in Mexico's actual living constitution. As we have already said, in the last third of the nineteenth century there were scant conditions for constitutional government and democracy to flourish and consolidate in Mexico. In 1877, General Porfirio Díaz became president of the Republic and remained in power for more than 30 years.

Díaz's rule was dictatorial. During his several administrations elections were far from fair and truly competitive. Civil liberties prescribed in the Constitution were de facto strictly limited (particularly those related to democratic participation, ie freedom of the press, freedom of association). Moreover, there is evidence of massive violation of human rights in some regions of the country, and particularly against some indigenous communities.[8]

Nevertheless, the overthrow of Díaz as a consequence of the Mexican revolution in 1911 did not mean that democracy would reign at last all around the country. The political system that emerged from the revolution could hardly be called truly democratic. Against the background of

---

[7] Quotations taken from article 12, sections III and VIII of the Second Constitutional Law of 1836.

[8] As shown by the book written by the American journalist JK Turner, *Barbarous Mexico* (Chicago IL, Charles H Kerr & Co, 1910).

anarchy that characterised Mexican politics during and immediately after the revolution, by the late 1920s a 'logic of control' began to emerge. The group of generals who had won the civil war introduced gradually and pragmatically, in a process of trial-and-error, a set of mechanisms for regulating the political participation of all groups, for controlling their confrontations, and for reducing the level of conflict. Even though they were backed by military power, the introduction of these controls entailed a great deal of negotiation, compromise and alliance formation between the governing group and the most relevant social forces. The result of those negotiations was the coalition that formed the basis for the political stability which Mexico enjoyed for more than 70 years. Mexican political leaders regarded as their most important responsibility the maintainance of the coalition by using all the mechanisms of control and negotiation they were able to devise. Paramount in this system was the 'official' party, PRI (*Partido Revolucionario Institucional*), whose actual leader was the incumbent president of the Republic. This party won all presidential elections between 1929 and 1994 and for decades controlled the majority of State governorships as well as federal and State legislatures and municipal governments. It is important to mention that federal, State and municipal elections were regularly held, but electoral processes were neither competitive nor fair. Changing this situation has been the great challenge of Mexico's transition to democracy. In Chapter 2 of this book, we analyse the constitutional reforms that were required to achieve fair and competitive elections, and thus open up the possibility of rotation in government. Moreover, we examine some of the main issues, debates and tensions that can be identified in Mexico's attempt to consolidate its incipient democracy.

III. REPUBLICANISM

Just after independence from Spain in 1821, the new nation had to choose what form of government it would adopt. Some groups preferred the option of a constitutional monarchy, while others wanted a republic. While a constituent assembly was discussing these two options, General Agustín de Iturbide organised a coup in 1822 and forced the assembly to appoint him as Emperor of Mexico. He promised to govern under the principles of a constitutional monarchy, but failed to do so in actual practice.

This first experience with the monarchic political form resulted in a complete failure. From his very proclamation as Emperor, Iturbide had intense conflicts with the forces represented in Congress, as well as with those forces based in the different regions of the country, which could foresee the centralising trends that the monarchy would set. In the end these forces, allied with a group of dissatisfied generals, forced the abdication of Iturbide. A new constituent assembly was elected and installed on 7 November 1823. This assembly drafted the first constitution of independent Mexico: the Constitution of 1824 (officially called 'Federal Constitution of the United Mexican States'). Before doing that, the assembly produced the so-called 'Constitutive Act of the Mexican Federation',[9] which was a sort of provisional statute to organise government while the constituent assembly was drafting the Constitution. The main purpose of this document was to reach a compromise in the sense that the republican, representative and federal principles would be the basis of the constitutional arrangement in the making (all of which were confirmed by the Constitution of 1824).

Subsequently, the republican principle was confirmed by the Constitution of 1857, which was also liberal and federal, and established freedom of religion and equality before the law (thus prohibiting special jurisdictions of the clergy). As one might suppose, the Constitution of 1857 was fiercely opposed by the Catholic Church and the conservative political group.[10] Civil war broke out, in what later on would be known as the 'Reform War'. During this time the liberal group drafted the so-called 'Reform Laws' (examined below), which targeted the Catholic Church, intending to undermine its power and influence in Mexican politics and social life.

In this context, the monarchic principle appeared again in Mexico's political scenario, when anti-liberal and conservative groups, noting that under the existing balance of forces they would never succeed in preserving the old order, sought to turn the balance in their favour by appealing to the support of a foreign power.

---

[9] 31 January 1824.

[10] On 17 December 1857, a general of the conservative group, Félix Zuloaga, proclaimed the 'Plan of Tacubaya', the most important points of which were: the non-recognition of the Constitution of 1857 as legitimate; and the calling of a new constituent assembly.

The historical context was this: the 'Reform War' ended in 1860, with a defeat of the conservative group and the Catholic Church.[11] Following the war, the country was devastated. In particular, the external public debt was very high and the newly elected government of President Benito Juárez was unable to pay and suspended debt payments for two years. The navies of Spain, England and France were sent to Mexico to collect, but the government of Juárez was able to reach an agreement (*Agreement of La Soledad*) to avoid the invasion.

The situation was seized by some members of the conservative group to convince Napoleon III, Emperor of France, that the moment was apt for the establishment of a reign loyal to France in the Americas. Thus, France broke the *Agreement of La Soledad*, and the invasion started on 19 April 1862. In this context, with the support of Napoleon, a group of conservative notables offered the throne of Mexico to Archduke Maximilian of Habsburg, brother of Franz Joseph, Emperor of the Austro-Hungarian Empire, and son-in-law of King Leopold of Belgium, who ultimately accepted the offer, travelling to Mexico in 1864.

Maximilian I of Mexico issued a 'Provisional Statute of the Mexican Empire' on 10 April 1865, establishing a 'moderate monarchy of a Catholic prince'. Yet, in the end the French Army, the only real source of support of Maximilian,[12] was defeated by the Mexican armed forces loyal to President Juárez (and to the Republican principle). Maximilian was captured, judged and sentenced to death. He was shot on 19 June 1867.

Within the republican framework, Mexico has opted for the presidential form of government and not for a parliamentary one, but the path towards this alternative has not been straight forward. For example, the Constitution of Apatzingán (1814) established a collegiate form of Executive. Moreover, in the discussions within the constituent assembly of 1824, the pros and cons of a collegiate Executive were considered by deputies, but in the end they decided to vest power in one person only.

[11] It was called the Reform War because the liberals, who eventually won it, proposed a programme of reforms to the Constitution of 1857 that sought to establish the separation of the State and the Catholic Church.
[12] Maximilian had entered into conflict with the Catholic Church, because of his liberal ideas, such as freedom of religion, and disagreements on Maximilian's policy towards the Church's properties and the weight of the conservative group in his government.

As Valadés says, this was a decision of historic transcendence and implications because it determined the frame of subsequent political struggles and developments.[13]

For its part, the Constitution of 1857 also established a presidential system. Yet, since it had been drafted after years of fighting a dictator, its drafters decided to create a constitutional design based on a strong Congress that would be able to control the Executive. Thus, that constitution established one chamber only (that is, no Senate, a chamber common to federal systems). Furthermore, the president did not have the power to veto legislation.

In this context, President Benito Juárez, who during the 1857–60 civil war and the foreign invasion had consolidated personalised exercise of the presidential power, alleged in 1867 that it was not possible to govern the country under the arrangement established by the Constitution of 1857. In his view, the president was at the mercy of Congress. Therefore, he proposed a return to bicameralism and granting the veto power to the president, to give the latter room for political manoeuver vis-à-vis Congress. The Constitution of 1857 was amended in 1874[14] in order to incorporate both proposals. These two features are still present in the current Constitution of 1917.

During the successive administrations of General Díaz (1877–1911), the presidential system was conditioned by the realities imposed by the personal exercise of power by the president-dictator. But as we mentioned before, General Díaz was overthrown in 1911 by the social movement that later would be known as the Mexican revolution. In the context of this movement, the constitutional assembly that gathered in 1916 discussed whether to preserve the presidential form or to shift to some sort of parliamentarian form of government. In his address to the assembly, the main revolutionary chief, President Venustiano Carranza, suggested that Mexico required a strong president. In his view, to succeed, parliamentarianism required two features that Mexico lacked: a well-developed deliberative body and strong, well-organised political

---

[13] D Valadés, 'Problemas y Perspectivas del Sistema Presidencial Mexicano' in A Ellis, J Orozco and D Zovatto (eds), *Cómo hacer que funcione el sistema presidencial/Making Presidentialism Work* (Mexico, UNAM and IDEA, 2009) 529–75.

[14] Under article 127 of the 1857 Constitution, the amendment procedure required the approval of two-thirds of each chamber of the federal Congress, and the approval of the majority of State legislatures. This procedure is reproduced in article 135 of the 1917 Constitution.

parties. In the end, the presidential form prevailed. Yet, discussions on the convenience of introducing in Mexico the parliamentary form of government have occurred at several points: in 1917 (just after the new constitution had been approved); then, in 1921; and more recently, in the context of discussions on what is the proper constitutional design that Mexico requires in the new democratic context. These discussions are reviewed in Chapter 4 of this book.

IV. FEDERALISM

The struggle between federalism and centralism deeply divided Mexican society during the nineteenth century. These were not just labels, but were connected to concrete interests and groups.

The road towards the federal form is the result of: a) the administrative reform implemented in New Spain by Charles III of Bourbon in the late eighteenth century (which divided the colony into 12 territorial jurisdictions called *intendencias*); b) the regime of the Cádiz Constitution that established '*diputaciones provinciales*' in New Spain (which were local representative bodies); and c) the political-economic development of relevant regions of the country that were far away from the capital (Mexico City) and were to some extent self-sufficient.[15]

These processes created local political groups scattered around the country that soon started to claim increased political autonomy within their regions. Subsequently these claims were transformed into a demand for the adoption of the federal form. As stated by Reyes Heroles, this was not a struggle between concepts, but between centralised interests and de-centralised interests. There was a centralised oligarchy (formed of groups of landowners and merchants that controlled imports and exports of Mexico's traditional products), mostly based in Mexico City. They were allied with the top hierarchy of Catholic Church and the Army. The former was interested in preserving its properties, its sources of income (particularly the *diezmo*, which was a sort of tax that could be collected coactively), its influence, a regime of religious intolerance and its privileges (especially, the existence of a special jurisdiction to hear cases in which members of the clergy were involved). For its

---

[15] NL Benson, *The Provincial Deputation in Mexico* (Austin TX, University of Texas Press, 1992).

part, the Army was interested in maintaining its special jurisdiction (cases in which members of the military were involved were heard by military courts, and not by ordinary civil courts) and securing a generous and regular payment.

On the other hand, de-centralised interests could be found in local oligarchies (made of landowners dispersed all around the territory), allied with a small, educated and also dispersed middle class, which had the expectation of social mobility through having access to power (an expectation opened up by independence and the adoption of republicanism and democracy). In turn, these groups connected with popular sectors by way of appealing to the concrete needs of the population, for example, equality between the Spanish and native population; or the abolition of different sorts of duties and levies that had to be paid to the Church.[16] These popular sectors formed the local militias that confronted the centralised interests mentioned above, in the struggle to establish in Mexico a type of federalism.

In relation to the adoption of the federal form of state, a crucial point in history is the above mentioned 'Constitutive Act of the Mexican Federation' of 1824. With this document, political forces dispersed around the country made it clear that the federal form was a condition sine qua non of constituting the new state. The Constitution of 1824 confirmed this, but political struggle led to derogation from the federal principle by the aforementioned Seven Constitutional Laws of 1836. In turn, this provoked a violent reaction on behalf of the States, some of which separated from the Union in those years, either indefinitely (like Texas) or temporarily (like Yucatán, which returned when federalism was re-established).

In the end, the groups that proclaimed the federal principle prevailed. The Constitution of 1857 established federalism as the form of the Mexican state, which was confirmed by the Constitution of 1917, currently in force. Nevertheless, as with other institutions foreseen in Mexico's constitution, 'living federalism' was not effective, in the absence of a true constitutional government and rule of law under the regime of Porfirio Díaz. Moreover, it also was subordinated to the logic of political centralisation and control of the hegemonic party system for most of the twentieth century. The way in which this happened, and

---

[16]   See J Reyes Heroles, *El Liberalismo Mexicano*, vol I (Mexico, Fondo de Cultura Económica, 1973) VII–XIX.

also how today Mexico is trying to reinvigorate and make functional its federal system, are examined in Chapter 5 of this book.

V. SEPARATION OF STATE AND CHURCH

A central theme in the struggles related to the formation and consolidation of a polity in Mexico during the nineteenth century was the conflict between the Catholic Church and the liberal groups that were seeking to create a secular and laic state. The power, influence, privileges and huge wealth of the Catholic Church formed the core of the colonial order that the liberals were trying to transform. As argued by Reyes Heroles,[17] the liberals' fight against the Church was not merely a form of anti-clericalism. The opposition to the Church was grounded on the principles and goals of the liberal political programme. Against the principle of equality, the Church wanted to retain its privileges (eg special jurisdiction for members of the clergy), and to increase them by denying to the new state the power that the King of Spain had exercised over it for centuries, the so called *Patronato Real*. But the Church also wanted to maintain religious intolerance as well as restrictions of freedom of thought and expression. Moreover, to back its vision of the country the Church had close allies (like the top Army officials), and most importantly, its own economic power: in the 1820s the Catholic Church was the most important owner of real property in Mexico, the most important banker and the most important owner of schools and institutions of health and charity.

Nevertheless, the Constitution of 1857 introduced a series of rules that intensified the conflict between the state and the Catholic Church. For instance, article 5 prohibited contracts that implied the loss of freedom in respect of work, education or religious vows. In addition, article 12 prohibited 'special tribunals', which implied that ecclesiastic courts (and also military courts) would no longer have power to hear civil-ordinary cases. That is to say, only the civil courts of the state would be able to hear cases that fell within the scope of civil matters (contracts, civil liability, marriage, inheritances, etc). For its part, article 27 established that religious bodies would not be able to have legal capacity to acquire or administer real property, with the exception only of the buildings that were immediately and

[17] *ibid.*

directly used for the service or object of the institution. Finally, article 123 established the exclusive power of federal authorities to create rules on public manifestations of religious belief, according to the laws passed by Congress on the matter. All these constitutional rules have to be read in the context of the struggle between the state and the Catholic Church: the latter, with its money and economic power, had supported the conservative group and the dictatorship of General Santa Anna, that in turn had led to the 1853–56 civil war.

As one might suppose, the Constitution of 1857 was fiercely opposed by the Catholic Church and the conservative group; hence, as we already mentioned above in our discussion on republicanism, civil war broke out (the so-called 'Reform War'). During this time the liberal group drafted the so-called 'Reform Laws', which targeted the Catholic Church, intending to undermine its power and influence in Mexican politics and social life.

There were eight 'Reform Laws':

1. Law on Nationalisation of Church Properties (12 July 1859).
2. Law on Civil Matrimony (23 June 1859).
3. Law on Civil Status of Persons (28 July 1859).
4. Decree that prohibits the intervention of the Church in the administration of cemeteries (31 July 1859).
5. Decree Severing Relations with the Vatican (3 August 1860).
6. Law on Freedom of Religious Worship (4 December 1860).
7. Law on the secularisation of hospitals and charitable institutions (21 February 1861).
8. Decree declaring the extinction of all religious communities in the Mexican Republic (26 February 1863).[18]

In 1873, these laws were incorporated into article 127 of the Constitution of 1857, which in turn was the basis of article 130 of the current Constitution of 1917. This article established a series of restrictions on all religious institutions,[19] specifically in their capacity to own real property and on their participation in politics. These issues and the way in which they have evolved since 1917 are examined in Chapter 7 of this book.

[18] With the exception of the 'Sisters of Charity', which performed an important service to the community at that time.
[19] The main target was the Catholic Church, but in fact the restrictions applied to all religious institutions.

VI. FUNDAMENTAL RIGHTS

The forces that pushed for independence were impregnated with the ideals of political liberalism, which included separation of powers, democracy, supremacy of the law, and also respect for fundamental rights. All these principles can be seen in different constitutional documents drafted in Mexico during the nineteenth century. However, it was not until the Constitution of 1857 that a large and detailed catalogue of such rights was incorporated into the constitutional text.

These rights acquired a particular meaning in the struggle against those who opposed the implantation of a state based on liberal principles. In this way, equality meant the removal of privileges and special prerogatives of bodies such as the Catholic Church and the Army; due process was essential to put an end to the arbitrary exercise of political authority prevalent in Mexico since its time as a colony; and freedom of religion, of thought and of expression were all necessary to establish the conditions that make possible a democratic and representative form of government.

Yet, I also have mentioned that during the dictatorship of General Porfirio Díaz the fundamental rights recognised by the Constitution of 1857 were de facto restricted and selectively respected or violated, depending on the dictator's perception about the regime's needs to maintain political control.

Subsequently, and after the Mexican revolution, the Constitution of 1917 recognised basically the same catalogue of fundamental rights in the 1857 Constitution, but introduced a series of what we know today as social rights. It is possible to find some antecedents of this concern for social issues and for taking redistributive measures under conditions of extreme social inequalities from the very beginning of Mexico's political-constitutional development. This can be seen, for example, in article 5 of the already mentioned *Sentimientos de la Nación* of 1813; and also in the debates of the constituent assembly that drafted the Constitution of 1857.[20]

What today we call 'social rights' were incorporated at the constitutional level only in 1917, thanks to the initiative of the groups that

---

[20] Deputy Ponciano Arriaga, after making a critical examination of the system of property prevalent in Mexico, proposed land redistribution through agrarian reform.

participated in the Mexican revolution, which were present in the constituent assembly gathered that same year. In this way, the Constitution recognised social rights such as the right to education, the right to land, and workers' rights. Specifically, article 3 of the Constitution established that primary public education would be free, and that all public education as well as private education at the primary, elementary and superior levels would be secular too. Moreover, article 27 of the Constitution established a series of rules related to agrarian reform, defining precise limits to the amount of land that can be owned by private owners; and established different procedures to expropriate the land that exceeded those limits in order to distribute it to landless peasants. For its part, article 123 established a long and detailed list of the rights of industrial workers such as: an eight-hour working day, the right to a day's rest per week, the right to proper compensation after an unjustified termination of the working relationship by the employer, the right to strike and the right to form unions, among many others. These rights, and the way in which the regime that emerged after the revolution 'administered' the exercise of those rights in connection with ample sectors of the population (peasants and industrial workers), served to constitute the social bases that gave legitimacy to the hegemonic party system for decades.

At the same time, the promise of social rights found in the Constitution represented an effort to overcome the deep social divisions that Mexico inherited from colonial rule. This promise forms part of the foundations that have made possible Mexico's political community and, since 1917, it has become an essential element of the country's constitutional identity.

The emergence of a hegemonic party system conditioned the efficacy and scope of the catalogue of fundamental rights, which was subordinated to the logic of political control of the regime. In Chapter 6, I examine how the breakdown of the hegemonic party system has meant an increasingly relevant role for the Supreme Court, which has started to produce constitutional criteria that are more protective of fundamental rights. I refer to the new dynamic in which the country is engaged, as a consequence of Mexico's incorporation into the Inter-American System for the Protection of Human Rights (IASHR), and especifically as a consequence of the recognition of the contentious jurisdiction of the Inter-American Court of Human Rights.

VII. THE NATION'S OWNERSHIP OF MINERAL RESOURCES

The economic policies implemented by Díaz between 1877 and 1911 created the conditions that later would result in a violent social explosion (the Mexican revolution). Basically, these policies consisted of two things: the concentration of land ownership in a few hands (promoting a pattern of production based on very large '*Haciendas*'); and a very generous policy of concessions granted to foreign companies for the exploitation of Mexico's mineral resources and the promotion of an incipient industrial sector. Moreover, at the basis of the economic system promoted by General Díaz was the maintenance of very poor conditions of workers, and the establishment of harsh mechanisms for maintaining labour discipline, both in the agrarian and industrial sectors.

One of the main social demands of the forces that participated in the Mexican revolution concerned the redistribution of land, that is, agrarian reform. The issue was widely debated in the constituent assembly of 1917. For some, including President Carranza, the power of expropriation as established in the Constitution of 1857 was enough to carry out the agrarian reform programme that had been promised during the revolution. Article 27 of that constitution established the power to expropriate property for reasons of 'public utility' and 'prior compensation'. However, a group of legislators within the assembly thought otherwise. For them, agrarian reform had to be based on the rights of the nation over all the land and water within the national territory. In the end this concept prevailed, which explains a series of concepts and principles incorporated into article 27 of the Constitution of 1917 that strengthened the state vis-à-vis private owners, nationals and foreigners.

This conception is connected with the history of land concentration that was promoted since colonial times, which intensified during the regime of Porfirio Díaz. It is also linked to the history of the country as a colony, the exploitation of mineral wealth of the country during the colonial period, and the policy of Díaz that allowed foreign companies to take control of that wealth. It is also linked to the extremely poor conditions of the labour force that worked in the *haciendas* and in the mines, and to the harsh mechanisms of social and political control established by the regime in order to maintain labour discipline.

Thus, the Constitution of 1917 tried to break with the past experience, making mineral resources the exclusive property of the nation. In this way, some minerals can only be exploited by the federal government, while others can be exploited also by private companies, under a regime of concessions granted by the government in exchange for royalties. In Chapter 7 we examine some relevant aspects of this regime and how it evolved after 1917, as well as current debates in the context of economic reform that Mexico has been experiencing since the 1980s.

VIII. CONCLUSION

Mexico has had a turbulent and troubled political-constitutional evolution. Yet, throughout this evolution a series of principles have been defined as essential elements of its constitutional identity and structures. As we have seen in this introductory chapter, the definition of those principles has been the product of struggles between the interests and ideologies of different groups within Mexico's society, which had different political visions concerning the new independent state that was being formed.

The context of a fragmented society, with little social cohesion, with little or no experience of self-government, with no civic-democratic culture, explains to a great extent the difference between what we have called the formal constitution and the living constitution. Overcoming that difference is the great challenge of Mexico's society and political forces today.

FURTHER READING

Cockcroft, JD, *Intellectual Precursors of the Mexican Revolution 1900–1913* (Austin TX, University of Texas Press, 1968).

Cosío Villegas, D, *La Constitución de 1857 y sus Críticos* (Mexico, Fondo de Cultura Económica, 1998).

González, M (ed), *La Formación del Estado Mexicano* (Mexico, Porrúa, 1984).

González Oropeza, M, 'Recent Problems and Developments on the Rule of Law in Mexico' (2005) 40 *Texas International Law Journal* 577.

Hale, CA, 'The Civil Law Tradition and Constitutionalism in Twentieth-Century Mexico: The Legacy of Emilio Rabasa' (2000) 18 *Law and History Review* 257.

McHugh, JT, 'Mexican Constitutional Tradition' in *Comparative Constitutional Traditions* (New York, Peter Lang, 2002) ch 11.

Rabasa, E, *La Constitución y la Dictadura*, 10th edn (Mexico, Porrúa 2006).

Reyes Heroles, J, *El Liberalismo Mexicano*, volumes I, II and III (Mexico, Fondo de Cultura Económica, 1973).

Tena Ramírez, F, *Derecho Constitucional Mexicano*, 20th edn (Mexico, Porrúa, 1984).

Villegas Moreno, G, *México: Liberalismo y Modernidad 1876–1917* (Mexico, Fomento Cultural Banamex, 2003).

2

Democracy and the Electoral System

Introduction – Institution-building and the Transition to Democracy – The Judicialisation of the Electoral-Political Process – The Impact of the Inter-American System on Human Rights – Conclusion

I. INTRODUCTION

The key to Mexico's transition to democracy has been electoral reform. Democratisation has required the removal of the hegemonic party system's capacity to manipulate and control electoral results. Hence, the transformation of the party system took the form of a series of constitutional and legal reforms that established the basis for having fair and competitive elections at the federal and State levels. In turn, these reforms created institutions whose task is to guarantee impartiality and neutrality in the organisation of electoral processes and in the resolution of electoral disputes. This chapter explains this process of institution-building, which has played a major role in Mexico's transition to democracy. It addresses some of the constitutional issues, debates and tensions that can be identified in Mexico's democratisation process, which are linked to the evolution of the electoral system and, more precisely, to the progressive judicialisation of electoral politics.

II. INSTITUTION-BUILDING AND THE TRANSITION TO DEMOCRACY

The main issue required by democratisation was the removal of the hegemonic party system's capacity to manipulate and control electoral results. This required two things: first, the creation of institutions that could guarantee impartiality and neutrality in the organisation of electoral processes; and secondly, the creation of institutions for the resolution of electoral disputes, operated by courts and not by politically-biased organs. Two institutions have been central to achieving these two tasks: they are the Federal Electoral Institute (IFE) and the Federal Electoral Tribunal (TRIFE).[1]

1. The Federal Electoral Institute (IFE)

The IFE is an autonomous agency in charge of organising federal elections under the principles of certainty, legality, impartiality, objectivity and professionalism.[2] It is directed by a General Council of nine councillors designated by the vote of a two-thirds majority of the lower house of Congress, on the basis of proposals of its parliamentary groups following 'broad consultation with society' (Constitution, article 41.V). The term of office of the councillors is nine years, except for the 'president councillor', who serves a term of six years. The councillors are the only ones with the right to speak and to vote in the decisions of the Council, notwithstanding the fact that the Council also includes representatives of parliamentary groups in Congress and representatives of each national political party (who have the right to speak only).

The key element in the creation and evolution of the IFE has been the construction of its autonomy from the government and the 'official' party: under the hegemonic party system the latter were able to manipulate electoral results, since they controlled every step in the organisation of electoral processes.

The general election of 1988 was a watershed in the process of Mexico's democratisation. In that process, the 'official party' (the PRI) was deeply divided. Eventually, one of its factions, led by a popular leader (Cuauhtémoc Cárdenas), broke with the PRI and managed to form a broad electoral coalition that shook the entire system to its very foundations. The PRI candidate won, but the results of that election were highly contested and not credible for a significant proportion of

---

[1] I am using the acronyms in Spanish.

[2] These principles are expressly mentioned in article 41 of Mexico's Constitution, as amended in 1990.

the electorate,[3] fostering an increased demand for free and fair elections. In this manner, the post-electoral conflict of 1988 led to a reform process that sought to guarantee credible, legitimate, free and fair elections at the federal level. The IFE was the centrepiece of that reform.

In the year of its creation (1990) the IFE was still subject to the influence of the government, since its Council was chaired by the Minister of the Interior. Moreover, the (then called) 'magistrate-councillors' were designated by the Chamber of Deputies after a proposal made by the president of the Republic. The turning point took place in 1996, when the General Council of the IFE was significantly modified. In the first place, the Minister of the Interior stopped being the chair of the Council. Instead, the Council would be headed by a 'president councillor', and formed of eight councillors, designated through the procedure I explained in the first paragraph of this section. This was intended to guarantee the autonomy of the entity which has the power and responsibility for organising federal elections.

Apart from the IFE's autonomy, the other big concern of actors involved in Mexico's transition to democracy has been equity (in terms of access to financial resources and to the media). This has to be understood in the context of the hegemonic party system, in which the 'official party' had disproportionate advantages in electoral contests.

In turn, this concern with equity has led, in the first place, to a party-finance system in which public resources prevail over resources that come from private donors. Under this system, the IFE has the power to distribute public funds to national political parties (article 41.II of the Constitution). The formula for distributing public funds, intended to pay for the parties' ordinary and permanent activities, is based on a 30/70 rationale, that is to say, 30 per cent is allocated in equal measure, and 70 per cent in proportion to each party's share of the vote in the previous election of the Chamber of Deputies.

In the second place, concern for equity has also involved the introduction into the Constitution of a series of limits and prohibitions relating to the origin of funding that comes from private donors. Roughly speaking, this kind of funding cannot exceed an amount equivalent to 10 per cent

---

[3] The way in which votes were counted and the way in which electoral authorities informed the public in connection with the counting of votes (in the context of an electoral system that clearly favoured the candidate of the 'official' party) raised suspicions about the legality of the entire process.

of public funding. Moreover, article 41 of the Constitution empowers the federal Congress to define by statute limits to political parties' expenditure in electoral campaigns; caps on the contributions of supporters; and procedures to control the origin and use of all the financial resources of political parties. Again, the IFE has the power to monitor the way in which political parties comply with all these rules and limitations, and can also impose sanctions on those who do not comply.[4]

Since the constitutional reform of 2007, the Constitution has also stated that statute law shall establish the limits concerning political parties' expenditure in their internal processes for the nomination of candidates.[5] The reason for this was to reduce the importance of money in these processes and thus reduce the incentive to seek illegal sources of finance. With this reform, the power of the IFE to inspect the finances of political parties has increased, creating within the IFE itself a technical bureau specialising in these matters, which is not limited in its investigations by 'banking, fiduciary or fiscal secrecy'.[6]

Another key aspect of Mexico's electoral system is political parties' access to the mass media. On the one hand, the Constitution states that statute law shall guarantee that political parties have permanent access to the mass media (article 41.II). Before the constitutional reform of 2007, this access was achieved either through broadcasting time that belonged to the state (which was allocated to political parties), or through the latter's purchase of broadcasting time in direct deals with private TV and radio companies.

The reforms of 2007 introduced new rules on access to radio and television broadcasting: political parties will not be able to purchase electoral publicity through electronic mass media (radio and TV) in addition to the time controlled and distributed by the IFE. The IFE is the only agency with the power to administer the time that corresponds to electoral processes, and shall distribute that time to political parties according to a detailed list of rules found in article 41.III.A of the Constitution. The reasons for this reform were the perceived need to reduce the costs of electoral processes and to reduce the power and influence of TV and radio companies in the light of complaints on the

---

[4] 'Equity' in electoral competitions is a principle established in article 41.II of the Constitution.

[5] Article 41.II.C of the Constitution.

[6] Article 41.V of the Constitution.

partiality of some of companies in favour of or against some of the candidates in the general election of 2006.[7]

Moreover, since the reform of 2007, article 41.III.A of the Constitution states that no person,

> by himself or on account of third parties, will be able to purchase propaganda in radio and TV, directed to influence the electoral preferences of the citizens, either in favour of or against political parties or candidates running in a popular election.

This rule was introduced to satisfy the demands of the leftist party PRD, whose candidate was the subject of a hostile media campaign financed by some business organisations during the presidential election of 2006. Notably, the rule was challenged through a writ of *amparo*,[8] for being contrary to freedom of expression and other fundamental rights, which in turn has led to a debate on the possibility of unconstitutional constitutional reforms.

Is this restriction an undue limit on freedom of expression? Or is it a legitimate limit to the freedom to purchase space for transmission of party-political spots on radio and TV, as a contribution to bring about equity in electoral competition (a context in which some individuals have a disproportionate capacity to purchase time on radio and TV)? On 28 March 2011, the Supreme Court, in a split decision of 7 votes to 4, declared that the action of *amparo* was not the 'proper legal device' (*vía idónea*) to review the constitutionality of a constitutional reform, and thus dismissed the case.

This constitutional question was examined again by the Supreme Court in the Action of unconstitutionality 61/2008 and accumulated ones 62/2008, 63/2008, 64/2008 and 65/2008,[9] filed by four political parties: *Convergencia, Partido Verde Ecologista de México* (PVEM), *Alternativa Socialdemócrata* (AS), *Partido del Trabajo* (PT) and *Partido Nueva Alianza* (PANAL). Specifically, PANAL challenged the constitutionality of article 49 of the federal electoral code (COFIPE), which replicated the rule contained in article 41.III.A of the Constitution referred to above,

---

[7] In the presidential election of 2006, around US$153 million, that is, equivalent to 95 per cent of public funds the IFE granted to political parties to finance their campaigns, went directly into the purse of radio and TV companies.

[8] The writ of *amparo*, as a judicial proceeding to protect fundamental rights, will be discussed in chapter 5.III.

[9] Actions of unconstitutionality, as a judicial proceeding to challenge statute laws, will be examined in chapter 5.V.

arguing that the rule was an undue restriction on freedom of expression. According to PANAL, the rule contained in article 49 of the federal electoral code implied that in political-electoral matters, only political parties would have the freedom to express themselves through the media, and no citizen or organisation of civil society, would have the right to do so. Moreover, PANAL argued that this norm meant that political parties had a monopoly on political propaganda, and no one else would have the right to defend his or her opinions, not even if a party or a candidate directly attacked them. Finally, the plaintiffs argued that the challenged norm was contrary to the freedom to seek, receive, and impart information and ideas of all kinds, as established by article 13 of the American Convention on Human Rights.

A unanimous Supreme Court was of the view that article 49 of the federal electoral code was not unconstitutional, because it was basically a replication of article 41.III.A of the Constitution, which in turn had been the product of a decision legitimately made in November of 2007 by Mexico's *pouvoir constituent* (constituent power).[10]

Other measures that have been taken in order to reduce the costs of electoral campaigns (thus reducing incentives for seeking illegal sources on behalf of political parties) include limits on the duration of electoral campaigns and 'pre-campaigns' (article 41.IV of the Constitution). In this way, campaigns in the year of a presidential, Senate and deputies election (every six years) are limited to 90 days; in mid-term deputies election, the limit is 60 days. Moreover, the same article establishes that under no circumstances may 'pre-campaigns' exceed the equivalent of two-thirds of the time established for electoral campaigns. According to this article, federal and State electoral statutes shall establish the rules on the periods in which nominations of candidates, pre-campaigns and campaigns shall take place. In turn, this norm has given rise to a series of legal disputes over alleged 'anticipatory' acts of campaigns.[11] For example, just recently the Federal Electoral Tribunal (TRIFE) confirmed a State electoral court decision stating that the fact that a candidate attended a meeting with political councillors, leaders and activists of the party-coalition that was nominating him, could not be considered as an anticipatory act of campaign. To conclude otherwise would

---

[10] SCJ, Action of unconstitutionality 61/2008 and accumulated actions 62/2008, 63/2008, 64/2008 and 65/2008, Federal Official Gazette, 3 October 2008.

[11] That is, those organised before the authorised periods.

produce the absurd result of deeming that a candidate is not allowed to participate in political events internal to his party, which would be contrary to the freedom of political activism. The implication is that 'anticipatory' acts of campaign are those directed to the electorate at large (not only to party activists) before the period allowed by the law to start campaigning.[12]

Finally, and related to the topic of the electoral system and the media, it is also important to mention that the 2007 reform introduced a rule in Section III.C of article 41 of the Constitution, by which political parties must abstain from employing expressions that denigrate institutions or political parties themselves or that slander individuals. This rule was introduced to satisfy the demand of the leftist party PRD, whose candidate was the object of a harsh 'negative campaign' in the presidential election of 2006. In turn, the rule has provoked a national discussion on whether this constitutes an improper limitation of the freedom of expression.

What is the meaning of 'denigration' in the context of this provision? In a number of cases the TRIFE has stated that expressions that are not aimed at making reasoned criticism but rather seek only to associate a series of immoral and illegal practices with a given party constitute denigration. According to the Tribunal, the Constitution protects the expression of ideas and opinions of those who are involved in political debate, provided that, seen in their context, they contribute to the formation of a free public opinion, the consolidation of the party system and the promotion of a democratic culture. For the Tribunal, the purpose of the 2007 reforms (which introduced the provision in question) had been to avoid 'excesses' that weaken democracy. The implication is that expressions that do not make proposals and do not contribute to a serious and reasoned debate in society may constitute the kind of denigration that is forbidden by the Constitution.[13]

For its part, article 134 of the Constitution states that propaganda on governmental programmes and actions shall have an institutional character (and should be linked to informative, educative or social orientation purposes), thus prohibiting its use for personal promotion of a public servant. This means that in propaganda spots broadcast through the mass media, neither the image, the voice, or the name of a public servant should appear in governmental propaganda. The motive for the

---

[12] TRIFE, SUP-JRC-193/2011.
[13] TRIFE, SUP-RAP-81/2009 and SUP-RAP-99/2009, respectively.

introduction of this rule has to do with the abuse by some public servants who use public resources to promote their image in the mass media. In turn, this rule has led to a discussion on the extent to which State governors' duty to present an annual report can be used as an instrument of personal promotion.[14]

As I said above, the IFE has the power (and the duty) to monitor, whether or not political parties and public servants comply with all the constitutional rules concerning the organisation of elections. This has created problems of work overload in the IFE, since the new rules imply a responsibility to monitor and inspect almost every action of political parties and candidates.

2. The Federal Electoral Tribunal (TRIFE)

The creation of the Federal Electoral Tribunal (TRIFE) sought the removal of the power to certify elections and resolve electoral disputes from politically-biased entities (the so-called 'electoral colleges' formed of legislators).[15] Today, the TRIFE forms part of the federal judicial power, and is formed of seven magistrates appointed by a two-thirds majority of the Senate, after proposals made by the Supreme Court of Justice. These magistrates serve a term of nine years without the possibility of re-election. Furthermore, the Tribunal comprises a permanent Superior Chamber, as an appeal court, as well as five regional chambers.

The origins of the TRIFE can be traced back to the constitutional reforms of 1986, which created an electoral court[16] with the power to hear disputes that may arise out of federal elections. Yet, the decisions of that court could be reviewed and modified by the electoral colleges of each chamber, which remained the final instance arbiter in the certification of

---

[14] The rule has inspired some politicians to find creative ways to cover personal promotion under the façade of legitimate institutional communication programmes.

[15] Originally, article 60 of the 1917 Constitution established that each chamber of Congress would be able to certify the election of its own members, and would have the power to resolve any doubts that may arise concerning the validity of the relevant elections in specific districts. The way in which this certification occurred was through the so-called 'electoral colleges' formed in each chamber, with groups of would-be-legislators, elected in the same electoral process they were called to validate (principle of self-certification). Moreover, article 60 also stated that the decisions of the electoral colleges of both Chambers would be definitive and unchallengeable.

[16] In Spanish, this court was called the *'Tribunal de lo Contencioso-Electoral'*.

elections. In the end, and after a series of reforms, the TRIFE became the only entity with the power to check the legality and constitutionality of acts and resolutions produced by the agencies in charge of organising elections in Mexico. It can do so in relation to both federal and State agencies that organise elections.[17] Importantly, the TRIFE also hears actions brought by citizens to challenge acts and resolutions of electoral authorities that violate their political and electoral rights.[18]

In addition, we also have to mention that in 1996 the Supreme Court of Justice was granted the power to review the constitutionality of federal and State electoral laws, through the so-called 'action of unconstitutionality'. This action can be brought in order to solve a possible contradiction between 'general norms' (a concept that encompasses State constitutions as well as federal and State electoral statute laws) and the federal Constitution. This action must be filed within the period of 30 days after the publication of the challenged norm and it can be brought by the national leadership of the political parties registered with the IFE, in connection with federal and State electoral laws; or by the State leadership of the political parties registered at the State electoral authorities, with respect to electoral laws passed by the respective State legislature.

Moreover, this action, which is an 'abstract' mechanism for the control of constitutionality,[19] can be seen as a relevant element of the dynamic of democratisation described above. By solving cases brought through this action, the Supreme Court of Justice has applied the federal constitutional standards for the organisation of State elections, thus forcing democratisation at the State level (we will discuss this in more detail in section III.1 of this chapter). In addition, it is an example of the increasing importance of courts both in the resolution of electoral disputes and, more broadly, in shaping the rules and principles that constitute the arena for political-electoral confrontation, both at the federal and at the State levels.

The TRIFE has also been a key element in this dynamic of democratisation in which courts have been playing a central role. Its contribution

[17] Through the so-called *Juicio de Revisión Constitucional* (Proceeding of Constitutional Revision), which shall be examined in the next section of this chapter.
[18] The so-called *Juicio para la Protección de los derechos político-electorales del ciudadano* (Proceeding for the protection of political-electoral rights of the citizen), also examined in the next section of this chapter.
[19] It is 'abstract' because to file the action does not require a 'concrete' act of application of the challenged norm.

has taken place mainly through the solution of cases brought under two proceedings created in 1996: the Proceeding for Constitutional-Electoral Revision and the Proceeding for the Protection of Political-Electoral Rights of the Citizen, which will be analysed in the following section.

III. THE JUDICIALISATION OF THE ELECTORAL-POLITICAL PROCESS

A relevant element of the dynamic of democratisation described above is the increasing importance of courts in the resolution of electoral disputes. This evolution has taken place against a historical background that long resisted the intervention of courts in electoral matters.

The role of the Supreme Court and the TRIFE in the performance of their new functions has not been without tensions (both between these courts and between them and other actors). The judicialisation of political-electoral confrontations has produced responses on behalf of different actors participating in the political process, who have tried to set up limits to the Tribunal's increased powers. In the present section we shall examine how this has taken place, focusing first on the way in which the Supreme Court has applied the standards established in the federal Constitution to the rules for organising elections at State level; secondly, we shall study how the TRIFE has exercised its power to review, through the proceeding for Constitutional-Electoral Revision, the constitutionality of acts and decisions of State agencies that organise State elections; and thirdly, we shall analyse how the TRIFE has defined the scope of political rights through the so-called proceeding for the Protection of Political-Electoral Rights of the Citizen.

1. Federal Constitutional Standards and State Rules for Organising State Elections

Since the end of the 1980s the federal government has gradually recognised opposition victories in State and municipal elections as a way of deflecting dissent from the national arena.[20] The recognition was the

---

[20] A Selee and J Peschard, 'Mexico's Democratic Challenges' in A Selee and J Peschard (eds), *Mexico's Democratic Challenges, Politics, Government and Society* (Washington, DC, Woodrow Wilson Center Press/Stanford CA, Stanford University Press, 2010) 12.

consequence of political negotiation, bargaining and give-and-take, rather than of the plain acknowledgment of the results in fair and truly competitive elections. For this reason opposition parties pushed for finding a formula that allowed democratisation at the State and municipal levels.

In this way, in 1996, article 116.IV of the Mexican Constitution was amended in order to introduce a series of standards that State constitutions and electoral laws have to follow. According to the long and detailed list of standards established in article 116.IV:

- the guiding principles in the organisation of State elections shall be 'certainty, impartiality, independence, legality and objectivity';
- the authorities that organise elections and those that resolve electoral disputes in the States shall be autonomous in their functioning and independent in their decisions;
- State law shall establish remedies and proceedings to challenge illegal electoral acts and resolutions;
- State law shall also establish mechanisms to guarantee equity in the access of political parties to mass media;
- State law shall establish criteria to define limits to expenditure by political parties in political campaigns; as well as limits on money contributions by supporters;
- State law shall define which acts constitute electoral crimes and the corresponding penalties.[21]

Apart from these standards, the constitutional reform of 1996 also opened up the possibility of filing actions of unconstitutionality to challenge State constitutions and statutes that contradict those standards (as we already explained above). The use that political parties have made of this mechanism for control of constitutionality of State electoral laws, has served to shape the latter according to the standards established in the federal Constitution.

In this way, for instance, the Supreme Court has concluded that:

A. A reform of the Constitution of the State of Chiapas which sought to extend the term of the incumbent State legislators and municipal authorities beyond their regular term in order to homologate State and federal elections was unconstitutional. The reason was that this decision violated the principle of no-re-election, the right to universal,

---

[21] The constitutional reform of 2007 amplified this list of standards, which today is formed of 14 paragraphs.

free, secret and direct suffrage to elect authorities, and the right to political participation of citizens, all of which are granted by the federal Constitution.[22]

B. The reform of the Constitution of the State of Jalisco that sought to remove the members of that State's Electoral Council was contrary to the federal Constitution, whose article 116 states that the members of those State authorities shall enjoy autonomy and independence.[23]

C. A constitutional reform in the State of Sonora related to re-districting for the purposes of State elections was unconstitutional. The reason was that the criteria used for re-designing electoral districts was a geographic one, rather than one that takes into account the proportion of the State population in each district, as ordered by article 116.II of the federal Constitution.[24]

In sum, since 1996, standards of the federal Constitution and the action of unconstitutionality have teamed (so to speak) in order to foster democratisation at State level. Yet, after 16 years of this reform, it is possible to say that democratisation has occurred in an asymmetric manner. Some States have truly democratised, while in others powerful authoritarian interests have been able to block the emergence and consolidation of political pluralism and fair electoral competition. Equity in elections is a pending matter in many States.

2. The Proceeding for Constitutional-Electoral Revision

The reform of 1996 introduced into the Constitution the so-called *Juicio de Revisión Constitutional Electoral* (Proceeding for Constitutional-Electoral Revision), through which the TRIFE can hear claims against final acts and resolutions of the competent electoral authorities of the States charged with organising and certifying elections; or to resolve disputes that arise from them, which may be relevant for the development of the respective electoral process or for the final result of the election. This proceeding originates in article 99 of the Constitution and is regulated

---

[22] SCJ, Action of unconstitutionality 47/2006 (and related actions 49/2006, 50/2006 and 51/2006).

[23] SCJ, Action of unconstitutionality 88/2008 (and related actions 90/2008 and 91/2008).

[24] SCJ, Action of unconstitutionality 18/2005.

in its details in the Law on Contesting Electoral Matters.[25] In essence, its goal is to challenge the unconstitutionality of acts and resolutions of electoral authorities of the States in the election of governors, State legislatures, and chief of government of the Federal District and members of the latter's legislative assembly, as well as elected members of municipalities and local authorities of the Federal District. In practical terms, through this proceeding, political parties have standing to seek revision (by the TRIFE) of decisions of State electoral authorities potentially 'captured' by State Executives.

Specifically, this proceeding has been used to review decisions of State electoral courts rendered in connection with disputes arising out of State elections. Nevertheless, as pointed out by Berruecos, the increased power of the TRIFE has created tensions associated with federal intervention in local conflicts, especially as the Tribunal has broad scope to interpret State legislation and to review its application by State electoral courts.[26]

A manifestation of this tension can be seen in the debate concerning the so-called 'abstract cause' to nullify an election, which has been a creation of the TRIFE case law, and has no base on an express text of the Constitution. Essentially, it means that the TRIFE can nullify State elections when it has found that a constitutional principle concerning the organisation of elections has been violated in a widespread way, creating reasonable doubt over the legitimacy of the relevant electoral process, even if the State legislation does not expressly foresee the possibility of nullifying the relevant election. This concept emerged in the context of a challenge against the election of governor of the State of Tabasco, filed by the PRD in 2000. The result was that the decision of the Tabasco Electoral Tribunal was reversed and the election for governor in the State of Tabasco was declared void by the TRIFE, which also ordered the Tabasco legislature to appoint an interim governor, who was in turn to call a new election within six months.[27]

The creation and use of the 'abstract cause' to nullify State elections by the TRIFE (as it happened in Tabasco, 2000, in Yucatán, 2001 and in

[25] Articles 86–93.
[26] S Berruecos, 'Electoral Justice in Mexico: The Role of the Electoral Tribunal under New Federalism' (2003) 35 *Journal of Latin American Studies* 802.
[27] Superior Chamber of the Electoral Tribunal. Thesis S3ELJ 23/2004. *Compilación Oficial de Jurisprudencia y Tesis Relevantes 1997–2005*, pp 200–201. TRIFE, SUP-JRC-487/2000.

Colima, 2003) fuelled an intense debate on the proper scope of the Tribunal's powers to interpret and apply the constitutional principles contained in the Constitution relating to the organisation of elections at State level. In fact, this debate led to an amendment to article 99 of the Constitution (as a part of the reform package of 2007), which today explicitly states that: 'The Superior and Regional Chambers of the [Electoral] Tribunal shall only declare the nullity of an election on the basis of the causes expressly established in the statute laws'.

Yet, this addition to the Constitution, which intended to limit the TRIFE's power to nullify elections, has not ended debate on this issue. On the one hand, in several cases,[28] the Superior Chamber of the TRIFE determined that the reform of 2007 meant that no longer could it nullify a State election invoking the 'abstract cause'. On the other hand, in 2007 the Superior Chamber of the TRIFE confirmed the decision of the Electoral Tribunal of Michoacán which nullified the election in the municipality of Yurécuaro, State of Michoacán, on account of the use of religious symbols and elements during the campaign of the winning candidate, which violated State electoral legislation as well as both the federal and State constitutions.[29] In this case, the winning candidate of the PRI challenged the decision of the Tribunal of Michoacán, alleging that the nullification of the election had been based on the 'abstract cause', which since the 2007 constitutional reform could no longer be applied. In response, the TRIFE concluded that Michoacán's Electoral Tribunal had not decided the case on the basis of the 'abstract cause', but had directly applied the principle of separation of state and Church of article 130 and article 35.XIX of the Electoral Code of Michoacán, which specifically prohibited the use of religious symbols and expressions in electoral propaganda.

The debate is far from settled and is a manifestation of a tension between the Electoral Tribunal's own conception of its role and scope of its power of constitutional interpretation; and attempts by political actors to set up limits on the Tribunal through the political process.

---

[28]   TRIFE, SUP-JRC-497/2007, SUP-JRC-500/2007 and SUP-JRC-165/2008.
[29]   TRIFE, SUP-JRC-604/2007.

3. The Proceeding for the Protection of Political-Electoral Rights of the Citizen

The 1996 reform introduced another novelty into the Constitution that has had an impact on the electoral system: the Proceeding for the Protection of Political-Electoral Rights of the Citizen, which grants individual citizens an action to challenge acts and resolutions of electoral authorities (and also of political parties) that violate their political and electoral fundamental rights.

Indeed, article 99, paragraph four, section V of the Constitution states that it is the power of the TRIFE to solve, in a definitive and final way, challenges against acts and resolutions of the electoral authorities that infringe citizens' political and electoral rights to vote, to be elected, and to freely and peacefully join political organisations in order to participate in Mexico's political affairs.[30] In addition, this action can also be brought by party members, against their own parties, when the latter perform acts or make decisions that infringe their members' political rights. Since the reform of 2007, article 99 of the Constitution also states that before a citizen can file an action against the political party to which he is affiliated (for alleged violation of his political electoral rights) he must exhaust first the remedies foreseen in the party's internal regulations.

An example of the application of these proceedings to review acts and resolutions of political parties can be found in a 2000 case in which two affiliates to the *Partido del Trabajo* (PT) brought an action against the party, alleging that the latter's leadership had violated internal regulations governing the expulsion of members. The Superior Chamber of the Electoral Tribunal considered that this had been the case, finding that such conduct was against the generic right of association and the plaintiffs' specific right to political affiliation. Thus, the Superior Chamber ordered the party leadership to restore the plaintiffs' use and enjoyment of their rights as affiliates, without prejudging the party's right to decide whether to initiate a new procedure of expulsion or not, but ordering that if this was the case, it should do so according to the party's internal regulations.[31]

---

[30] Article 79, paragraph 1 of the Law on Contesting Electoral Matters, states that a citizen can also use this proceeding to challenge the acts and resolutions that affect his/her right to be a member of the local electoral authority.

[31] TRIFE, SUP/JDC/021/2000.

An interesting development concerning this proceeding has to do with the power of the TRIFE to establish standards concerning the 'internal affairs' of political parties. Through these proceedings, the Tribunal has defined what elements are required for a political party to be considered democratic and therefore, able to obtain its registration.[32] An example how the TRIFE has defined democratic standards for political parties can be seen in the following case. In January 2001 a political organisation applied to the IFE to obtain registration as a political party. In July of the same year the General Council of the IFE denied registration to that organisation, among other reasons, because its Internal Regulations lacked the minimum elements established by the law to be considered democratic.[33] The political organisation (*Partido Popular Socialista*, PPS) sought a revision of that decision (SUP-JDC-781/2002), and the TRIFE confirmed the IFE's resolution. In this case, the Tribunal established the parameters to determine whether the internal regulations of political parties in Mexico are democratic or not:

A. There must be an assembly or an equivalent organ, as the main decision-making centre of the party, which shall be formed of all the affiliates, or when this is not possible, with a big number of delegates or representatives. The internal regulations must establish the formal rules to call the assembly, both to ordinary sessions by the leadership of the party, or to extraordinary sessions by a reasonable number of members. Furthermore, internal regulations must also establish the periodicity within which ordinary sessions shall be called, as well as the quorum necessary to hold valid meetings.

B. Internal regulations must guarantee the protection of fundamental rights of the affiliates, as well as the highest degree possible of participation, such as active and passive vote under conditions of equality, the right to information, freedom of expression, and free access and exit as party affiliates.

C. Internal regulations must establish disciplinary proceedings, with minimum due process guarantees, such as the establishment of a procedure that includes the right to be heard and to defend one's

---

[32] Registration implies access to public financing and other prerogatives.

[33] Article 27.1 of the federal electoral code (COFIPE) states that political parties have the duty to establish in their internal rulings, democratic proceedings for the formation and renewal of their leaderships. Yet it does not define the concept of 'democratic proceedings'.

case, the definition of what constitutes a fault, as well as the establishment of proportional sanctions. Resolutions must be justified, and internal regulations must have rules on the competence of the organs that impose sanctions (including rules that guarantee these organs' independence and impartiality).

D. Regulations must foresee procedures for the election of party leaders and candidates, with rules that guarantee equality, direct vote of affiliates, or indirect, but in every case under the principle of a free vote.

E. Regulations must adopt the majority rule as the basic criterion to make decisions within the party, so that, with the participation of a significant or considerable number of its members, binding decisions can be made (no super-majorities shall be required, save in relation to matters of 'special transcendence').

F. Finally, internal regulations of parties must establish mechanisms of control of power, such as, for example, the possibility of revoking the mandate of party leaders; the establishment of well-defined causes of conflict of interest between the different party positions or between the latter and public office, as well as the establishment of short terms for party leaders.[34]

There is another interesting case that illustrates the context and the manner in which the TRIFE has solved cases brought under the proceeding examined in this section. I am referring to a 2007 action brought by 20 citizens of the indigenous community of Tanetze (State of Oaxaca) to challenge Decree No 365 of the State legislature. This decree had confirmed a decision of the State electoral authority that declared the impossibility of organising elections in that community because of 'absence of conditions'.[35] In its answer to the complaint, the Oaxaca legislature argued that the statute of limitations excluded the late challenge under electoral law (that is, outside of five days after the decree's publication in the Official Gazette).

The TRIFE refused to strictly apply the statute of limitations rule against the plaintiffs, arguing that in cases in which plaintiffs are members of indigenous communities, it could not be assumed that the

---

[34] TRIFE, SUP-JDC-781/2002; SUP-JDC-021/2002 and SUP-JDC-803/2002.

[35] Since 2002 Oaxaca's legislature had declared the dissolution of municipal authorities, and the governor had appointed a Municipal Administrator to govern the community.

publication of the decree alone was an adequate means for the communication and diffusion of its content. The Tribunal reasoned that the decree should have been directly notified to the community in question. Because of their specific social, geographic, cultural and political conditions and the lack of proper communication and transport facilities, it could not be expected that the community would be aware of the acts and communications of State authorities made public through the State Official Gazette. Besides, the TRIFE considered that the challenged decree had been issued in violation of article 16 of the Constitution, according to which all acts of authority have to be founded and motivated.[36]

IV. THE IMPACT OF THE INTER-AMERICAN SYSTEM
ON HUMAN RIGHTS

Mexico acceded to the American Convention on Human Rights on 24 March 1981 and recognised as binding the adjudicatory jurisdiction of the Inter-American Court of Human Rights on matters relating to the interpretation or application of the Convention on 16 December 1998. Mexico's accession to the Inter-American system for the protection of human rights (IASHR) has entailed the country's immersion in a different and new dynamic for the interpretation and application of fundamental rights by national courts. In some instances, this dynamic has even produced changes to the text of the Constitution, as will be apparent after a brief examination of the *Castañeda* case.

On 5 March 2004, Mr Jorge Castañeda Gutman filed an application with the Executive Director of Political Rights and Parties of the IFE to register as a candidate for President of Mexico in the elections that would be held on 2 July 2006. The IFE denied the application, invoking a clause in the Mexican Constitution which states that 'the purpose of political parties is . . . to afford [citizens] access to public office', and a provision of the Federal Code of Electoral Institutions and Procedures (COFIPE) which states that 'only national political parties shall have the right to apply to register candidates for popularly elected office'.

After filing the domestic action of *amparo* to challenge this decision, and going all the way to the Supreme Court of Mexico only to lose on

---

[36] TRIFE, SUP-JDC-11/2007.

the grounds that *amparo* relief is inadmissible against decisions of electoral bodies, Mr Castañeda took his case to the IASHR. Eventually, the Inter-American Commission on Human Rights filed a claim before the Inter-American Court of Human Rights, alleging among other things the absence of a simple and effective remedy in Mexico's domestic legal system to challenge the constitutionality of decisions prejudicial to one's right to participate in government and the impediment thus created, which prevented Mr Jorge Castañeda Gutman from being registered as an independent candidate for the office of President of Mexico. For the Commission, this constituted a violation of the right protected under article 25 (right to judicial protection) of the American Convention on Human Rights, in relation to the state's obligation to respect and enforce the Convention.

For its part, in its analysis of the case, the Inter-American Court of Human Rights (IACtHR) examined two possible procedures foreseen in Mexico's domestic legal system that could potentially serve to challenge the constitutionality of acts issued by Mexico's electoral authorities. These procedures are: the *amparo* procedure and the proceeding for the protection of electoral-political rights of citizens.

After examining them, the IACtHR concluded that neither of them provided an effective remedy that allowed individuals to challenge the kind of acts of authority involved in the *Castañeda* case for being contrary to the Convention, the Constitution and the law.

In the case of the *amparo* procedure, it did not provide protection because according to article 73.VII of the Act on Amparo, its application was excluded from electoral matters. As for the proceeding for the protection of electoral-political rights of citizens, it was not an effective remedy for two reasons. On the one hand, according to article 79 of the Law on Contesting Electoral Matters, Mr Castañeda would have to have been postulated by a political party in order to claim a violation of the political right to be elected, in relation to the registration of his candidacy. On the other hand, and in spite of the Electoral Tribunal's competence explicitly granted by article 99 of the Constitution since the reform of 1996, the Supreme Court of Justice had decided in May 2002 that the Constitution did not allow the TRIFE to control the constitutionality of electoral laws in respect of acts and decisions in which they had been applied, 'because the only control of the constitutionality of laws allowed by the Constitution was control with general effect, which was the exclusive competence of the Supreme Court of Justice by means of the unconstitutionality proceeding'.[37] This meant that access to an effective judicial remedy by Mr Castañeda was denied.

By way of parenthesis, we should note that with the constitutional reform of 1996, the TRIFE had the power to declare the unconstitutionality of electoral statute laws and, therefore, to determine their inapplicability in concrete cases. This was congruent with the provision of article 41.IV which established that the system of mechanisms to challenge electoral acts and resolutions would be designed to guarantee the 'constitutionality and legality' of the latter; and it was also congruent with article 99, paragraph 4, section III which allowed the Electoral Tribunal to hear cases of potential violation of constitutional or legal norms. However, in 2002 the Supreme Court had issued an interpretative ruling that deprived the TRIFE of that power (in what appears to be a manifestation of a 'war between courts', with the Supreme Court refusing to accept another court in the land with the power it had traditionally and exclusively wielded: the power of constitutional control). According to the Supreme Court, the only way to challenge the unconstitutionality of electoral laws was the one established in article 105.II: the action of unconstitutionality, which is only heard by the Supreme Court of Justice, sitting *en banc*. In addition, the Supreme Court also said that in every case, the TRIFE had to apply and honour the interpretations that the Supreme Court had made relating to the Constitution.[38]

This decision established a significant limitation to the power and strength of the TRIFE and created a legal vacuum. The TRIFE, supposedly the highest electoral court in the land, could not perform an essential element of its functions: the examination of whether electoral laws, and the acts and resolutions issued on the basis of such statutes, were constitutional or not. In addition, the Supreme Court's decision also implied a reduction of the scope of protection of electoral-political rights of individuals, since the action of unconstitutionality cannot be filed by citizens, but only by the subjects specified in article 105.II of the Constitution. In other words, with the new rules, individuals were deprived of the right to challenge electoral laws for being contrary to the Constitution.

---

[37] *Castañeda Gutman v Mexico*, Inter-American Court of Human Rights, Judgment of 6 August 2008. See paras 122–25.

[38] Thesis PJ 23, 24, 25 y 26/2002. *Semanario Judicial de la Federación y su Gaceta*, vol XXXI, January 2010, pp 19–23.

Since the beginning, this criterion of the Supreme Court was highly controversial. The argument that supported it ran against express constitutional text, consolidated practice and even logic (as to the performance of the TRIFE functions and constitutional responsibilities). The legal vacuum thus created and its implications for Mexico's legal system became evident in the context of the *Castañeda* case, brought before the Inter-American Court of Human Rights. In this case, as we have seen, an individual citizen, such as Mr Castañeda, had no effective remedy to challenge the unconstitutionality of the resolution of the IFE that denied him the possibility of registering as an independent candidate for the presidential election that was due in 2006.

In the end, the IACtHR concluded:

> 131. Given that the application for amparo was not admissible in the case of electoral matters, the exceptional nature of the unconstitutionality proceeding and the inaccessibility and ineffectiveness of the judicial procedure for protection to contest the failure of a law to conform to the Constitution, at the time of the facts of this case, there was no effective remedy in Mexico enabling an individual to question the legal regulation of the political right to be elected established in the Constitution and in the American Convention. Owing to this, the Court concludes that, the State did not offer the alleged victim an appropriate remedy to claim the alleged violation of his political right to be elected and, consequently, violated Article 25 of the American Convention, in relation to Article 1(1) thereof, to the detriment of Mr. Castañeda Gutman.[39]

Thus, Mexico was found to be in violation of the right to judicial protection embodied in Article 25 of the American Convention on Human Rights and was ordered to complete the adaptation of its domestic law to the Convention, within a reasonable time. This required the legislature to adapt the secondary legislation and the norms that regulate the action for the protection of the citizen to the provisions of the constitutional reform of 13 November 2007. With this, citizens would be able to use that remedy to effectively challenge the constitutionality of statutes that might violate their right to be elected.[40] It is important to note that the Inter-American Court ordered Mexico 'to *complete* the adaptation of its domestic law to the Convention' (emphasis added), because as the Court was hearing the case (and anticipating the judgment),

---

[39] *Castañeda Gutman v Mexico* judgment, n 37 above, para 131.
[40] See Declaration and Orders of the judgment in the *Castañeda v Mexico* case.

Mexico passed the constitutional reform of 13 November 2007, which restored to the TRIFE the power to control the constitutionality of electoral laws in respect of acts and decisions in which they had been applied, in concrete disputes.

V. CONCLUSION

In the context of its democratisation process, Mexico has been able to create institutions that have contributed to ending the hegemonic party system, and establishing the foundation of a democratic regime. Today, the consolidation of this regime faces a series of challenges. One of them has to do with the relationship between money and politics. Crucial in this respect is the IFE's capacity to monitor the finances of political parties during electoral campaigns. In the country's recent experience, we have seen that political parties are able to build up parallel and illegal systems to finance campaigns (as in the 2000 presidential election with the experience of the so-called *PEMEXgate* and *Amigos de Fox* cases).[41]

For its part, the constitutional reform on the relation between mass media and politics has created a considerable amount of tension between the IFE and the TV corporations and big business who want to influence the electoral process. Evidently, the mass media, specifically the two TV companies, have been affected in their economic interests by that constitutional reform. And the private sector has been limited in its ability to influence politics using the mass media. To illustrate this tension, we can recall how in 2008 one of the TV corporations refused to transmit the political propaganda broadcasts in the terms requested by the IFE. In response, the IFE fined the corporation 2 million pesos.

Yet, another big concern is the potential influence of money coming from organised crime in electoral campaigns. On 31 May 2011 the three leaders of the biggest political parties issued a joint declaration on the necessity of working together in order to impede the use of money coming from organised crime to finance political campaigns. In turn,

---

[41] The '*PEMEXgate*' case involved the illegal deviation of resources from the state oil company PEMEX to support the PRI candidate in the 2000 presidential election. The *Amigos de Fox* case involved the creation of a network of individuals and enterprises that made contributions to the PAN presidential candidate in 2000 that exceeded the limits established by the law.

this requires strengthening the IFE in its ability to monitor the sources of party financing. However, there are signs that suggest that political parties do not have the intention to strengthen the IFE as an institution. On the contrary,

– Political parties in the lower house delayed the appointment of three of the nine electoral councillors for more than one year (from November 2010 to December 2011). Therefore, the General Council of the IFE was forced to work with six people only.
– Political parties promoted, through the constitutional reforms of 2007, the creation of the so-called 'General Comptroller' of the IFE who shall be designated by the vote of two-thirds of the Chamber of Deputies, after proposals presented by public universities. This 'General Comptroller' has the power to inspect all the revenue and expenditure of the IFE, and has been identified by some as a new (and negative) trend in the development of Mexico's democracy in the following sense: the Comptroller could represent an attempt by political parties to reduce the IFE's autonomy,[42] by creating this bureau whose head is appointed by parties' parliamentary groups in the lower house.[43] This is another manifestation of the tension between the IFE, which is supposed to check political parties, and these parties that resist IFE's inspection powers (and of course IFE's multi-million peso sanctions against them).

In the field of electoral justice, there is the debate on the scope of the TRIFE's powers to nullify elections and to establish standards on the 'internal affairs' of political parties, as we could see in our discussion on the 'abstract cause' to nullify elections. Therefore, we will continue to see the tension created by the increased power of the TRIFE associated with federal intervention in local conflicts, especially as the Tribunal has broad scope to interpret State legislation and to review its application by

---

[42] Political parties are worried about the IFE's power to impose multi-million peso fines on them, which has consistently happened whenever the IFE has found that parties have committed violations of electoral rules on, say, the transmission of party-political broadcasts in the mass media.
[43] The General Comptroller has already accused the IFE of misusing public funds allotted to it, and has asked the IFE to return to the Federal Treasury a substantial amount of money (348 million Mexican pesos) that were not used to finance IFE-approved programmes. For its part, the IFE has argued that such funds were saved in order to purchase a series of buildings needed by the institution, instead of having to pay rent for them.

State electoral courts. In all this, the TRIFE is at the centre of the stage, as political actors use different proceedings as tools for everyday political struggle, in the context of increased polarisation of Mexican politics in recent years.

Finally, we will continue to see tensions and debates derived from Mexico's incorporation into the Inter American system for the protection of human rights. The case of *Castañeda* puts forward a final issue I would like to address: one that has to do with the debate on the possibility and convenience of allowing non-partisan candidates (so-called 'independent candidates' or 'citizen candidates'). In a context in which political parties seem to have lost part of their credibility in the eyes of the public, this is an appealing option, which until the constitutional reform of 9 August 2012 was not allowed by federal electoral law (though it was allowed by some State electoral codes, like in the State of Yucatán). For some, independent candidates are necessary to give democracy back to citizens (by-passing political parties). For others, independent candidates would further weaken political parties, strengthen our old tradition of the personalised exercise of power and contribute to a fragmentation of representation in Congress, all of which would have a negative impact on democracy and governability.

The Supreme Court addressed this issue in Action of unconstitutionality 61/2008 and accumulated actions 62/2008, 63/2008, 64/2008 and 65/2008,[44] which challenged the constitutionality of article 281, paragraph 1 of the federal electoral code, that prohibited 'independent candidates' in federal elections. The argument of the plaintiffs was that the constitutional reform of 2007 had expressly prohibited that kind of candidacy at State level (article 116.IV.E),[45] but said nothing on the topic at the federal level. Therefore – the plaintiffs argued – the prohibition of article 281, paragraph 1 amounted to a violation of the right to be elected in article 35.II of the Constitution, in prejudice of citizens that seek elected office without being postulated by a political party in a federal election.

---

[44] See above, n 7.

[45] The main argument of the reformers was that 'independent candidates' ran against the logic of strengthening the multi-party system on which Mexico's incipient democracy was based. Yet, the rule of article 116, IV.E) has an exception: indigenous peoples have the right to designate the authorities of their traditional forms of government according to their norms, procedures and traditional practices, independently from political parties (article 2, Section A, III and VII of the Constitution).

In this case, the Supreme Court said that the right contained in article 35.II of the Constitution could not be interpreted in an isolated manner. On the contrary, it had to be interpreted in a systematic and harmonic way, in connection with other articles of the Constitution (particularly with article 41), seeking a point of equilibrium between that right and other values constitutionally protected, such as the constitutional system of political parties and the constitutional principles of the federal electoral functions.

For the Court, under a functional interpretation of articles 35.II and 41, the framers of the successive constitutional reforms in electoral-political matters in Mexico have intended to strengthen a plural and competitive system of political parties since they are central to the reproduction of a constitutional democratic state. In the light of this, the absence of an express prohibition of 'independent candidacies' with respect to federal elections could not be interpreted in the sense that they were allowed and that the federal legislative power had the duty to regulate them in the federal electoral code. This interpretation – the Court said – would run against the entire logic of the constitutional design for organising federal elections and would cause serious practical problems if implemented, for example, in connection with the system of financing political parties and the distribution of access of political parties to the mass media.[46] Therefore, the Court concluded that 'independent candidacies' were not allowed by the Constitution at the federal level.

On 9 August 2012 Mexico's Constitution was amended in order to allow 'independent candidates' at all levels. The reasons that justified this amendment had to do with the objective of strengthening citizenship; the need to expand the scope of political rights and to open up new channels of political participation, in order to strengthen Mexico's democracy. If the corresponding statutory reforms are passed in the next couple of years, we might see independent candidates running for different public offices in the elections of 2015.

---

[46] SCJ, Action of unconstitutionality 61/2008 and accumulated actions 62/2008, 63/2008, 64/2008 and 65/2008, Federal Official Gazette, 3 October 2008.

FURTHER READING

Ackerman, J (ed), *Nuevos escenarios del Derecho Electoral: Los Retos de la Reforma de 2007–2008* (Mexico, UNAM, 2009).

Córdova, L, 'La Reforma electoral y el cambio político en México' in D Zovatto and J Orozco (eds), *Reforma Política y Electoral en América Latina, 1978–2007* (Mexico, UNAM and IDEA, 2008) 653–703.

Córdova, L and P Salazar (eds), *Democracia sin Garantes: Las Autoridades vs. La Reforma Electoral* (Mexico, UNAM, 2009).

Klesner, JL, 'Electoral Competition and the New Party System in Mexico' (2005) 47 *Latin American Politics & Society* 103–42.

Orozco, J, 'The Mexican System of Electoral Conflict Resolution in Comparative Perspective' (2006) 2 *Taiwan Journal of Democracy* 51–60.

Orozco, J, *Justicia Electoral y Garantismo Jurídico* (Mexico, Porrúa, 2006).

Valadés, D, 'Problemas Jurídicos de las precampañas y las candidaturas independientes' in Cienfuegos D and López, MA (eds), *Estudios en Homenaje a Don Jorge Fernández Ruiz. Derecho Constitucional y Política* (Mexico, UNAM, 2005).

3

The Legislative Branch of Government

———————

Introduction – Bicameralism – Rules on the Integration of the
Two Chambers of Congress – Organising the Work of Both
Chambers of Congress – The Committee System of Congress –
Parliamentary Groups in Congress – The Permanent Committee
of Congress – The Powers of Congress – The Legislative Process
– Congress's Powers to Check the Executive – Jurisdictional-like
Functions of Congress – The 'Superior Audit of the Federation'
– Conclusion

I. INTRODUCTION

THE TRANSFORMATION OF the hegemonic party system
into a multi-party system had primarily an impact on the integration of the federal Congress. This transformation started with
the reform of 1977, which introduced new electoral rules allowing
minority political parties to have a good number of seats in the lower
house of Congress. With the years, this representation increased until
the hegemonic party lost its majority in that house, in 1997. These
changes, in turn, forced a series of constitutional reforms concerning
the rules for organising Congress's work, and they also influenced the
way in which bicameralism works in practice.

Article 49 of Mexico's Constitution establishes the principle of separation of powers, stating that the supreme power of the Federation is
divided, for its exercise, into legislative, executive, and judicial branches
of government. Moreover, this article states that two or more of these
powers shall never be united in one single person or corporation, nor
shall the legislative power be vested in one individual except in two

cases: a) the case of extraordinary powers granted to the Executive, in accordance with the provisions of article 29 of the Constitution (analysed in the next paragraph); and b) the case of Congress's authorisation allowing the president of the Republic to increase, reduce or cancel export and import tariffs approved by Congress, or to create new tariffs, as well as to restrict or prohibit imports, exports and the transit of products when he deems this urgent for the benefit of the country's economy. In this case, the president has to report to Congress (in his yearly budget proposal) on the use that he has eventually made of this power (article 131 of the Constitution).

Indeed, article 29 of the Constitution allows for the restriction or suspension of constitutional rights and guarantees (those 'which present an obstacle to a rapid and ready combating of the situation' in the event of 'invasion, serious disturbance of the public peace, or any other event which may place society in great danger or conflict'). The procedure for the suspension or restriction of rights was reformed significantly in June 2011. Today, article 29 of the Constitution contains a list of rights that cannot be suspended or restricted under any circumstance; it also establishes that the suspension or restriction of other rights must be justified and be proportionate to the threat in question. Besides, it establishes that all the legislative and administrative measures taken by the Executive under the decree of suspension of rights shall lose validity immediately at the end of the period of suspension or restriction of rights. This reform took place in the context of the federal Executive 'war on drugs', which by early 2012 has resulted in more than 50,000 deaths. The reform enhances the protection of human rights at the constitutional level, while 'on the ground' there seems to be evidence of human rights violations perpetrated by the armed forces against the civilian population in the war against drug cartels. According to Human Rights Watch, efforts of the Mexican government 'to combat organised crime have resulted in a significant increase in killings, torture, and other abuses by security forces, which only make the climate of lawlessness and fear worse in many parts of the country'.[1]

Moreover, article 29 allows Congress to grant 'authorisations' to the president, so that he can deal with the situation. This is actually an authorisation to legislate, which has only been granted once under the

---

[1] See Human Rights Watch, Mexico Report 2012, January 2012: (www.hrw.org/sites/default/files/related_material/mexico_2012.pdf).

Constitution of 1917, when Mexico declared war on Nazi Germany and its allies during the Second World War. Notably, it was used by the president to issue legislation that had little to do with the participation in the war, ie the 1942 presidential decree that 'froze' rents in certain kinds of dwellings in Mexico City.[2]

The latter is just one example of the way in which the principle of separation of powers actually worked under the hegemonic party system. This principle, which has been written down in all the constitutional texts Mexico has had, has been far from being a real feature of the living constitution. Yet, under the new conditions, with the formation of a multi-party system, and within the framework of a presidential political regime, the principle has started to acquire new life, shaping the dynamic of governance. In turn, the new dynamic has posed its own challenges to the different actors of the political process, who have had to adapt themselves to this novel situation, not without tensions and conflicts.

II. BICAMERALISM

Article 50 of the Constitution states that the legislative power of the United Mexican States is vested in a General Congress, which shall be divided into two chambers, one of deputies and the other of senators. This is the basis of Mexico's bicameralism, a feature that has been present throughout the country's constitutional history, with the exception of the original version of the 1857 Constitution, which suppressed the Senate (which was re-established with the reform of 1874, for reasons relating to the perceived need to introduce checks and balances within the federal legislative power, and strengthen the Executive vis-à-vis Congress).[3]

Traditionally, bicameralism has been identified with federalism. This link was established with the Constitution of 1824, according to which senators would be designated by the State legislatures, by majority vote. Because of this designation procedure, the prevailing conception was that senators represented the States and not the nation (as was and still is the case with deputies). Nevertheless, there are some elements in

---

[2] Decree promulgated on 24 July 1942.
[3] See above, chapter 1.III.

Mexico's constitutional development that have weakened the link between federalism and bicameralism, one of them being the fact that the constitutional laws of 1836 established a two-chamber system (Chamber of Deputies and Senate), but abolished the federal political form ('States' were transformed into 'Departments'), creating instead a centralised state. This did away with the idea that the Senate was necessarily a chamber of territorial representation associated to the federal form. In addition, today senators are no longer designated by State legislatures, but are elected by direct popular vote (just like deputies); and 32 senators (out of 128) are elected by proportional representation (PR), on the basis of closed and ranked lists nominated by political parties, which are assigned in proportion to each party's share of the national vote. These senators have no 'electoral connection' with any specific State. Finally, the logic of representation that prevails in the Senate is dominated by political party identity, rather than by territorial concerns. In spite of this, senators still consider themselves as the guardians of State interests at the federal government level.

During the time of the hegemonic party system, bicameralism was subjected to the logic of party discipline and loyalty to the hegemonic party leader, who was the president of the Republic. Nevertheless, under the current multi-party system and due to the president's lack of a clear majority in either chamber of Congress, bicameralism has entered into a new dynamic that demands negotiation and compromise between the two chambers, as well as between Congress and the president.

III. RULES ON THE INTEGRATION OF THE TWO CHAMBERS OF CONGRESS

Political-electoral reforms passed in Mexico since the 1970s, sought to strike a balance between the majority principle for the election of federal legislators, and the need to allow the participation in Congress of political forces that had been excluded or significantly reduced in their ability to get representation in the federal legislature. The result was the creation of a 'mixed system', which is predominantly majoritarian, but that also has an important component of PR in both chambers of the federal legislative power.

In this way, today the Chamber of Deputies is formed of 500 legislators, elected through two different systems of representation: 300 are elected in single-member district contests through the first-past-the-post principle (FPTP); and 200 are elected through PR, by lists of 40 candidates presented and rank-ordered by registered national political party for each of the five regional districts into which the country was divided for this purpose.[4]

For its part, the Senate has a total of 128 seats. 64 are elected according to the traditional system (FPTP system, two per State); 32 seats are elected in each State, and are allotted to the party that gets the second place in the corresponding senatorial election (the first minority), while the remaining 32 are elected by PR, on the basis of closed and ranked lists nominated by political parties, which are assigned in proportion to each party's share of the national vote.

In both houses of Congress, the reason for the introduction of PR seats has to do with concessions granted by the hegemonic party to opposition parties in the context of increasing political instability, social unrest and economic crisis which forced a gradual transition to democratic rule in the late 1970s. The aim of the PRI-government was to co-opt dissenters and ensure the legitimacy of the one-party dominant system by expanding the boundaries of electoral competition.[5] With PR, opposition parties had access to Congress, but the PRI did not lose control of either house for a long time (until 1997, in which it lost the majority in the Chamber of Deputies).[6]

Moreover, article 54 of the Constitution establishes a ceiling of 60 per cent on representation in the Chamber of Deputies: no party may be allotted a number of seats that exceeds that percentage. This rule can be understood against the background of a hegemonic party system which for decades controlled the vast majority of seats in the federal Congress. Its purpose is to guarantee plural representation in the Legislature.[7]

---

[4] See article 52 of the Constitution.

[5] A Selee and J Peschard, 'Mexico's Democratic Challenges' in A Selee and J Peschard (eds), *Mexico's Democratic Challenges, Politics, Government and Society* (Stanford CA, Stanford University Press/Washington, DC, Woodrow Wilson Center Press, 2010) 13.

[6] Interestingly, and after the constitutional reforms of 1977, 1983 and 1987, the members of State legislatures and of municipal councils must be elected through this mixed formula that combines plurality and PR.

[7] Similar rules can be found today in most State constitutions, related to the election of the members of State legislatures.

A characteristic that distinguishes Mexico's Constitution from most constitutional systems (concerning the integration of Congress) is the principle of no re-election of federal legislators for the immediate period contained in article 59. This rule was not present in the original text of the 1917 Constitution, but was the result of a reform introduced in 1933 (which also extended the 'no immediate re-election' principle to state legislators and to municipal presidents). This reform had its origins in the 1932 Convention of the *Partido Nacional Revolucionario* (the grandfather of the PRI), which sought to return to the principle of absolute no re-election of the president of the Republic (which had been changed in 1928 to favour the return of Obregón to a second term as president).[8] The Convention promoted the idea that the no re-election principle had to be established with respect to all elected offices; an idea that was taken up by the president of the Republic and by Congress, resulting in the constitutional reform of 1933 mentioned above. With hindsight, it can be argued that this rule was functional to the hegemonic party's need to assure a constant rotation of loyal political groups, in a regular process of distribution of political positions that was part of the regime's strategy of control and generation of support.

Since the mid-1960s there have been proposals to change this rule, in order to allow the re-election of both federal and State legislators. The main argument in favour of this proposal is that immediate re-election would have an impact on the quality of representation of Mexico's legislative branch of government, since it would strengthen the 'electoral connection' between legislators and their constituencies: re-election would empower voters to punish or reward their representatives in Congress on the basis of the evaluation of their performance, an option they do not have under the existing rules. In other words, with the possibility of re-election, legislators can be accountable with respect to their constituencies. Yet, this proposal is opposed by those who fear that, in the context of Mexican politics and political-civic culture, re-election would work in favour of political bosses who would take over congressional seats indefinitely.

---

[8] See below chapter 4.IV.

IV. ORGANISING THE WORK OF BOTH
CHAMBERS OF CONGRESS

Increased pluralism in both chambers of Congress has required the modification of its internal rules for the direction and organisation of parliamentary tasks, responsibilities and powers. In this way, since the 1980s Congress has passed from a form of organisation that assumed the existence of a clear majority party, to a scheme that assumes the existence of pluralism and balance amongst the different political parties with representation in Congress. In turn, this new situation has forced negotiation and compromise for the sake of achieving coordination and order in the performance of legislative tasks.

The re-organisation of Congress's rules has taken place through a series of reforms to the Organic Law of Congress (OLC) which, according to article 70 of the Constitution, cannot be vetoed by the president and does not require promulgation by the Executive in order to be valid. One of the main features of these reforms was the creation of the so-called '*Junta de Coordinación Política*' in each chamber of Congress, which is formed of the coordinators of each of the parliamentary groups (in the Senate, the *Junta* is also formed of 2 senators of the party that holds the majority of the house's seats and 1 senator of the largest minority in the house). Interestingly, the antecedent of this *Junta* was a committee that was created in the Chamber of Deputies in the LV Legislature (1991–94) by a parliamentary agreement of the leaders of the different political parties in that house.[9] This agreement put aside express mandates of the OLC and its Internal Regulations (which presupposed the lack of plurality in the political composition of the house), for the sake of pragmatically accommodating opposition parties, and incorporating their leaders in decisions relating to the house's governance.

The OLC was later reformed, and today both houses of Congress have a *Junta de Coordinación Política*, whose president shall be the coordinator of the parliamentary group which controls the absolute majority in the respective house; yet, if no group holds that majority, the law establishes a rotation system for the designation of the president: in the lower house, the presidency of the *Junta* has a yearly term and shall correspond successively to the coordinators of the three largest parliamentary groups, in the

---

[9] The 'Committee on Internal Regime and Political Concertation'.

order determined by the *Junta* itself.[10] Since 1997 no party has had an absolute majority of seats in the Chamber of Deputies, which means that the presidency of the *Junta* has rotated in the terms I have just described.

In the Senate, the presidency of the *Junta* is also of one year's duration, and shall be occupied by each in turn of the coordinators of the parliamentary groups that control a number of seats that amount, at least, to 25 per cent of the total (the order shall be determined by the coordinator of the parliamentary group with more seats in the Senate).[11] Furthermore, the decisions of the *Junta* are taken by absolute majority, through a system of weighted voting, that is, each coordinator has as many votes as the number of seats his or her party controls in the Senate. Moreover, in this house only two parties have reached 25 per cent of the seats since 2000 (PAN and PRI), so they have taken turns in controlling the presidency of the *Junta*.

The main responsibilities and powers of the *Junta* are to reach agreements related to the pieces of legislation debated in Congress that require a vote in the 'house floor' (plenary session), as well as making proposals to the house floor in order to place members on committees and determine who shall chair them.

In addition to the *Junta*, each chamber also has another organ in charge of guiding the work of the plenary sessions of the two chambers of Congress: the so-called '*Mesa Directiva*' or 'Presiding Board'. The evolution of this office, which also has the institutional role of representation of each house, through its president, reflects the need for institutional adaptation in the context of increased pluralism in both chambers. In this way, and after the reforms of 1994 and 1999 to the OLC, in the Chamber of Deputies, the Presiding Board shall be elected by the house floor in plenary session, and shall be formed on of one president (who represents the unity of the house), three vice-presidents and one secretary for each parliamentary group. The members of the Board are elected by the vote of two-thirds of the deputies present in the corresponding plenary session[12] for one year and can be re-elected.

In the Senate, the Presiding Board is formed of a president, three vice-presidents and four secretaries, elected for a one-year term by absolute majority of the senators present in the corresponding plenary

[10] Article 31.4 of the OLC.
[11] Article 81.5 of the OLC.
[12] Article 17 of the OLC.

session, and they can be re-elected.[13] In both chambers, the Presiding Board has the duty to direct the work of the relevant house under the principles of impartiality and objectivity and shall make its decisions by consensus. Yet, if a consensus is not reached, decisions shall be taken by the rule of majority in the lower house and by absolute majority in the Senate, through the system of weighted votes. In case of a draw, the president shall have a casting vote.[14]

Congress has two periods of ordinary sessions. The first one starts on 1 September and normally ends on 15 December, except for the year in which the president takes office (1 December every six years). In this case, the period can extend up to 31 December of the respective year; the second period starts on 1 February and ends on 30 April of every year.[15] In addition, extraordinary sessions of Congress or of a single house can be called by the Permanent Committee on its own motion or on the proposal of the Executive (we will discuss the structure and powers of the Permanent Committee below, in section VII of this chapter). In any case, the Congress gathered in extraordinary sessions shall be restricted to debating and deciding on the issues for which the sessions were called.

V. THE COMMITTEE SYSTEM OF CONGRESS

Legislative committees are an essential part of the structure and functions of Mexico's legislative power. They introduce the principles of division of labour, of specialisation and order in the work of Congress and, to the extent possible, seek to guarantee the quality of the results of legislative work. Most importantly, they are smaller fora for reaching agreements that can be later transported to the house floor. In sum, the work in committees determines the result of the houses and Congress as a whole.

The membership and the chairs of the committees are decided by the house floor, on the basis of the proposals of the *Junta de Coordinación Política* of each house. In determining this membership, the *Junta* and the house have to take care to integrate into the committees the

---

[13] Article 62 of the OLC.
[14] Articles 20, 21, 62 and 66 of the OLC.
[15] Articles 65 and 66 of the Constitution.

different political parties, reflecting to the extent possible the proportions that exist in the house floor.[16] Ordinary committees are thus formed and remain as such during all the period of the corresponding legislature.

Committee presidents are important actors in the work of Congress. They are responsible for the study of bills and the production of legislative reports for the consideration of each house's floor; for the setting of the committees' agenda; and the calling of committee sessions. Furthermore, in actual practice they function as conveyor belts for petitions and demands by social groups, and make political statements on matters of public relevance and concern.

Importantly, the presidents of congressional committees have the power to request from the federal Executive information and documents relating to the matters examined and studied in the committee, unless the information is classified according to the applicable statutes. Moreover, apart from in those circumstances, federal authorities have to hand in the requested information 'within a reasonable time frame'. If the information is not provided, then the committee president shall officially address a complaint to the head of the corresponding agency or to the president of the Republic.[17]

Articles 39 and 90 of the OLC list the committees that must exist in each house of Congress: 40 in the Chamber of Deputies and 30 in the Senate. In general terms, their competence corresponds to the subject areas of the entities and agencies that form the federal public administration. Moreover, each chamber can decide on the creation of more committees when deemed necessary. That is why today the lower house works with 56 committees and the Senate with 62.

VI. PARLIAMENTARY GROUPS IN CONGRESS

Parliamentary groups form part of the organisation of modern legislatures, and are formed of the legislators that belong to the same political party. Seen as part of the congressional machinery, they contribute to better performance of parliamentary tasks. In the case of Mexico, as pointed out by Manuel González Oropeza, the legal recognition of

---

[16]　Articles 43.3 and 104.3 of the OLC.
[17]　Articles 45 and 97 of the OLC.

parliamentary groups is relatively recent (it dates back to 1977), in spite of the fact that in actual practice they have always existed.[18] The constitutional and legal recognition of parliamentary groups involved the establishment of a series of requirements and conditions for their formation.[19] In turn, once recognised as such every parliamentary group is entitled to a series of rights, prerogatives and resources, and has to comply with certain duties relating to its role in the work of Congress.

The idea of integrating legislators in parliamentary groups led by a coordinator[20] responds to the need to organise complex congressional tasks, through agreements on specific actions that guarantee better performance. This concern can be seen in article 71 of the OLC, which mandates that the Senate's parliamentary groups shall seek the formation of common criteria for the deliberations in which their members participate.

The OLC leaves room for the eventual decision of deputies and senators to quit a parliamentary group without joining another one. In that case, the corresponding legislator does not lose his/her prerogatives and rights to participate in the work of the respective house. However, these legislators with no party affiliation do not have the right to participate in the discussions and decision-making of the *Junta de Coordinación Política*.

In actual practice, parliamentary groups are able to guarantee an important level of party discipline. Valencia has reported high levels of party discipline among Mexican federal legislators, but she also has noted that this discipline is not absolute: there seem to be different sorts of factors that explain why some legislators decide to vote against the instruction of the party coordinator in Congress. Among those factors, Valencia identifies: structural factors and factors associated with a political party's internal rules. For example, PR based on lists proposed by political party leaders, and the prohibition on immediate re-election,

---

[18] M González, 'Grupos Parlamentarios' in Instituto de Investigaciones Jurídicas, *Diccionario Jurídico Mexicano*, vol V (Mexico, UNAM, 1983) 305–7.

[19] For example, a minimum of five members is required to form a group, whose members must formally apply to be recognised as such. In addition, when applying they must attach the By-Laws or statute that will govern the group's relations and forms of action.

[20] The designation of parliamentary groups' coordinators and their relationships are not matters that fall within the scope of the OLC, but rather the internal rules and guidelines agreed by each parliamentary group.

favour party discipline in Congress; as do the rules for the selection of candidates and on the financing of campaigns.[21]

Moreover, as reported by a former senator, the coordinators of parliamentary groups have access to and control of relevant financial resources granted by the house to each group. The discretionary and unchecked use of those resources is an important element for the construction of strong leadership and maintaining party discipline. Coordinators thus distribute those resources with total discretion and opacity not only towards the public but also with respect to the members of their own parliamentary group. Thus, the leadership of coordinators is linked to their capacity to respond to the political needs of their members through the resources they control. This allows an anti-democratic handling of the groups, concentrating power in a few leaders, who can freely negotiate with the Executive whatever they may deem convenient, even out of the eyes of both the public and the legislators of their own group.[22]

VII. THE PERMANENT COMMITTEE OF CONGRESS

We also have to mention the so-called Permanent Committee of the General Congress, which responds to the need to guarantee the institutional presence of the federal legislative power in the country's political affairs, during Congress's recess.

Since the constitutional reform of 1987, the Permanent Committee is formed of 37 legislators (19 deputies and 18 senators). They are designated by the respective house on the eve of Congress's recess. Notably, and in spite of the fact that no rule states that the Permanent Committee should have a plural composition, the body includes legislators of all parties represented in Congress.

Most of the powers of this committee are listed in article 78 of the Constitution and include, among others, the power to receive the bills introduced during Congress's recess and proposals addressed to the chambers, and to turn them over to the relevant committees; to call the

---

[21] L Valencia, *La Disciplina Parlamentaria en México: LVIII Legislatura de la Cámara de Diputados* (Mexico, UNAM, 2005) 207–16.

[22] M Bartlett, 'Perspectivas de la Auditoría Superior de la Federación como Organo Constitucional Autónomo' in J Ackerman and C Astudillo, *La Autonomía Constitucional de la Auditoría Superior de la Federación* (Mexico, UNAM, 2009) 89–98.

Congress or a single house, on its own motion or on the proposal of the Executive, to extraordinary sessions (in both cases the vote of two-thirds of the legislators present is required); to grant a leave of absence for 30 days to the president of the Republic and to appoint a president ad interim during such absence; and to ratify a series of high-office appointments made by the president of the Republic.

In addition, other powers of the committee can be found scattered around the constitutional text. Examples include the power to approve, during congressional recess, the president's designation of the members of the public agency in charge of organising the National System of Statistics and Geography; of the judges of the agrarian courts; and the members of Mexico's Central Bank (all these functions in principle correspond to the Senate).[23]

In practice, the Permanent Committee works as a forum of political deliberation, debating issues that are of concern to public opinion at specific junctures. As a result of these debates, it regularly makes requests or exhortations directed to the federal Executive, to adopt certain courses of action.[24]

VIII. THE POWERS OF CONGRESS

Congress has a series of powers scattered around different parts of the Constitution. It has the power to legislate in connection with a broad set of matters listed in article 73 of the Constitution. It has the so-called power of the purse (on which I will elaborate later on). It has powers to designate an interim president in cases of temporary or absolute absence of the incumbent according to article 84 of the Constitution, and it has powers to check the Executive (some of which shall be discussed in section X of this chapter).

Some of these powers are exercised by the two chambers of Congress, but some others are exclusive to one or the other chamber. For example, the Chamber of Deputies has the exclusive power to approve the budget proposed by the Executive; and it also has the exclusive power to designate the councillors of the IFE and the top official of the Superior

---

[23] Articles 26.B, 27.XIX and 28, para 7 of the Constitution.
[24] For example, the Permanent Committee's Agreement of 29 August 2005, exhorting the Executive to start a campaign against homophobia.

Audit of the Federation, as well as to 'coordinate and evaluate the performance' of this office (see below, section XII of this chapter). For its part, the Senate has the exclusive power: to designate Justices of the Supreme Court (on the basis of three-name lists presented by the president of the Republic); to approve international treaties negotiated by the president; and to approve the 'friendly agreements' to resolve conflicts of territorial limits between different States, among others.

Under the period of the hegemonic party system, the exercise of Congress's powers was subordinated to the president's programme and political needs. Today, in the context of a multi-party system that has been developing since the late 1970s, political actors in Congress tend to align themselves on the basis of political party identities and memberships, developing practices of cooperation and conflict depending on the political conjuncture and the different issues.

In this way, on the one hand, it is relevant to notice that cooperation is not uncommon. In her analysis of Executive-Legislative relations under divided government in Mexico, Casar reports that legislative activity has not suffered quantitatively: the number of bills presented in Congress and the number of bills passed have been growing in absolute terms; the time taken to pass a bill has not been substantially altered; the rate of rejection of bills has not increased; and while the rate of approval of the Executive's bills has diminished greatly, it is still high for a divided government.[25]

It is true that this kind of multi-party consensus has not been present in all policy areas and subject matters: from a qualitative perspective, most initiatives of Mexican presidents under divided government which have been crucial to the pursuance of their main economic projects (taxation, energy, labour, pensions and telecommunications) were defeated.[26] Nevertheless, divided government has not produced legislative paralysis or systematic opposition to the president's legislative agenda.

On the other hand, it is also possible to identify a pattern of conflict in connection with the relationship between the president and Congress.

---

[25] The rate of approval for the Executive's bills declined from an average of 98 per cent during the hegemonic party system to just above 80 per cent during the second half of Zedillo's administration (1997–2000), to an average of 65 per cent during the Fox administration (2000–2006). See MA Casar, 'Executive-Legislative Relations: Continuity or Change?' in Selee and Peschard (2010), n 5 above, 127–29.

[26] *ibid*, at 129.

This pattern has emerged as the result of the 1994 reforms that strengthened the Supreme Court in its functions as a constitutional court,[27] in the context of divided government and of a Congress ready to use recently created judicial procedures to challenge some decisions of the Executive.

The first notorious challenge to Executive power consisted of a constitutional controversy (26/99) brought by the Chamber of Deputies against the president's refusal to disclose information that was required by an accountancy firm hired by that Chamber to conduct an audit of a special fund (FOBAPROA, which stands for Banking Fund for the Protection of Savings) created in 1990. This fund was used in 1995 in order to support banks that were in trouble as a consequence of the financial crisis that erupted in December of 1994. Basically, the FOBAPROA was a public trust which assumed the performance of loans by banks that were at risk of insolvency when a massive number of people and companies were unable to pay as a consequence of skyrocketing interest rates. Since this amounted to converting an amount of 552 billion pesos into public debt, Congress decided to order an audit to investigate FOBAPROA's operations.

Yet the Ministry of Finance and other financial regulatory agencies refused to disclose the required information, and the Executive refused to order those agencies to do what the Chamber of Deputies required. Therefore, the latter filed a constitutional controversy, alleging an 'indirect violation' of the Constitution: the constitutional principle of legality was violated because the Executive had contradicted a series of rules established in different statutes, which imposed on the president the duty to disclose the information requested by the Chamber of Deputies.[28]

The Supreme Court (comprising 11 Justices), using its power to 'supplement the complaint' (*suplencia de la queja*), decided unanimously in favour of the plaintiff, but on reasons that were different on those alleged by the latter. For the Court: a) the Chamber of Deputies had 'the widest powers' to review the public account of the federal government under article 74.IV of the Constitution, and these powers included the power to request all the information that was required to achieve its goals; b) Congress had the power to 'recognise and order the payment'

---

[27] This topic will be analysed in more detail in section V of chapter 5 of this book.
[28] 'Indirect', because the constitutional violation is the result of a legal violation.

of the national debt, as well as the power to request all the information that was necessary to evaluate if the recognition of public debt was appropriate or not; and c) all Secretaries of State had the duty to inform Congress on any matter of their competence, according to article 93 of the Constitution. In view of this, the refusal of the Executive to disclose the information prevented Congress from exercising its constitutional powers. For that reason, the Court declared that the refusal was invalid, and ordered the Executive to disclose the information.[29]

This case illustrates a pattern of conflict between the Executive and Congress, mediated by the Supreme Court. We will see another example of this pattern of conflict in connection with the dispute between two different public-policy views on the management of the so-called 'strategic areas' of the economy; that is, certain areas of economic activity that the Constitution reserves to the federal government, with the exclusion of the private sector (see Chapter 8 of this book on 'The Constitution and the National Economy').

IX. THE LEGISLATIVE PROCESS

One of the most important changes in Mexico's political system in recent decades has been the shift of power from the Executive to the federal Congress, both in terms of agenda-setting and policy-making. In short, Congress has become a locus of power.[30] However, I would qualify this statement saying that it is applicable more in connection with the legislative process than with the Legislature's power to check the Executive.

According to article 71 of the Constitution, the power to introduce bills for consideration is vested in: the president of the Republic; deputies and senators of the federal Congress; State legislatures; and a number of citizens that is equivalent to no less than 0.13 per cent of registered voters.[31] Moreover, it has to be noticed that the president of

---

[29] SCJ, Constitutional controversy 26/99. *Chamber of Deputies of the Congress of the Union v Federal Executive, Semanario Judicial de la Federación y su Gaceta*, Ninth Epoch, Plenary session, XII, August 2000, pp 575–962.

[30] MA Casar, 'Executive-Legislative Relations: Continuity or Change?' in Selee and Peschard (2010), n 5 above, 117.

[31] 'Popular legislative initiative' was introduced into the Constitution by the recent reform of 9 August 2012.

the Republic has the exclusive power to introduce bills that refer to federal income and budget of each year.[32]

During the years of the hegemonic party system the Executive was the political actor that introduced most of the bills.[33] However, this situation has changed notably since the LVII Congress (1997–2000), which was the first in which the PRI did not have an absolute majority of seats in the lower chamber. As reported by Casar, of the 2,013 bills presented during the first three years of the Calderón administration (2006–09), only 37 were initiated by the Executive.[34]

With respect to deputies and senators, the Constitution does not foresee a specific number of legislators required to exercise the power to introduce bills; therefore, it is understood that this can be done either by individual legislators or groups of them. Finally, State legislatures also have power to introduce bills in the general Congress, but in practice they do not do so often.

The rules on the relationship between the Chamber of Deputies and the Senate in the context of the legislative process can be found in article 72 of the Constitution. Essentially, both chambers of Congress must agree on the text of a bill, both in general and article-by-article, in order to refer it to the president of the Republic (who shall either promulgate the new statute or veto the bill). The approval of a report in general and article-by-article requires the majority of the legislators present.

A recent constitutional reform, published on 9 August 2012, has granted a new power to the president of the Republic in connection with the legislative process, known as the 'priority legislative procedure': at the opening of periods of ordinary sessions of Congress, the Executive can introduce up to two bills that shall receive preferential treatment. Each house of Congress has to discuss and vote on the bill in a specific time frame (within 30 days after introduction of the bill by the Executive or after the referral by the house that discussed and voted the bill in the first place).[35]

[32] Article 74.IV of the Constitution, paras 1 and 2.
[33] Victor Manzanilla reports that in the early 1980s, for instance, around 98 per cent of the bills came from the federal executive power. Quoted by J Orozco, 'Las Legislaturas y sus funciones de control sobre la actividad gubernamental' in Coloquio Senado de la República/UNAM, *Política y Proceso Legislativos* (Mexico, Senado de la República/UNAM/Miguel Angel Porrúa, 1985) 37.
[34] MA Casar, 'Executive-Legislative Relations: Continuity or Change?' in Selee and Peschard (2010), n 5 above, 132.
[35] See article 72 of the Constitution.

Finally, the president of the Republic has the power to veto legislation passed by Congress. Nevertheless, it can be overcome by a two-
thirds majority in each house of Congress, in which case the Executive
has to publish the new statute in the 'Official Gazette of the Federation'.[36]
Usually, the statute shall be valid as of the day of its publication or at
such later time as is outlined in the statute's 'transitory articles'.[37]

Divided government produced an unprecedented surge in legislative
activism. As explained by Nacif, the number of bills introduced by
opposition parties increased substantially at the same time that the
amount of Executive-initiated legislation decreased. All actors made an
adjustment in their law-making behaviour as the balance of power
changed. Legislators anticipated that their capacity to influence the process of legislation had increased substantially, and they responded by
introducing bills in areas of legislation in which only the Executive had
formerly taken the initiative.[38] Contrary to the expectation that divided
government would produce legislative gridlock, Mexico's federal legislative process is now highly productive, as the result of multi-party coalitions formed to approve bills. Notably, the most common legislative
coalition formed in Congress – regardless of the bill's origin – has been
that of all parties.[39]

X. CONGRESS'S POWERS TO CHECK THE EXECUTIVE

1. Investigation Committees

Apart from the power of ordinary committees to request information
and documents from the agencies and entities of the federal public
administration in the terms explained above, both houses of Congress
have the power to constitute committees of investigation. This possibility was introduced as part of the 1977 constitutional reform, which created 100 PR seats in the Chamber of Deputies, in addition to the already

[36] The veto power of the Executive will be examined in more detail in section V
of chapter 4 of this book.
[37] 'Transitory articles' are rules established in the final part of statutes, which
refer to the conditions for the statute's entrance into force.
[38] B Nacif, 'The Fall of the Dominant Presidency: Lawmaking under Divided
Government in Mexico', *Cuaderno de Trabajo No 185* (Mexico, CIDE, 2006) 11.
[39] MA Casar, 'Executive-Legislative Relations: Continuity or Change?' in Selee and
Peschard (2010), n 5 above, 128–29.

existent 300 plurality (FPTP) seats, in order to give access to opposition parties in that house.[40] The reform package also empowered one-quarter of the deputies and half of the senators to request the formation of investigative committees in order to investigate matters related to specific kinds of federal public agencies: the so-called 'de-centralised' agencies[41] and enterprises in which the federal government holds the majority of the stock.

Between the date of this reform (1977) and the end of the hegemonic party system in 2000, few investigative committees were formed (7), and when they were, their work was delayed and hampered in different ways. The issues they had to investigate included, for example: accusations that the telephones of social, political and business leaders had been tapped; illegal practices in the liquidation of the National Bank of Fishing and Ports (BANPESCA); corruption charges against the brother of a former president of the Republic in connection with operations of a state-owned commercial food enterprise where the accused had been planning director; and illegal financial operations of the Federal Electricity Commission.[42] Yet, as reported by Ugalde, the activities of those investigative committees had lacklustre results. Either because they were undermined from within (as PRI legislators controlled the majority of the committee's seats and therefore were able to work in favour of the government officials who were under investigation); or because authorities under investigation were able to hide information that was required by the committees to do their job properly, in the absence of legal mechanisms and procedures to enforce disclosure and transparency.[43]

Indeed, the end of the hegemonic party system has not meant a strengthening of investigative committees, since they still show institutional weakness, at the same time as the agencies and persons implicated in investigations have shown their power to resist them.

---

[40] In 1986 the number of PR seats was increased to 200.

[41] These are basically public enterprises that are governed by rules that to some extent resemble those of private companies, rather than those of the public administration and bureaucracy.

[42] LC Ugalde, *The Mexican Congress, Old Player, New Power* (Washington DC, The CSIS Press, 2000) 66–91.

[43] *ibid.*

2. President's Duty to Inform

Before the reform of 15 August 2008, article 69 of the Constitution stated that the president had the duty to attend the opening of the first period of ordinary sessions of the Congress, in order to submit a report, in writing, on the general state of the country's administration. Under the original text, the president did not have the duty to actually read the report before Congress; though this happened in practice, in a tradition that went back to the very origins of Mexico's constitutional history.

The reform of 2008 removed the duty of the president to attend the opening session of Congress. The reason given was that the format of the presidential report did not correspond to the new democratic and multi-party era. Indeed, the original provision had been criticised for many years, mostly because under the hegemonic party system, the reading of the report by the president before Congress had transformed itself into a ceremony to show devotion and loyalty to the chief of the Executive. In turn, this kind of criticism eventually had led to a series of reforms to the OLC which had sought to make of this act a Republican ceremony in which the president and Congress could publicly find themselves face-to-face, in order to exchange points of view on the evaluation of the state of the Union and the performance of the president's administration in the respective year. For instance, one of those legal reforms established a procedure by which prior to the president's arrival at the Congress session, a legislator of each of the parliamentary groups with representation in the federal Legislature would be able to take the Congress floor in order to make explicit his party's political position towards the government.

Nevertheless, the reform of 2008 broke with this logic by removing the president's duty to attend Congress. No doubt, this reform was influenced by recent historical experience of presidential reports, in which, rather than an exchange of different political views, what prevailed was a culture of no-dialogue and even insults among the different political parties and between the Executive and some legislators, in the context of the increasing polarisation of Mexican politics.

In addition, the 2008 reform introduced a second paragraph into article 69, according to which both houses of Congress would be responsible for making an analysis of the president's report (this is hardly a novelty, since it was already allowed under the text of article 69 before the 2008 reform); and empowered federal legislators to request from the president the production of additional information related to the report, through questions filed in writing. Moreover, this new paragraph also empowered each house of Congress to summon the secretaries of state, the Attorney General and the heads of public enterprises, who must attend the call (this is not new either) and must produce the requested reports under oath (this is a novelty).

Mexican legislators have posed many parliamentary questions to the Executive since the reform of 2008 opened this possibility. For example, in the context of the review and debates of the 2008 presidential report on the state of the Union, the different parliamentary groups of the Chamber of Deputies formulated 68 questions to the Executive, related to most matters of the federal government's competence. All the answers were published in the Parliamentary Gazette of that house.[44]

XI. JURISDICTIONAL-LIKE FUNCTIONS OF CONGRESS

The chambers of Congress perform a jurisdictional-like function through two procedures that resemble what in other countries is known as impeachment. These two procedures are: a) the so-called 'political trial'; and b) the declaration to allow the prosecution of certain public servants (listed in article 111 of the Constitution). Both procedures are foreseen in Title Four of the Constitution, which refers to the 'Responsibilities of public servants and the patrimonial liabilities of the State'.

The current shape of the rules of this Title comes from the constitutional reform of 28 December 1982, which was proposed by President Miguel de la Madrid as part of a strategy of reconciliation with the private sector (harmed by the expropriation of private banks decreed by the previous president in September 1982). This reconciliation strategy had two main elements: on the one hand, the establishment of clear limits on the kind of areas, activities and responsibilities of the public and the private sectors respectively (we will review this topic in Chapter 8 of this book); and on the other hand, the introduction of new constitutional rules on the liability of public servants, to respond to the private sector's accusations of widespread corruption and waste of government officials.

---

[44] *Parliamentary Gazette*, Year XII, no 2643, Chamber of Deputies, 27 November 2008.

1. Political Trial

At a general level, this procedure is governed by article 110 of the Constitution, but all its details can be found in the Federal Act on the Responsibilities of Public Servants. In our account of the procedure we shall examine what is established in the Constitution, without reference to the Act, but at least a couple of references to the Act have to be made, in order to understand the kind of conduct that may lead to political responsibility.

In this way, article 6 of the Act states that a political trial may be initiated whenever acts or omissions of public servants referred to in article 110 of the Constitution produce harm to 'fundamental public interests'. In turn, article 7 of the same statute defines as conduct that causes harm to 'fundamental public interests': an act of aggression against democratic institutions; serious and systematic violations of fundamental rights; acts of aggressions against the freedom to vote; undue use of public authority; acts or omissions that produce violations of the Constitution or to federal statutes whenever they cause serious damage to the Federation, to one or more States, or to society, or that produce a disruption in the normal functioning of institutions; and the systematic or serious violations of plans, programmes and budgets of the federal public administration or of the Federal District, and to the statutes that determine the handling of federal and Federal District's economic resources.

Furthermore, article 7 states that the mere expression of ideas shall not give rise to a political trial, and that the federal Congress shall assess the existence and gravity of the acts or omissions referred to as the conduct under examination, clarifying that if it is found that a crime has been committed, the procedure of declaration to allow the prosecution of public servants shall be activated.

The public servants that can be the subject of a political trial are listed in article 110 of the Constitution. In summary, the list includes all the top federal public servants of the legislative, executive and judicial branches of government, plus the heads of other 'autonomous constitutional entities' (such as the IFE). Notably, the president of the Republic is not included in this list: he cannot be subjected to political responsibility by the procedure examined here.

State governors, State legislators, Magistrates of State superior courts of justice and members of State councils of the judiciary may be the subject of political trial under the Constitution and the corresponding federal statutes. However, in this hypothesis the resolution shall only have a declaratory effect, which shall be communicated to the corresponding State legislature, so that it may proceed in the way that it may consider proper, according to its own constitution and competences.

In this procedure, after taking notice of an accusation, the Chamber of Deputies has to assess whether or not the public servant in question has committed any of the acts or omissions defined in article 7 of the Federal Act on the Responsibilities of Public Servants. If, after a procedure that grants due process rights to the accused as required by article 110 of the Constitution, the lower house decides by the vote of an absolute majority of the deputies present that this has been the case, it shall proceed to sustain the charges before the Senate.

For its part, and after hearing the accusation and giving the accused public servant the opportunity to defend himself, the Senate shall declare by the vote of a two-thirds majority of the senators present, either that the accused is innocent or guilty, and, in the latter case, the sanction that shall be imposed on him. Finally, the sanctions shall consist of the dismissal of the public servant from his position, and it can also include his disqualification from public office for a period of up to 20 years.[45] In this procedure, the declarations and resolutions of the two chambers of Congress are final and cannot be challenged.

In Mexico's political process, it is relatively common to make requests for political trial against adversaries or to threaten to make them. It is part of the language of confrontation that has been developed in Mexico during recent decades, but in actual practice political trials conducted by the federal Congress have seldom occurred.

At State level there are a few cases, in which the Supreme Court has had the opportunity to produce a couple of interesting criteria. For instance, in 1998, the Congress of the State of Morelos filed an accusation against the governor of that State, Jorge Carrillo Olea,[46] alleging that he was liable for causing serious harm to fundamental public interests, as a consequence of his failure to comply with his constitutional duties to fight organised crime, and for having allowed the operation of criminal groups related to drug-trafficking and several cases of kidnapping.

---

[45] Articles 110 of the Constitution and 8 of the Federal Act on the Administrative Responsibilities of Public Servants.
[46] Notably, Carrillo Olea had been the head of the intelligence agency of the federal government between 1989 and 1990.

As required by the Constitution of Morelos, the State legislature filed the petition to the Superior Tribunal of that State, seeking the governor's removal and disqualification as a public servant for the maximum period allowed by State law, as well as an order prohibiting him from leaving the State territory. Yet, the Superior Tribunal dismissed the petition, reasoning that the Constitution of Morelos did not expressly subject the governor to the possibility of a political trial. Against this decision, the Congress of Morelos filed a constitutional controversy (21/99) to the Supreme Court alleging that the federal Constitution *did* subject all governors to the possibility of political trials. The Supreme Court decided in favour of the Congress, stating that article 137 of Morelos's Constitution had to be interpreted in a systemic way, that is to say, in connection with article 135 of that Constitution which stated that the governor and other public servants of Morelos shall be responsible in terms of Title Four of the federal Constitution. Moreover, the Supreme Court also was of the opinion that Morelos's Constitution had to be interpreted in a harmonic way, that is, in the light of article 109 of the federal Constitution, according to which the sanctions established in article 110 of that Constitution (removal and disqualification as a public servant) shall be imposed on the public servants mentioned in that article (which includes State governors). At the end of the day, this meant that State governors can be subject to a political trial, even if State constitutions do not expressly allow that possibility.[47]

The consequence of this decision was the invalidation of the decision of the Morelos Superior Tribunal that dismissed the petition of political trial. In the end, the procedure went on, leading to the removal of Carrillo Olea as governor and his disqualification from occupying any public office for 12 years.[48]

---

[47] SCJ, Constitutional controversy 21/99, published in the *Semanario Judicial de la Federación y su Gaceta*, vol XI, February 2000, p 516.

[48] On the criminal trial front, on 29 January 2004, Carrillo Olea was found not guilty by the Second Chamber of the Morelos Superior Tribunal of Justices in connection with the crimes of 'non-fulfilment of public functions' and 'undue exercise of public functions' of which he had been accused by the State attorney general.

2. Declaration that Allows the Prosecution of Certain Public Servants

This procedure is governed by article 111 of the Constitution. Basically, it implies that certain public servants (who are listed in this article)[49] have the privilege of being relatively immune to criminal prosecution. The immunity is relative because it can be removed by the procedure established in article 111, whose purpose is to create an obstacle to the possibility of politically-motivated criminal accusations and prosecutions against certain public servants. The intention is to protect the public function they perform from these kinds of pressures.

According to this procedure, if criminal charges are brought against a public servant listed in article 111, the prosecution cannot proceed in the absence of a declaration by the Chamber of Deputies allowing this possibility. This declaration has to be approved by an absolute majority of the deputies present, and its effect consists of the deprivation of the public servant's immunity, his removal from public office for the duration of the criminal trial he is supposed to face, and his submission to the jurisdiction of the corresponding criminal court. However, if the trial concludes with an acquittal, the public servant in question shall be allowed to return to his office.

Interestingly, the president of the Republic *can* be subjected to this procedure, in which case the Constitution has established a procedure similar to the one described above for political trial: the Chamber of Deputies would have to sustain the charges against the president, acting like a prosecutor, and the Senate would decide, acting as a court, whether the president were guilty or not and, given the case, the appropriate sanction (removal from office and the penalty foreseen in the criminal code (Federal Criminal Code) for the crime that was committed). In spite of this, we have to recall that according to article 109, the president can only be prosecuted for 'treason to the country' or for 'serious crimes'. The former is a crime foreseen in the military criminal code (Code of Military Justice) and involves helping the county's enemies in time of war; while the latter is a vague and ambiguous term, not well

---

[49] The list essentially coincides with the one of article 110 examined above. However, the Directors General or their equivalents of de-centralised organisations, enterprises of State participation, societies and associations assimilated into the latter, and public trusts are not covered by this immunity.

defined by the Constitution, or by statute law, or by legal doctrine, a situation that further shelters the president from congressional mechanisms of accountability.

Since 1917, this procedure has been put into practice on four occasions: a) against Senator Jorge Diaz Serrano, for acts of corruption committed during the time he had been General Director of the public petroleum enterprise, PEMEX. He had also been a candidate for the presidency against of the incumbent president, and at least partly responsible for the huge public debt acquired by Mexico in the presidential administration of 1976–82; b) against Rene Bejarano in 2004, accused of using illicit funds to finance electoral campaigns; c) in 2005, against the Chief of government of the Federal District; and d) against federal Deputy Julio Cesar Godoy in 2010, for alleged money laundering in favour of one of the drug cartels that operate in Mexico.

In spite of the constitutional and legal provisions on public servants' responsibility described in this section, Mexico ranks low in terms of the honesty of its public servants. According to Transparency International's corruption perception index of 2011, Mexico ranks 100th with a score of 3.0, in a list in which New Zealand ranks 1st with a score of 9.5 and Somalia ranks 182nd with a score of 1.0. This is an indication that the beautiful words put into the Constitution do not work well in actual practice. The reasons for this are many, one of them being powerful resistance to making the instruments of political and administrative accountability truly work, as the experience of the SAF shows.

XII. THE 'SUPERIOR AUDIT OF THE FEDERATION'

In 1999, and in a context in which the hegemonic party had lost the absolute majority in the lower house of Congress for the first time in more than 60 years, the Mexican Constitution was reformed in order to create a new system for the supervision of public expenditures. This reform created the Superior Audit of the Federation (SAF), an entity with autonomy granted by the Constitution,[50] which was assigned broad powers to review the annual Federal Account and to determine damage in the use of public federal funds, as well as to hold specific public servants responsible for the misuse of public funds.

---

[50] Article 79 of the Mexican Constitution.

Later on, social demands for increased accountability and for better use of public funds led to a second round of constitutional reforms (promulgated on 7 May 2008) that, in summary, empowered the federal Congress to pass legislation to homologate public accountings at the federal, State, municipal and Federal District levels; defined with more precision the subjects under supervision (including federal, State, municipal and Federal District authorities that receive and expend federal funds,[51] but also every other entity, be it a physical or juristic person, public or private, that receives and expends federal funds).

Moreover, the constitutional reform of 7 May 2008 also established the duty of the subjects under supervision to follow specific criteria determined by the corresponding statute law in their own accountancy,[52] in their patrimonial and budgetary control systems, and in their registry of the federal funds transferred to them; in addition, the reform also empowered the SAF to carry out audits of performance, that is, audits that go beyond the logic of accountancy, that seek to determine whether the subjects under supervision have complied with the objectives and goals of approved plans and programmes or not. In this case, the SAF can issue recommendations directed to improve the performance of the supervised entities.

Yet, a review of the SAF's recent activities, reveals the existence of powerful resistances against the full and efficacious performance of its duties and functions. For example, in 2004 the SAF asked the Ministry of Energy and the Regulatory Commission of Energy to review their procedures for granting permits to national and foreign private enterprises to produce electric power. The SAF gave both public entities 45 days to comply with its 'observations' and 'recommendations', stating that in case of failing to do so, it would proceed to request the reposition of the administrative procedures related to the granting of the permits. In essence, what the SAF argued was that these permits were unconstitutional, taking into consideration that article 27 of Mexico's Constitution states that

---

[51] With the exception of 'federal participations', which will be explained later in this book.

[52] *Ley de Fiscalización y rendición de cuentas de la Federación* (Act on Inspection and Accountability of the Federation) published on 29 May 2009. This statute derogated from the previous *Ley de Fiscalización Superior de la Federación* (Act on Superior Inspection of the Federation), which had been published on 29 December 2000.

It is of exclusive competence of the Nation to produce, transmit, transform, distribute and supply electric power that has the object the provision of public service. In this matter concessions shall not be granted to private entities and the Nation shall benefit from the goods and natural resources that are required for that purpose.

From the SAF's perspective, the unconstitutionality derived from the fact that in some permits private entities were allowed to sell electric power to entities other than the Federal Commission of Electric Power. The actual goal of the recommendations was to modify the way and conditions under which the permits were being granted by the federal government; and to determine possible responsibilities of public servants that granted those permits in an 'irregular' way.[53]

According to the Executive this intervention of the SAF violated the principle of separation of powers, and constituted an undue and unconstitutional extension of SAF's powers. From the Executive's perspective, the SAF was trying to replace the Executive in what constituted exclusive powers of the Executive (that is, granting the permits), and was also replacing the federal judicial power, issuing recommendations whose goal was to invalidate administrative acts for being contrary to the Constitution.

In a 6-5 vote, the majority of the Justices considered that the SAF had gone beyond its powers granted by the Constitution which, in short, were referred to the revision of the annual account of the federal government in what has to do with the State's 'financial management'. In turn, this concept did not imply the power to review the administrative acts that had led to grant the permits related to the production of electric power. The Court stated that all the acts related to granting the permits for the production of electric power (applications forms, the examination of applications, the collection of royalties, the issuing of the permit title, the revision of how a licensee complies with the conditions and terms of the permit, and the imposition of sanctions) were of the exclusive competence of the Union's Executive, and corresponded to the Regulatory Commission on Energy.

The recent history of the SAF, in this and other cases that we have not discussed in this work, shows that some political actors at the highest level of Mexico's political system have played in favour of limiting

---

[53] This dispute is related to the constitutional battle explained in section VIII of this chapter.

the supervision capabilities and powers of an agency that was supposed to strengthen accountability in the use of federal funds.

XIII. CONCLUSION

The breakdown of the hegemonic party system produced the need to make structural changes in Congress. Pluralism in its two houses required the creation of new rules for the organisation of legislative work and activities. Moreover, the new context has also induced the search for a new role of the different branches of government and new patterns of relation in the constitutional system. With respect to the federal Congress, some modifications have already taken place, but still the new powers face serious limitations in actual practice.

The agenda for the reform of Congress is wide. One of the most important issues has to do with the removal of the prohibition of immediate re-election of federal legislators. With this measure, the quality of representation would improve, as legislators would be directly accountable to their constituencies every three (deputies) or six years (senators). Constituencies would be able to punish or reward bad or good legislators. In addition, this measure could provide job stability to 'good' legislators (those who work for their constituencies and are rewarded for doing so), which in turn could have an impact on the quality of their work within congressional commissions, thanks to accumulated experience.

Other reform proposals imply deeper structural changes, under the assumption that while electoral institutions have been fundamentally modified, the institutions of government have remained basically the same. In this way, some analysts have argued that in the new context, the structure of Mexico's presidential system must change: what the country's constitutional system needs is a parliamentarisation of the presidential system.[54] This would mean, among other measures, granting Congress the power to ratify some or all of the secretaries of the cabinet and some form of congressional power to manifest its disapproval of secretaries of state. The assumption behind this kind of proposal is that in the context of 'divided governments' presidents need to build up coalitions in

---

[54] Valadés, Diego, *La parlamentarización de los sistemas presidenciales*, 2nd edn, (Mexico, UNAM, 2008).

order to have a solid base of support in Congress. In turn, this requires the negotiation and design of a coalition governmental programme and the introduction of parliamentary-like institutions and mechanisms into the logic of the still presidential system of government.

FURTHER READING

Mora Donatto, C (ed), *Relaciones entre el Gobierno y el Congreso* (Mexico, UNAM, 2002).

Mora Donatto, C, 'Oposición y Control Parlamentario en México' (2010) 23 *Cuestiones Constitucionales* 121.

Pedroza de la Llave, Susana Thalía, *El Control del Gobierno: Función del Poder Legislativo* (Mexico, UNAM/INAP, 1996).

Rodríguez Lozano, A, *La Reforma del Poder Legislativo en México* (Mexico, UNAM, 1998).

Serna de la Garza, JM, 'Derecho Parlamentario' in *Enciclopedia Jurídica Mexicana* (Mexico, UNAM/Porrúa, 2002).

4

The Executive Branch of Government: Presidencialismo

Introduction – The Formation of the Tradition of a Strong Executive Power – Social Change, Economic Reorganisation and Constitutional Reform: The End of the Hegemonic Party System – Election of the President and his Position as Both Head of State and Head of Government – The President and the Legislative Process – The President and the Fiscal Process – Conclusions

I. INTRODUCTION

MEXICO'S PRESIDENTIAL SYSTEM, in which executive power has been exercised under conditions of authoritarian government, has been known as *presidencialismo*.[1] This was the form of government that prevailed during the successive administrations of General Porfirio Díaz (1877–1911), as well as during the days of the hegemonic party system (1929–2000). In those years, in spite of having a formal constitution ascribed to the principles of political liberalism and democracy, the political process was decidedly unbalanced in favour of the federal Executive. Constitutional principles such as separation of powers and federalism remained, as it were, dormant, as Mexico's presidents were able to subordinate the legislative and judicial branches of government, as well as State governors.

The transformation process of the hegemonic party system in the terms I have explained in the previous chapters has deprived the president

---

[1] See S Zamora and JR Cossío, 'Mexican constitutionalism after *presidencialismo*' (2006) 4 *International Journal of Constitutional Law* 412.

of some of the powers that made of him the undisputed centre (or apex) of the entire political system. This does not mean that he is at the mercy of the legislative and judicial powers. Rather, a new balance among the different branches of government has been under construction in the last decades, characterised by a pattern of negotiation and conflict between the executive and legislative powers, mediated by an increasingly important Supreme Court of Justice.

In this chapter I shall analyse this process, in the following order. First, I shall examine the formation of what can rightly be identified as the tradition of a strong executive power in Mexico or *presidencialismo*; secondly, I will explain how social change, the economic re-organisation of the country and constitutional reform created the basis for the end of the hegemonic party system, thus creating the need to define a new role for the Executive under the new circumstances. Thirdly, I will refer to the rules on the election of the president and examine his position as both head of state and head of government. Fourthly, I will review the president's role in the legislative process (mainly through the power to introduce bills and the power to veto legislation). And, finally, I shall study the president's powers relative to the fiscal process, and the emerging pattern of relationships with Congress in connection with the legislative process.

II. THE FORMATION OF THE TRADITION OF A STRONG EXECUTIVE POWER

When studying the history of political institutions of contemporary Mexico, there is a theme that emerges again and again, at every step of their process of formation: the issue of political control. By this I mean that, vis-à-vis powerful factors pushing for fragmentation, secession and polarisation, Mexican political leaders have had as their most important priority the construction of mechanisms to counteract the tendencies that have posed actual or potential threats to the existence of every possible kind of political order.

In fact, this concern with political control has been present since the earliest attempts to construct a nation state in Mexico. We find it in the 'Restored Republic' (restored after the French imperial adventure), when President Juárez had to resort to permanent 'extraordinary' powers in order to be able to govern in the face of the constant threats posed by the regional '*caciques*' to the federal Executive. And we find it too in General Díaz's dictatorship, which established a system of political control based on concessions to regional elites, limitations to their capacity to compete for political positions, and on the use of military force to subjugate both them and the impoverished masses. This concern for maintaining political control was also present in the construction of the post-revolutionary political regime, as the new political leaders tried to pacify the country and establish a nation-wide political order.

It is important to point out that the emphasis on control, as I am using it here, has appeared in the context of specific patterns of political participation and social conflict. That is, the characteristics of participation and conflict prevalent in Mexico have been fundamental in explaining the mechanisms of control that have been introduced. For instance, in the nineteenth century, political participation was dominated by the regional elite, that is, the large landowners and their middle-class allies, who controlled access both to the federal and local bureaucracies, and to the federal Congress. Conflict over the formation of a nation-state was set, on the one hand, in terms of the struggle between the local '*cacicazgos*' (whose main institutional base at the federal level was the Congress), and the federal Executive. On the other hand, the other major source of conflict was the struggle of popular sectors of the population to break with a harsh system of domination.

It is also relevant to mention at this point the work and thought of Emilio Rabasa, who wrote an influential analysis published in 1912, on the predominance of the executive power in Mexico's constitutional history. In his seminal book *The Constitution and Dictatorship*, he tried to demonstrate that dictatorship had been the result of a wrong constitutional design. In his view, the Constitution of 1857 had established a fundamental unbalance between the Legislature and the Executive, giving supremacy to the former, and limiting the latter. Nevertheless, the specific circumstances of Mexico, which had to do with its formation as an independent state and the difficulties of achieving national unity, required a strong Executive capable of resisting forces that pushed for disintegration and dispersion. In turn, the lack of compatibility between constitutional forms and urgent political needs had led the Executive to overrun the constitution. The logical consequence – Rabasa argued – was dictatorship, whose highest expression was found in the regime of General Porfirio Díaz, who stayed in power for more than 30 years. Yet, as a remedy against this trend and outcome, Rabasa proposed to adjust the Constitution to Mexico's reality: the Constitution has to establish an active and strong Executive, with a broad (but clearly defined) area of competence.[2] Importantly, this diagnosis and recommendation influenced the constituent assembly that designed the Constitution of 1917.[3]

At the beginning of the twentieth century, the Mexican revolution set in motion social forces that sought the creation of a political space for their social and economic demands. Peasants and workers, who had been previously denied the right to participate meaningfully in the political process, mobilised militarily to assure some recognition of their needs and claims. This came to broaden once more the scope of conflict in Mexico to a very large extent. Even after the civil war had finished, the country displayed dispersed and powerful social forces, divided in terms not only of region, but also of class, cultural traditions, personal loyalties, and political ambitions. Integration was low and the level of conflict was very high. Under such conditions, it is not surprising that during the 1920s, every government failed to maintain definite political stability in the country at large.[4]

It is against this background of anarchy that we can understand the emergence of the 'logic of control', again, as a dominant factor of Mexican politics. The group of generals who had won the civil war introduced gradually and pragmatically, in a process of trial-and-error, a set of mechanisms for regulating the political participation of all groups, for controlling their interactions, and for reducing the level of conflict. Even though they were backed by military power, the introduction of these controls entailed a great deal of negotiations, compromise and alliance formation between the governing group and the most relevant social forces. The result of those negotiations was the coalition that was

---

[2] E Rabasa, *La Constitución y la Dictadura* 10th edn (Mexico, Porrúa 2006) 112–14.

[3] For an examination of Rabasa's influence on México's twentieth-century constitutionalism see CA Hale, *Emilio Rabasa and the Survival of Porfirian Liberalism, The Man, his Career, and His Ideas, 1856–1930* (Stanford CA, Stanford University Press, 2008).

[4] President Carranza was assassinated in 1920 as a result of the '*Agua Prieta*' rebellion; in 1924 there was another rebellion organised by a group of generals who supported former President de la Huerta, which finished in a blood-shed; between 1926 and 1928 there was the civil war generated by the state-Catholic Church conflict; and as a result of the presidential elections of 1928, the three main contenders, Generals Serrano, Gómez and Obregón were assassinated (the latter being already the president elect).

the basis of the hegemonic party system that existed in Mexico for most of the twentieth century. During that period, Mexican political leaders regarded it as their most important responsibility to maintain such a coalition together, by using all the mechanisms of control and negotiation that they were able to devise (even if this had a negative impact on democracy and constitutional government).

Recapitulating, since the 1920s the main concern of Mexican national political leaders has been to bring under their control the main aspects of political participation of groups and individuals: elite competition, formulation of demands, generation of support, agenda-setting. To do so, they managed to build a very complex and expansive structure governed by the president of the Republic, that subordinated regional powers, limited competition from the political elite, regulated the political participation of other influential groups (ie businessmen, the Catholic Church) and of the popular sectors and the formulation of their demands, and that also assured the unity and obedience of the bureaucratic apparatus. This was achieved through the utilisation of the following modes of political action:

a) The particularistic and discretionary distribution of rewards (or their retention), such as money, patronage, privileges, status and political positions.

b) The control of elite political competition. The expectations of access to political power and of rotation in public office were constantly held through a system of elite circulation managed by the 'official' party and ultimately controlled by the president; the system promoted a high turnover rate, and avoided the appropriation of power by a single group.

c) The gradual and partial fulfilment of the social reforms contained in the Constitution. The implementation of programmes such as those of agrarian reform, social security and housing, and regulation of industrial relations, specifically targeted towards the most organised and mobilised sectors of the population, was conducive to the integration of these elements into the governing coalition.

d) The intervention of the government in the constitution of social representative bodies either by creating the organisations themselves, or by encouraging competition within and between the existing associations in order to bring about a leadership more akin with the government's programmes. The government could use all the

resources of the public administration to co-opt leaders and to iso-
late radical and reluctant elements.

e) The provision of controlled channels of access to policy-making in
areas of public activity relevant to the organised groups of society.
These were formal and informal mechanisms of consultation, advice
and communications that gave special interest associations an
opportunity to make their voice heard by the government in the formulation of policy. With this, a sense of participation was achieved,
thus enhancing integration in the coalition.

f) The use of a general and all-inclusive 'ideology of the Mexican revolution', that legitimised the governing group a priori, and to which all
the members of the coalition were committed in one way or another.

g) The threat of the use of force to bring into line the elite who refused
to join or stay in the coalition, or to eliminate radical elements who
refused to play under the system's rules.

Following to some extent Kaufman and Purcell's line of argument,[5]
we could say, thus, that working within the existing formal institutions
of the political regime, these practices were employed by political actors
to govern Mexico; and that the overlapping of institutions and practices
structured the peculiarly 'Mexican way' of dealing with political and
social conflict during the years of the hegemonic party system. Needless
to say, the president of the Republic sat at the apex of this complex
structure, which allowed the subordination of both the legislative and
judicial branches of government.

III. SOCIAL CHANGE, ECONOMIC REORGANISATION AND
CONSTITUTIONAL REFORM: THE END OF THE
HEGEMONIC PARTY SYSTEM

What distinguished Mexico's *presidencialismo* throughout most of the
twentieth century was the constant common party-political identity
between the president of the Republic and the majority in the federal
Congress, as well as the control that the former exercised over the latter.
In turn, the formation and maintenance of that identity can only be
understood as a result of the hegemonic party system that emerged

---

[5] S Kaufman, Purcell and J Purcell, 'State and Society in Mexico: Must a Stable
polity be Institutionalized?' (1982) 32 *World Politics* 195.

after the Mexican revolution. The special relationship between the president of the Republic and the hegemonic party (the PRI), was the axis of a complex political system that guaranteed governance in Mexico in terms of stability, efficacy and legitimacy. The crucial factor was the president's leadership of a party that incorporated most of the more important political and social forces in the country (eg trade unions and peasants' organisations); a party that in turn controlled the majority in Congress for many decades.

Notably, some of the bases on which the structure of power mentioned above was constructed underwent a series of relevant changes by the end of the twentieth century. This opened up the possibility of a change in the pattern of relations between the president and the federal Congress.

One of those changes was the transformation of the social and cultural context of the political system. For instance, the increase of Mexico's population was paramount: between 1917 and 1990, it increased from 14 million to 81.2 million people.[6] Moreover, in 1917, 71.2 per cent of the population lived in the rural areas; but by 1990 the same percentage lived in urban areas.[7] Finally, in 1917, 65.2 per cent of the population was illiterate but in 1990 this figure had been reduced to 12.4 per cent.[8]

The result of this transformation was a more complex and heterogenous society, whose political and social demands could neither be contained nor channelled by the traditional mechanisms of political control. In addition, since the early 1970s Mexico's strategy of economic development started to show signs of exhaustion: the period between 1958 and 1970 was characterised by high rates of economic growth and low inflation; yet the 1970s were characterised by economic slowdown, inflation, devaluation, increased public indebtedness and dependence on oil revenues, which in turn increased social and political unrest in the country at large.

In this context, PRI governments were forced to implement an ambitious programme of economic reforms in an attempt to establish the basis for renewed economic growth and stability. Yet, some of these reforms had an impact on the practices and strategies that Mexican presidents used to become the lynchpin of the political system, allowing

---

[6] In 2011 the population of Mexico amounted to 123.3 million persons.
[7] By 2011 78 per cent of Mexicans lived in urban areas.
[8] In 2011 6.9 per cent of the Mexican population remained illiterate.

the integration of major political and social forces into the hegemonic party system. Two examples of these reforms have to do with the modification of the rules on agrarian reform and the central bank, which will be explained below.

1. The New Agrarian Constitutional and Legal Rules of 1992

Before the reform of that year, the president was considered by article 27 of the Constitution as the 'highest agrarian authority'. That is to say, he was at the top of a structure of administrative authorities in charge of implementing the agrarian reform programme mandated by the Constitution. In practice, this meant that the president had the last word in connection with the expropriation of land and the division and redistribution of '*latifundios*'.[9]

These powers gave Mexican presidents a formidable instrument to build broad bases of support in the peasant sector. Indeed, Arnaldo Córdova has explained how the instruments and procedures derived from article 27 of the Constitution were the basis of an alliance formed between the president of the Republic and peasants' organisations, mostly during the 1930s.[10] In short, the terms of that alliance were these: the president would implement the agrarian reform programme using his broad powers in that area, and in return peasants' organisations would deliver political support to the president and the 'official' political party. This pact allowed the incorporation of most peasant organisations into the PRI. In this way, Mexican presidents had the direct support of these organisations, that were ready to mobilise in defence of the president's agrarian policies or his policies on other subject areas.[11]

However, in 1992 the constitutional and legal rules on the agrarian reform programme were changed.[12] Basically, the programme was can-

---

[9] '*Latifundios*' are extensions of land that exceed the limits allowed by the Constitution in its article 27.

[10] A Córdova, *La Ideología de la Revolución Mexicana*, 7th edn (Mexico, Era, 1979).

[11] Notably, Presidents Cárdenas (1936–40) and Echeverría (1970–76) resorted to peasant mobilisations to consolidate power and to strengthen themselves in their conflict with Mexico's private sector.

[12] The promoter of the constitutional amendment was President Carlos Salinas (1988–94).

celled, under the argument that there was no more land to distribute. Moreover, the constitutional right of peasant communities to 'apply' for land was taken out of the constitutional text; peasant communities, known as '*ejidos*', were allowed to transform part of their land from the collective to the private ownership regime (and thus set it up as collateral for obtaining credit) and to enter into association with private investors, under certain conditions. Significantly, the president of the Republic ceased to be recognised as the 'highest agrarian authority'.

The reforms of 1992 were justified in terms of economic convenience and the physical impossibility of continuing with land distribution. The goal was to bring about certainty and legal security to ownership in Mexico's rural areas, in order to increase investment and thus agricultural production. Yet, as a by-product, the new rules had an important impact on the instruments that presidents used to gain political strength, getting the support of peasants' organisations.

2. The Creation of an Autonomous Central Bank in 1993

Since its creation in 1925, the Bank of Mexico has tried to achieve a balance between the government's aim to control and subordinate it to its political needs, and the need to guarantee autonomy by detaching itself from the short-term financial requirements of the executive power. The concern for autonomy of the Bank can be seen in the three statutes that organised its structure and powers (of 1925, 1936 and 1941). In spite of this, in general terms the president's interest in subordinating the Bank usually prevailed, thanks to his power to designate the Bank's president and the majority of its board.

For decades, the Executive's power to influence the central bank had a political use, particularly in moments perceived as 'critical' by Mexican presidents. For instance, monetary expansion and increased public spending were used by Presidents Cárdenas and Echeverría, as part of their attempt to mobilise popular sectors in their interaction with the private sector.

This subordination was enhanced when the government of President López Portillo (1976–82) decided to expropriate all Mexican private banks in 1982. In this context, the central bank became the government's instrument to organise credit policy in the country, which by then would be implemented by a public-only banking system.

Nevertheless, with the constitutional reform of 20 August 1993, this trend was reversed. The Bank of Mexico was granted autonomy, by virtue of paragraph 6 of article 28 of the Constitution, according to which:

> The State shall have a central bank which shall be autonomous in the exercise of its functions and in its administration. Its priority objective shall be to guarantee stability of the national currency's value, strengthening thus the State's conduct of national development. No authority shall order the bank to grant financing.

The main reason put forward by the reform proposal of President Salinas in 1993, was the need to establish the institutional conditions to guarantee low levels of inflation. This was important in view of the previous experience with high inflation rates that Mexico (and most Latin American countries) suffered during the 1980s.

Importantly, article 28 of the Constitution and the Organic Law on the Bank of Mexico of 1993, established an appointment system that granted job stability to the governor of the Bank, strengthening this officer's position in the eventuality of a president who would try to subordinate the Bank and its constitutional 'anti-inflation' objective to the political interest of the incumbent government. In this way, the five members of the Bank's board are appointed by the president with the approval of two-thirds of the Senate. The president has the power to appoint the governor of the Bank, for a term of six years that does not coincide with the six-year term of the president of the Republic. Thus, Mexican presidents will have to co-exist for several years with a central bank governor that was appointed by the previous chief of the federal Executive. Moreover, the governor can only be removed for the specific reasons established in article 43 of the Organic Law on the Bank of Mexico, and after a procedure in which the other members of the Bank's board play an important role (preparing a report), with the Senate having the final decision.

With this reform, the Bank of Mexico would be able to resist pressures coming from a president 'too' oriented towards the expansion of public spending as happened in the past. Today, the Bank has a constitutional mission to keep inflation low. From a historical perspective, this has deprived Mexico's president of a key instrument used in the past to strengthen the presidency.

In sum, it can be argued that social, cultural and economic factors have changed the stratum on the basis of which Mexico's *presidencialismo* was constructed, and this has induced changes at the institutional level that have deprived presidents of instruments that in the past were central to building wide bases of political support. All these factors and changes were crucial to fostering the terminal crisis and eventual breakdown of the hegemonic party system.

IV. ELECTION OF THE PRESIDENT AND HIS POSITION AS BOTH HEAD OF STATE AND HEAD OF GOVERNMENT

Mexico's presidents are directly elected by the people every six years.[13] Yet, re-election is absolutely prohibited. This prohibition can only be understood from a historical perspective: one of the main devices of the Mexican revolution that started in 1910 was to put an end to the re-election of dictator Porfirio Díaz (who had governed Mexico through successive re-elections between 1877 and 1911). Ironically, Díaz himself had led a revolt in 1871 proclaiming his *Plan de la Noria*, the main device of which was no re-election of President Benito Juárez; and another one in 1876, to impede the re-election of President Sebastian Lerdo de Tejada.

In spite of its centrality as a principle of the Mexican revolution, once in power, the group of generals that controlled Mexican politics in the 1920s tried to weaken it. Mexico's strong-man, General Alvaro Obregón, who had already been president between 1920 and 1924, organised a movement that eventually led to a constitutional reform (article 83) that allowed non-successive presidential re-election for just one term.[14] In that way, he was able to run for the presidency for a second time in 1928. He won the corresponding election but never took office: he was shot dead whilst president elect. After this, article 83 of the Constitution was reformed again, to re-establish the absolute prohibition on re-election for the presidency.[15]

The president of the Republic is both head of state and head of the federal government. As head of state, he is Commander in Chief of the

---

[13] Originally, the presidential term was of four years. However, this was charged with the reform of 24 January 1928, extending the term to six years, under the argument that presidential elections put the country in situations of such political agitation and stress, that it was convenient to extend the time between elections.

[14] The reform was enacted on 22 January 1927.

[15] The reform was enacted on 24 January 1928.

armed forces (article 89.VI of the Constitution); and is in charge of the state's foreign relations (article 89.X of the Constitution). Unlike in parliamentary systems, the president does not have the power to dissolve Congress.

As head of the federal government, the president is also the head of the federal public administration, which is divided into two structures: the 'centralised' agencies and the 'parastate' agencies.[16] The former consists of the different ministries of state, headed by the corresponding secretaries, who are appointed and removed freely by the president. The exception to this rule is the federal Attorney General, who is appointed by the president with the approval of the Senate (but he can be removed freely by the president).

For its part, the 'parastate' public sector is formed of state enterprises, whose number decreased significantly since the economic reforms (privatisations) that started in the early 1980s. In this way, if in 1983 there were 2155 public enterprises, by 1993 they were only 213. This reduction has also had a political impact, since apart from their contribution to the country's economic development, they performed political functions: they allowed the president to create and maintain diverse political 'clienteles', thus widening his base of support.[17] A reduction of the 'parastate' sector has weakened the president's capacity to build up domestic political support.

V. THE PRESIDENT AND THE LEGISLATIVE PROCESS

In chapter three we studied the legislative process from the perspective of both chambers of the federal Congress. In this section, we will make some general remarks on the role of the president of the Republic in this process, specifically addressing the president's veto power.

Indeed, the Constitution grants the Executive the power to veto legislation. This power dates from the reform passed in 1874 to the Constitution of 1857, which originally cancelled this possibility with the aim of designing a presidential system in which Congress had broad

---

[16]   Article 90 of the Constitution.

[17]   The president has the power to appoint and remove freely the public servants that will head federal public enterprises.

powers vis-à-vis the Executive.[18] Interestingly, the reasons put forward in 1917 in favour of the preservation of the president's veto power connect directly with the interpretation of Emilio Rabasa of the constitutional evolution of Mexico during the nineteenth century that I mentioned above.[19]

For the 1917 constituent assembly, the original version of the 1857 Constitution had been too restrictive of the powers of the Executive, to the extent that the president had no influence on the legislative process that allowed him to force a reconsideration of a bill by the houses of Congress. This situation

> which has faced our presidents with the difficult choice of becoming dictators, dissolving the popular Chambers, or finding in one of them a systematic opposition that leads to their unavoidable downfall, has revealed a great vice in our fundamental law for the lack of the veto power.[20]

Besides, the constitutional framers of 1917 thought that without the super-majority of two-thirds of both chambers of Congress required to override the veto of the president, the institution would lose its purpose as an instrument to avoid hastiness in the legislative process and as a tool with which the Executive could defend itself against the possible invasion of competences carried out by the legislative power.[21]

As reported by Carpizo in his classic study on Mexico's presidential system, the veto power was used dozens of times during the twentieth century.[22] Nevertheless, in those cases it was used in the context of a hegemonic party system, more for the purpose either of a president who had second thoughts on a piece of legislation that he himself had designed and introduced in Congress, or for that of an Executive which wanted to impose discipline on Congress.

In the context of a plural system, the veto has been used by Mexico's Executive a number of times. Evidently, and in contrast with the past, this power has been exercised in the spirit of true separation of powers. In this way, the first non-PRI president of the Republic in more than

---

[18]   For this reason, the Constitution of 1857 also created a Congress of one chamber only: the Chamber of Deputies.

[19]   See above, section II of this chapter.

[20]   Second Commission of the Constituent Assembly of 1917.

[21]   J Carpizo, *El presidencialismo mexicano*, 18th edn (Mexico, Siglo XXI, 2004) 85.

[22]   In the hegemonic party system, the last time the president used his veto power was in 1969. See *ibid*, at 90–91.

70 years, Vicente Fox, vetoed the Act on Rural Development in March, 2001 which, among other things, established: the participation of farmers' organisations in the decision-making process for the regulation of imports; a mechanism for the revision of international commercial agreements with the potential to harm national farmers' interests; and the duty of the federal government to create an official agency to support commercialisation and training, in favour of farmers.[23]

Furthermore, Fox also vetoed the Act on the Tax Administration System (SAT) on 15 March 2003, an act that sought to incorporate two ministers of finance of State governments into the federal 'Tax Administration System' board, and established the duty of the federal government to compensate taxpayers for losses caused by federal tax authorities.[24]

In this book we will examine one veto in particular, which is relevant because it redefined the relations between Congress (and particularly the Chamber of Deputies) and the president, in connection with a crucial subject: the budget. Moreover, this case is relevant because the Supreme Court made important rulings on separation of powers and the supremacy of the Constitution. Finally, it is an example of the use the Supreme Court has started to make of innovative interpretation techniques, in the context of its consolidation as a constitutional court.[25]

Indeed, the 2005 Budget approved by the Chamber of Deputies was vetoed on 30 November 2004 by President Vicente Fox. He alleged that the budget had to be corrected, since several allocations (to federal programmes) approved by that chamber affected the operation of various secretaries of state and the implementation of the main social policy programmes of the federal public administration.

The Chamber of Deputies rejected the veto, alleging that according to the Constitution the president was not allowed to veto the budget. In view of this, and to avoid a constitutional and a budgetary crisis, the presidency promulgated the budget as approved by the Chamber of Deputies, but it also brought a constitutional controversy before the Supreme Court (which was registered as 109/2004) challenging the

---

[23] In this case, Congress yielded and passed a statute omitting the elements that had been objected to by the Executive's veto.

[24] In this case, the veto was not overridden and eventually Congress passed a legislative reform that took into account the observations made by the president in his veto, which was published on 12 July 2003.

[25] This will be further explained in chapter 5.

Chamber's refusal to consider the veto under the procedure established in article 72 of the Constitution, on the grounds that it was contrary to the principle of separation of powers (article 49) and also to article 72 itself.[26]

To resolve this case, the Court had to opt between a literal reading of the Constitution[27] and one that took into account historical and functional factors. In the end, the Supreme Court decided that a literal reading of articles 72 and 74 of the Constitution was not enough to determine whether the president can veto the budget approved by the Chamber of Deputies or not.[28] According to the Court, a systematic interpretation of articles 70 to 75 of the Constitution allowed it to determine that the president did have the power to veto the budget. Specifically, the rules of article 72 (including those on the veto) applied both to unicameral and bicameral legislative procedures.

In addition, giving a historical interpretation of the genesis of the Constitutions of 1857 and 1917 with respect to the legislative process and the budget, the Court noted that there was never the intention to exclude the budget from the scope of the veto. Finally, the Court engaged in a 'genetic' and 'teleological' interpretation, which sought to uncover the rationale of the veto in the constitutional system. In summary, the Supreme Court said that the purpose of the introduction of the veto in Mexico's Constitution, since the reform in 1874 of the 1857 Constitution, was to achieve a just balance between the legislative and executive powers in the creation of statutes. In Mexico's history, the absence of that balance had resulted in political crises that ended up in institutional and constitutional breakdown (echoes of the Rabasa doctrine on *presidencialismo* in Mexico). With this argument, the Court was implying that to understand that the budget could not be vetoed amounted to a distortion of the just balance between the legislative and the executive powers.

---

[26] Article 72 contains the rules on the federal legislative process.

[27] On its face, article 72 of the Constitution seems to apply to legislative procedures in which both houses of government intervene in a successive way.

[28] For the Court, the veto is a means of collaboration between the executive and the legislative branches of government, by which the former is able to give the latter additional information and objections that may have not been taken into account by Congress when it debated on the bill, in the corresponding legislative process. See the judgment on Constitutional controversy 109/2004, published in the Federal Official Gazette on 24 October 2005.

In conclusion, the Supreme Court was of the opinion (in a 6-5 decision) that the president did have the power to veto the congressional decree that approved the budget. Therefore the Chamber's decree that refused to consider the president's observations on the budget approved by the Chamber of Deputies was nullified. Moreover, the Court clarified that the parts of the budget that had not been vetoed remained valid, but those that had been the subject of the Executive's observations had to be considered and discussed by the Chamber of Deputies (this required that the Permanent Committee of Congress had to call the Chamber of Deputies to extraordinary sessions, so that it could consider, discuss and vote on the observations made by the president on the 2005 Budget which it approved on 14 December 2004.[29]

Today, it seems that political actors are aware that, in the context of a new pattern of relations between the executive and legislative powers and of a multi-party system, the rules on their interaction within the legislative process have to be 'modernised', changing some of the rules that govern the president's veto power found in article 72 of the Constitution. In this way, in 17 August 2011, those rules were amended in three important ways: first, the ability of the president to 'freeze' statutes approved by Congress simply by not publishing them, was eliminated. Under the new rule, if the president does not publish a statute within 10 days after its approval, the president of the Chamber that first discussed and approved the statute will be able to do it; secondly, the time limit for exercising the president's veto power was extended from 10 'working' days, to 30 'calendar' days. Finally, the 2011 amendment established that those time limits should not be interrupted because of a congressional recess. In this hypothesis, the president has to address the veto to the Permanent Committee of Congress, which has the duty to turn it over to the corresponding congressional committees for examination and further treatment by both chambers of Congress, as soon as they start their ordinary sessions.

[29] Judgment of 17 May 2005. Published in the Official Gazette of the Federation of 25 October 2005.

VI. THE PRESIDENT AND THE FISCAL PROCESS

1. The Budget

According to Gutiérrez et al, one of the policy arenas that has been most affected by the transition from a hegemonic party system to a multi-party system, has been the budgetary process. In spite of this, the constitutional rules that govern that process have remained precarious and ambiguous, producing uncertainty.[30]

The power to introduce the budget for consideration is vested in the president alone (article 74.IV of the Constitution). For its part, the only chamber that discusses and eventually approves or not the budget is the Chamber of Deputies. The reason for this has to do with the division of labour between both chambers that was decided with the reform of 1874 to the Constitution of 1857, which re-established the Senate: the only chamber that existed under the 1857 Constitution (that is, the Chamber of Deputies) accepted the creation of a Senate, but refused to waive its exclusive power to approve the budget. This circumstance has been criticised on the grounds that it breaks the unity of the budgetary process, which is composed of the budgetary and revenue sides (the Senate does have the power to approve tax laws); and that it weakens the ability to control the Executive, excluding one of the chambers of Congress from the discussion and approval of the budget.

The Constitution establishes a precise time limit within which the president has to introduce his proposed budget and the bill on the Public Revenue Act (no later than 8 September of each year).[31] Moreover, it also establishes a precise time limit for the chamber to approve the budget (no later than 15 November).[32] However, the Constitution says nothing on the

[30] G Gutiérrez, A Lujambio and D Valadés, 'El Proceso Presupuestario y las Relaciones entre los Organos del Poder Una Perspectiva Histórica y Comparada' in D Valadés and R Gutiérrez (eds), *Economía y Constitución* (Mexico, UNAM, 2001) 71.

[31] In the inaugural year of a new presidential administration (1 December every six years), the time limit for the introduction of the budget proposal is 8 December.

[32] This is the result of the constitutional amendment of 30 July 2004 (in contrast with the uncertainty and ambiguity of the original text of the 1917 Constitution on this matter), which intended to force the president to introduce the budget project on a precise date, and give a reasonable time for the Chamber of Deputies to discuss and eventually approve the budget.

consequences of a presidential breach of this rule, either by the extemporaneous presentation of the project or by not introducing it at all.

Another issue, which is also related to the discussion on the presidential veto on the budget, has to do with the absence of a rule that resolves the eventuality of a lack of agreement on the budget between the president and the Chamber of Deputies. This hypothesis has the potential of paralysing the federal government (with all the implied economic and social consequences), since article 126 of the Constitution states that no payment shall be made by government if it is not prescribed in the budget.[33] In other countries there are rules that solve the problem of a potential budgetary deadlock (for example, by ordering the extension of the budget of the previous year until a new budget is approved). In fact, the majority of Mexico's State constitutions already foresee a rule of this kind, as is also the case in countries as diverse as Germany,[34] Chile,[35] Colombia,[36] Spain[37] and Finland.[38] It would be important to introduce rules like these into Mexico's federal Constitution, in order to avoid disastrous consequences that would ensue from the eventual governmental shutdown.

It is important to recall that since 1997 the president's party in the lower house has not had the required majority to approve the budget. This means that he has to discuss and negotiate on his budget proposals with political parties in the Chamber of Deputies, in order to determine the distribution of public spending among the different federal programmes. In turn, this situation has increased the political weight of the Chamber of Deputies within the whole system. Yet, this has to be significantly qualified, since it is still the president, through the Ministry of Finance, who designs the budget and therefore it is him who sets the terms and parameters of the budgetary debate, leaving to the deputies the secondary power to make observations on and modifications to a previously defined agenda. Moreover, legislators do not have the time, resources or technical expertise to propose alternatives or deeper

---

[33] Article 75 of the Constitution foresees an exception to this rule: in connection with public employments established by law, if for any reason their salary is not determined in the corresponding budget, the salary established in the previous budget or in the statute law that created the public office shall be applied.

[34] Article 111 of the 1949 Basic Law.

[35] Article 64 of the Constitution of 1980.

[36] Article 348 of the Constitution of 1991.

[37] Article 134.4 of the Constitution of 1978.

[38] Article 69 of the Finnish Constitution.

changes to the budget proposed by the Executive, and therefore lack the ability to have an impact on the general orientation of economic policy. Nevertheless, as one analyst has observed, the deputies' increased power in the budgetary process has contributed to a more technical and policy-oriented discussion of the budget, and less rhetoric and ideological, when compared with past experience.[39]

2. Public Revenues

On the public revenue side, the Constitution grants the power to introduce the project of the so-called Public Revenue Act to the president of the Republic but, in contrast to the budget, the approval of both chambers of Congress is required (yet, the bill has to be introduced first in the Chamber of Deputies, as stated by article 74.IV of the Constitution).

The Public Revenue Act is the piece of legislation that establishes the list of all the sources of public revenue of the federal government and the forecast of what will be collected from the different sources. It includes taxes, royalties, tariffs, profits from public enterprises, and also contains the authorisations relating to public indebtedness.[40]

Yet, there is another topic that is relevant in connection with taxation that I would like to examine in this section, that has to do with the ability of tax payers to challenge the constitutionality of tax laws through the writ of *amparo* (which will be analysed in more detail in Chapter 5 of this book), thanks to the interpretation that the Supreme Court has given to article 31.IV of the Constitution.

This article of the Constitution, which states that Mexicans have the duty to pay taxes in the 'proportionate and equitable way established by statute law', has its origins in the Constitution of 1857.[41] Importantly,

---

[39] LC Ugalde, 'La Supervisión Legislativa de las Finanzas Públicas en México: de la aprobación del presupuesto a la revisión del gasto público' in G Pérez and A Martínez (eds), *La Cámara de Diputados en México* (Mexico, Cámara de Diputados del H Congreso de la Unión, LVII Legislatura, 2000) 145–47.

[40] Through this Act Congress authorises the levels of indebtedness of the federal government for each year, as established by article 73.VIII of the Constitution. This rule was the result of the constitutional reform of 25 October 1993, and was intended to put limits on the president's capacity to incur public debt (the background to this being the irresponsible increase of Mexico's public debt during the 1980s, which eventually led to default and economic crisis in 1982).

[41] In the Constitution of 1857, this norm was in article 31.II.

for the sake of our explanation, these words originally were not understood in the sense of granting Mexican taxpayers a constitutional right to 'proportionate and equitable' tax laws.

In fact, since the late nineteenth century (1877–82), the doctrine that prevailed stated that in connection with tax laws, courts could not judge Congress's decisions. According to that doctrine, legislators were representatives of the people, and as such they knew what measure of taxes had to be collected in order to satisfy public needs. In addition, for this doctrine the best guarantee against the potential abuse of Congress when deciding on tax matters, was the political process and, more specifically, the influence of public opinion and the people's electoral power. This doctrine was formulated by Ignacio L Vallarta, president of the Supreme Court between 1877 and 1882.[42] Interestingly, in his arguments on this issue, he explicitly referred to the influence of US Chief Justice Marshall.[43]

In turn, we have to point out that since public opinion and the electorate were controlled in the context of the dictatorial regime under consolidation in the years in which Vallarta produced this doctrine, the latter was perfectly functional to the regime's need of increasing public revenues, after years of public disorder and war that Mexico had experienced for most of the nineteenth century.[44]

This doctrine prevailed well into the first half of the twentieth century, in spite of taxpayers' insistence on challenging diverse tax laws for being 'disproportionate' and 'unequitable'.[45] In this way, even in 1954, the Court stated that it was not for the federal judicial power to decide

---

[42] The leading case was the *amparo* filed against the tax imposed on textiles factories, by the Law on Public Revenue of 5 June 1879. The plaintiffs challenged the tax, arguing that it was neither proportionate nor equitable, in terms of article 31.II of the Constitution of 1857, because it was directed specifically to said factories; therefore – they argued – it was not of general application, and did not give equal treatment in comparison to other tax payers. Yet, the Court said that it was general, since it did not address specific textile factories, but all textile factories of the country.

[43] IL Vallarta, *Cuestiones Constitucionales*, vol II, (Mexico, Porrúa, 1975) 16.

[44] In chapter 5 we shall reflect on the role of courts and specifically of the Supreme Court in the context of authoritarian regimes that have governed Mexico.

[45] In 1925, in the administrative *amparo* in revision 3173/22 filed by Aurelio Maldonado, the Court accepted that the Supreme Court could review, in *amparo*, a tax law that was notoriously abusive for ignoring the constitutional mandate according to which taxes must be proportionate and equitable. The Court admitted the case for consideration, but denied the *amparo* on the merits.

on the distribution of the tax burden. For the Court, this was a competence of the legislative power. Otherwise 'the Supreme Court would transform itself into the Superior Tribunal for the distribution of the tax burden in the entire Nation, which is absurd'.[46] Góngora Pimentel has suggested that this doctrine was linked to the context in which the state needed to consolidate its fiscal base.[47]

In the 1960s the Supreme Court started to develop a doctrine that eventually allowed litigants to obtain declarations of unconstitutionality of tax laws, through a writ of *amparo*, for being 'disproportionate' and 'unequitable'. In the first case in this line, the Supreme Court stated that the federal judicial power does have the power to review tax laws passed by the legislative power whenever it appears that the tax is 'exorbitant' and 'ruinous', or whenever the legislative power has exceeded in its constitutional powers.[48] Afterwards, in another case, the Court said that the ruinous and exorbitant character of a tax was part of the merits of the case, and not a matter by which to decide on the admissibility of a writ of *amparo*.[49]

These decisions of the Supreme Court removed the previously existing obstacles to challenging tax laws, opening up a period of intense and active litigation in which the issue was not whether the Court had the power to review tax laws, but the way in which article 31.IV had to be interpreted and applied in the revision of tax laws.[50] Basically, and under the current interpretation, the concept of proportionality is linked to the economic capacity of the taxpayer, under the rationale that the tax has to affect only a just portion of his income and profits; whereas equity means that tax laws should give equal treatment to all those that belong to the same category of taxpayers.[51] In practice, these concepts have given the Court a wide power to review and check the exercise of the taxation power of Congress and the Executive.

---

[46] Administrative *amparo* in revision 1785/49. *Compañía Mexicana de Hielo Seco, SA*, 7 May 1954.

[47] G Góngora Pimentel, *La Lucha por el Amparo Fiscal* (Mexico, Porrúa, 2007) 127.

[48] *Semanario Judicial de la Federación*, Sixth Epoch, Plenary session, First Part, XLVII, p 38. *Amparo* in revision 2742/57. *Inmuebles Continental, SA*, 2 May 1961.

[49] *Semanario Judicial de la Federación*, Sixth Epoch, Plenary session, First Part, XCIII, p 36. *Amparo* in revision 3280/50. *Antonio Fernández y coagraviados.* 16 March 1965.

[50] Góngora, *La Lucha por el Amparo Fiscal* (2007), above n 47, 195.

[51] Appendix to the *Semanario Judicial de la Federación* 1917–1995, volume I, First Part, Thesis 275, p 276.

What explains the fact that in the years in which the hegemonic party system was at its peak, the Supreme Court was able to produce an interpretation of the Constitution that directly affected the government's capacity to collect taxes and its ability to increase Mexico's historically low tax burden? Elizondo suggests that this was part of a sort of pact between the private and the public sectors, in the context of the model of economic development established in those years: high private investment rates in exchange for low taxation levels. In this way, it seems that Mexican presidents did not use their formal and informal powers to reform the Constitution to limit *amparo* in fiscal matters, nor did they put pressure on the Supreme Court to force a change in interpretation of article 31.IV of the Constitution which was less favourable to tax payers.[52]

In addition, it could also be argued that this was part of the stability of the authoritarian regime in the following terms: the admissibility of *amparo* to challenge tax laws allowed the formation of a safety valve that in actual practice was used by a relatively small number of tax payers, thus channelling tensions that might otherwise seek a resolution by way of demands of the private sector for improving the system of political representation.

The 'costs' of *amparo* against tax laws have been examined by Elizondo in the following terms: it increases enormously the workload both for judges and authorities that defend the treasury against *amparo* suits (between 2002 and 2007 a total of 134, 323 were filed against federal tax laws); in turn, workload induces errors and inefficiency by judges and authorities. Moreover, the enormous amount of time and attention devoted by them to these cases diverts resources that federal courts and specifically the Supreme Court could use to resolve other kinds of disputes (is the Supreme Court a constitutional court or a fiscal court?) Moreover, the amount of money that is lost by the federal treasury in *amparos* that are granted to plaintiffs is not insignificant. And finally, the way in which the writ of *amparo* in tax matters has evolved means that part of Mexico's tax policy has been transferred from the legislative power to the judicial power (specifically to the Supreme Court), particularly because the notions of proportionality and equity are so broad and undefined that the Court has had to develop very detailed accounts of their meanings

---

[52] C Elizondo Mayer-Serra, 'La Industria del Amparo Fiscal' (2009) XVI *Política y Gobierno* 356–59.

when examining challenged tax laws. In turn, this contradicts the theory of representation as the basis of taxation in a democratic state.[53]

Furthermore, we have to note that two characteristics of the writ of *amparo* have contributed to create the situation we are trying to explain in this section. First, judicial intervention to protect the Constitution through *amparo* can only take place as a result of the petition of a person whose constitutional rights have been infringed; secondly, the eventual declaration of unconstitutionality benefits only the party that obtained it in the concrete case. In practice, this has led to this scenario: highly specialised law and accountancy firms are able to get declarations of unconstitutionality of 'disproportionate' and 'unequitable' tax laws every year, thus protecting the select group of taxpayers who can pay for their services.

In turn, this has produced complaints against the unequal and discriminatory nature of the *amparo* against tax laws: large-scale tax payers and smaller tax payers receive different treatment concerning taxation, depending on their ability to successfully challenge the relevant statutes. This is so because due to the 'relative' or 'inter partes' effect of an *amparo* judgment, a declaration of unconstitutionality of a tax law obtained by one plaintiff does not benefit others if they did not litigate against the statute by filing an action of *amparo* themselves.[54] Also critical, Góngora has seen a problem in the abuse of the *amparo* on tax matters, since some taxpayers resort to it for the purposes of tax evasion, rather than as a tool to protect constitutional rights to just taxes.[55]

Finally, since in *amparo* proceedings district judges intervene at first instance, there are many cases in which some judges grant *amparo* and others deny it, a circumstance that creates distortions in economic competition and the structure of markets.[56]

---

[53] *ibid*, at 349–84.

[54] The recent constitutional reform, which under certain circumstances allows the Supreme Court to issue 'general declarations of unconstitutionality' of statutes (thus nullifying the challenged statute), explicitly excludes from this possibility tax laws. Inequities can be seen in the *Alsea* case. Alsea was a fast-food company which won a fiscal *amparo* against the Law on VAT, which allowed the company not to pay 15 per cent of the VAT on its sales; in contrast with its competitors (Kentucky Fried Chicken, McDonalds, Pizza Hut, etc). This produced distortions in the market in competition and loss of a good amount of public revenue, all derived from efficient and ingenious litigation in the field of fiscal *amparo*. See Elizondo, 'La Industria del Amparo Fiscal' (2009), above 52, 374–77.

[55] Góngora, 'La Lucha por el Amparo Fiscal' (2007), above n 47, 243.

[56] A Zaldívar, 'La reforma al amparo fiscal', *El Universal*, 5 April 2009.

VII. CONCLUSIONS

The distinguishing characteristic of Mexico's presidential system during most of the twentieth century was the political identification between the president of the Republic and the majority in both houses of Congress, and the control that the former had over the latter. In turn, the formation and reproduction of this identity can only be understood as the result of the way in which political power was reformulated after the Mexican revolution. Yet, many of the bases on which that power structure was built, experienced a series of changes during the final decades of the twentieth century. This situation opened up the possibility of a different pattern of relations between the Executive and Congress in Mexico.

Today there are several proposals for reforming Mexico's presidential system. Some of them refer to the possibility of introducing institutions that are typical of parliamentary forms of government (without changing the core presidential nature of the system).[57] Some others recommend the creation of mechanisms that allow the president minimal conditions for accomplishing his agenda, for instance, through the power to request from Congress preferential treatment of a limited number of bills introduced by the president every year.[58]

These proposals and recommendations apart, what is clear is that in the new political context, characterised by political pluralism and divided governments, Mexico's presidential system needs to be redesigned.

FURTHER READING

Carpizo, J, *El presidencialismo mexicano*, 18th edn (Mexico, Siglo XXI, 2004).

Carpizo, J, 'Mexico: Presidential or Parliamentarian System?' (2005) 23 *Mexican Law Review* 49.

Ellis, A, Orozco, J and Zovatto, D, *Cómo hacer que funcionen los sistemas presidenciales/Making Presidentialism Work* (Mexico, UNAM/IDEA, 2009).

Valadés, D, *La parlamentarización de los sistemas presidenciales*, 2nd edn (Mexico, UNAM, 2008).

---

[57] See the conclusions of chapter 3.

[58] The reform of 9 August 2012 introduced this preferential legislative procedure into the Constitution. See above, section IX in this chapter.

Zamora, S and Cossío, JR, 'Mexican constitutionalism after *presidencialismo*' (2006) 4 *International Journal of Constitutional Law* 411.

5

The Judicial Branch of Government: Courts and Judicial Review

Introduction – The Structure and Organisation of the Judicial Power in Mexico – Judicial Power, Control of Constitutionality and the Writ of *Amparo* in Mexico – Backlog as the Consequence of the *Amparo Casacion*: 'The Impossible Task of the Court' – Towards a Constitutional Court: The Reform of 1994 – The Court's Article 97 Investigative Power – Conclusion

I. INTRODUCTION

MEXICO'S COURTS SYSTEM is the product of the influence of two Western legal traditions. On the one hand, the Western-European tradition of Civil Law influenced the national conception on the role of judges in society and in politics. In short, and following Merryman's classic contrast between judges in the civil law and common law traditions, in the latter the judge is considered as a sort of 'cultural hero' fully legitimate to create law, while in the former judges are seen as public servants whose function is to apply the law as defined by the legislative power.[1]

On the other hand, the American constitutional model also influenced Mexico's Judiciary, particularly in connection with the organisation of courts in a federal system. Similar to the US courts system, Mexico has a dual structure of courts. There are federal courts which

---

[1] JH Merryman, *The Civil Law Tradition, An Introduction to the Legal Systems of Western Europe and Latin America* (Stanford CA, Stanford University Press, 1969) ch VI ('Judges').

apply federal law, and there are State courts that apply State law (though in some instances they also apply federal law, eg commercial law).[2] As we shall see, at the top of this whole structure there is a Supreme Court of Justice, which is not only the final interpreter of the Constitution, but also the guardian of the 'correct' application of both federal and State law (this shall be explained below, and is linked with the functions of federal courts as courts of cassation).

Jaime Cárdenas' description of the different stages in the evolution of Mexico's Supreme Court helps to create a 'big picture' to understand the role of this court in the country's constitutional system and its connection with the general political development of Mexico. Those stages are:

1. Stage of definition of the basic characteristics of the system (1824–82). In this period the influence of the US model was crucial. Yet, the Spanish and French traditions were also important, leading to judicial centralisation: in this period federal courts were assigned the power to review the decisions of States' superior courts applying State law.
2. Stage of subordination to a non-democratic and personalised regime (1882–1917). This was the phase in which dictator Porfirio Díaz consolidated in power. In this context, the Supreme Court did not effectively limit presidential power,[3] though it was able to protect at least some rights of non-political content.[4] Moreover, in this period courts had to struggle to be recognised as guardians of the law.[5] A good

---

[2] The Federal District, that is, Mexico City, also has its own system of courts, which apply law passed by the city's Legislative Assembly.

[3] For example, in this period the Court never opposed the unconstitutional use of delegated legislative powers by President Porfirio Díaz. A 'custom' which prevailed even under the Constitution of 1917, until the reform of article 49 of 28 March 1951, which expressly prohibited this practice with two exceptions: a situation of suspension of rights on account of a national emergency (article 29); and situations of urgency in the field of international commerce and problems in the balance of payments, in which the president is allowed to establish import and export duties, with later approval of Congress (article 131). See J Cárdenas, *Una Constitución para la Democracia* (Mexico, UNAM, 2000) 177.

[4] For instance, the Supreme Court granted *amparos* against statutes that violated the constitutional prohibition of retroactive statutes.

[5] During the 1880s resolutions of federal judges (injunctions in *amparo* proceedings) were not fulfilled by military chiefs around the country, whose usual answer was that they would wait for 'the respective orders issued by the Ministry of War and Navy'. Also, this was the time in which the Supreme Court denied religious and other 'corporations' the right to own property and to have standing before courts.

example of how the Supreme Court 'adapted' to a dictatorial regime was the development of doctrines of self-restraint, like the notion that the Court does not hear electoral-political disputes (which we shall review later in section III.2.A of this chapter).

3. Stage of relative independence (1917–28). After the military stage of the Mexican revolution, the Constitution of 1917 established the basis for judicial independence (for example, life tenure of Supreme Court Justices). Before the emergence and consolidation of the hegemonic party system the Supreme Court enjoyed a period of relative autonomy from political power.

4. Stage of subordination to a non-democratic and institutionalised regime (1928–44). In the phase of formation of the hegemonic party system, judicial independence was lost, with the removal of life tenure for Justices. With the constitutional reform of 1934, Justices would be in office for a period of six years (their term coincided with that of the Executive). In this way, each president was able to appoint 'his' Court.

5. Stage of 'alleviation' of backlog (1944–86). Life tenure of Supreme Court Justices was restored with the reform of 1944. This did not impede the president from exercising a strong influence on the Court, through the written and unwritten rules of the hegemonic party system which in this period was at its peak. The main concern in this stage was to solve the problem of the backlog created with the expansion of the Supreme Court's jurisdiction, as will be explained below (section IV of this chapter).

6. Stage of gradual recovery of autonomy (1986 till today). This period coincides with the gradual transition to democracy, and is characterised by the strengthening of the Supreme Court's independence and powers as a constitutional tribunal, and by the professionalisation of the federal judicial power.[6]

In this chapter we shall review some of the developments that shaped the identity of today's courts system of Mexico. First, I shall explain the

In turn, this affected indigenous communities (which qualified as 'corporations') which were not able to own and defend their land as communities. This was part of a process that took place during the end of the nineteenth century, which led to the high concentration of land ownership in the hands of very few people. L Cabrera Acevedo, *La Suprema Corte de Justicia en el Primer Periodo del Porfirismo (1877–1882)* (Mexico, Suprema Corte de Justicia de la Nación, 1990) 23.

[6] Cárdenas, *Una Constitución para la Democracia* (2000), n 3 above, 171–86.

structure and organisation of the federal and State judicial systems. Secondly, I will discuss the institution that forms the core of and gives identity to Mexico's courts system: the writ of *amparo*.[7] In this section we shall examine the origins of this institution, its raison-d'être, its main features and evolution.

Thirdly, I shall explain how the Supreme Court expanded its jurisdiction to hear cases that go beyond the control of constitutionality of acts and resolutions of other powers, and how this led to the serious problem of backlog. As we shall see, this issue dominated the institutional evolution of the federal courts system between 1917 and 1994, and was reflected in a series of constitutional reforms.

In fourth place, I shall examine the recent evolution of the Supreme Court and its consolidation as an independent power within the political-constitutional system. Indeed, this evolution has occurred in the context of Mexico's transition to democracy, to the point that, as suggested by Fix Fierro, today the Supreme Court represents the third branch of government, and is no longer the third-*class* branch of government that it used to be.[8]

Finally, I shall discuss the so-called power of investigation of the Supreme Court, granted by article 97 of the Constitution.[9] The way and the frequency with which this power was exercised between 1995 and 2011 provides evidence on how the Court has been playing an increasingly important role in mediating very difficult and complicated conflicts in Mexico's recent history.

II. THE STRUCTURE AND ORGANISATION OF THE JUDICIAL POWER IN MEXICO

1. Federal Courts

At the top of the federal courts system sits a Supreme Court of Justice, formed of 11 Justices appointed by two-thirds of the Senate, upon the

---

[7] In English, *amparo* means 'protection'.

[8] H Fix Fierro, 'La Reforma Judicial en México: ¿De Dónde Viene? ¿Hacia Dónde Va?' (2003) 2 *Reforma Judicial, Revista Mexicana de Justicia* 252.

[9] This power was eliminated from the Constitution with the reform of 10 June 2011, for the reasons that shall be examined in the corresponding section of this chapter.

proposal of the president of the Republic. Other federal courts are the Collegiate Circuit Courts, the Unitary Circuit Courts and District Judges, whose jurisdiction is defined in the *Ley Orgánica del Poder Judicial de la Federación* (Organic Law of the Federal Judicial Power) and the *Ley de Amparo* (Amparo Act), both passed by the Mexican Congress.

In general, and without getting into the details, Collegiate Circuit Courts have jurisdiction to review judicial decisions of States' superior courts (in *amparo casación* cases). For their part, District Judges hear on the one hand, *amparo* cases as *habeas corpus* and *amparo* cases as judicial review of statutes passed by federal or State legislatures, and of acts and resolutions issued by administrative authorities; on the other hand, District Judges hear federal civil and criminal cases. Finally, Unitary Circuit Courts hear federal civil and criminal cases on appeal.

Apart from the courts mentioned above, there are also other federal courts that decide different kinds of cases applying federal statute law: administrative courts (which hear disputes between private entities and individuals and the federal public administration); labour courts (which hear labour disputes applying the Federal Labour Act) and agrarian courts (which hear disputes connected with Mexico's peculiar agrarian regime derived from the Mexican revolution and its agrarian reform programme).[10] The final decisions of all these courts can be reviewed through *amparo casación* proceedings, by Collegiate Circuit Courts.

The formula for the designation of the Supreme Court Justices has changed over the years. Originally, the Constitution of 1917 stated that Justices of the Supreme Court would be designated by both houses of Congress (functioning as the Electoral College), upon the proposals of State legislatures.[11] Yet, Justices designated in 1917 would have a 'test' period of two years.[12] Those who were designated as Justices at the end

---

[10] The Agrarian Code is federal. Essentially, its rules refer to a collective-kind of land ownership which is called '*sistema ejidal*'. '*Ejidos*' are communities of peasants that own land as communities, rather than as individuals. More on this subject, below in chapter 8.V.

[11] In the debates on this topic, the constituent assembly considered different options. Some legislators were in favour of direct or indirect election of Justices. This was thought to be a condition to guarantee the democratic character of the Supreme Court. Yet, some others were for a system of collaboration between the existent powers, but with the exclusion of the Executive. This would guarantee both expertise and independence from the president.

[12] The constituent assembly of 1917 wanted to impose a probationary time period to check how the Justices would apply the new Constitution. Basically, the

of that period would be in office for a further four years. In 1923 a new process of appointment (or re-appointment) would take place, but from that moment onwards, Justices would have life tenure and could only be removed after the appropriate 'trial of responsibility' (also known as 'political trial', analysed above in Chapter 4, section XI.1) foreseen in article 111 of the Constitution (which involved the accusation of the Chamber of Deputies and the judgment of the Senate).

In spite of the original move towards strengthening the Supreme Court's independence, in 1928 and 1934 there were two reforms to the appointment system of its Justices, the effect of which was the subordination of the Court to the Executive. These reforms can be seen as part of the formation and consolidation of the hegemonic party system in Mexico. Indeed, the reform of 1928 was proposed by Mexico's revolutionary strongman, General Alvaro Obregón, being a candidate for the presidency.[13] In his proposal, he argued that the designation system was dominated by congressional politiquing. In turn, he proposed a system in which the designation would be the responsibility of the president with the ratification of the Senate. In addition, Obregón also proposed to grant the power to initiate the procedure for the removal of Justices for 'bad conduct' to the Executive, with the subsequent intervention of both houses of Congress (according to article 111 of the Constitution). The proposal succeeded and was published on 20 August 1928.[14] As stated by Cossío, this reform allowed the subordination of the judicial power to the Executive, by means of the latter's ability to remove Justices on the basis of a general concept such as 'bad conduct' and the control that the president already had in those years over the legislative branch of government.[15]

For its part, the reform of 1934, promoted by the president elect General Lázaro Cárdenas, targeted life tenure of Justices, which was seen by the sponsors of the reform as an improper denial of the people's sovereign right periodically to remove all public servants.[16] The

assembly did not want to have conservative Justices obstructing or distorting the application of the Constitution and its 'revolutionary' articles.

[13]   On Obregón, see above chapter 4.IV.

[14]   It also introduced the rule that still exist today, according to which the salary of Justices cannot be reduced during their time in office (article 94 of the Constitution).

[15]   JR Cossío, *La Teoría Constitucional de la Suprema Corte de Justicia* (Mexico, Fontamara, 2002) 37.

[16]   *ibid*, at 41.

reform was published on 15 December 1934: Justices would be designated for six years (just like the presidential term of office) and could be removed for 'bad conduct' by Congress upon the proposal of the Executive. The new Justices were designated on 26 December of that year.[17]

Life tenure was reintroduced with the reform of 21 September 1944 to article 94 of the Constitution, which was proposed by President Avila Camacho.[18] He considered that the system introduced in 1934 was a deficiency which harmed the Court's independence. As explained by Cossío, this reform seems to have been part of a strategy to 'de-ideologise' the Supreme Court,[19] initiating a period of stability that would last until 1994. In this period the Executive did not resort to the specific and ad hoc re-design (through constitutional reform) of the Supreme Court according to the political preferences of the incumbent president, but used instead the strong presidential powers to select and appoint Justices.[20]

In this way, and in spite of formal life tenure, in fact there was a high level of turnover in the Supreme Court. As reported by Fix, between 1958 and 1994 all Mexico's presidents were able to appoint at least 40 per cent of the Supreme Court Justices (and in five of the relevant presidential periods the percentage was equal to 50 per cent or more). In turn, this reflects the capacity that the Executive had during that period to grant political positions to Justices who 'voluntarily' quit the Court, and to influence the composition and orientation of the Court.[21]

---

[17] Cossío reports that only three of the Justices that had been designated under the 1928 rules were reappointed. The other 18 Justices (the 1934 reform also increased the number of Justices from 16 to 21), were appointed by the president with ratification of the Senate (already subordinated to the Executive): *ibid.*

[18] Yet, the presidential power to initiate the procedure to remove Justices for 'bad conduct' was preserved until 1982.

[19] Cárdenas was president between 1934 and 1940. He had a 'socialist' ideology which had an impact on many policy areas during his government. For example, on 13 December 1934, article 3 of the Constitution was amended, in order to establish that public education would embrace the ideology of socialism. Avila Camacho succeeded Cárdenas as president of the Republic in 1940. He took a series of explicit measures to take socialist ideology out of governmental programmes. In this way, under his leadership article 3 of the Constitution was reformed on 30 December 1946, to cancel the principle of socialist public education in Mexico.

[20] JR Cossio, *La Teoría Constitucional de la Suprema Corte de Justicia*, above n 15, at 50.

[21] H Fix Fierro, 'Poder Judicial' in M González and S López Ayllón (eds), *Transiciones y Diseños Institucionales* (Mexico, UNAM, 2000) 188–89.

2. State Courts

States and the Federal District have their own system of courts, which apply the statutes passed by their respective legislatures. In addition, State courts also hear commercial disputes applying commercial statutes, which are federal.[22] There are different kinds of courts within those entities. Typically, there are small-claims courts at the municipal level (normally with civil and criminal cases in the hands of the same judge); there are also courts of first instance (with jurisdiction to hear State law criminal and civil cases); and there is a Superior Court of Justice, which is the appellate level in the respective State (usually divided into several chambers, specialising in hearing on appeal criminal or civil cases, and in some jurisdictions family law cases). The *Tribunal Superior* of each State works in plenary sessions to resolve conflicts between its chambers.

As we can see, Mexico has a dual system of courts. Both systems are connected in the following way: the decisions of Superior Courts of the States and of the Federal District can be reviewed by federal courts (in general, by the so-called Collegiate Circuit Courts), through the writ known as *amparo casación*. This is one of the most important characteristics of Mexico's courts system, which has had an impact on the definition of our judicial federalism (highly centralised) and on the constitutional evolution of the Supreme Court of Justice, as will be explained and discussed in section IV of this chapter.

It is relevant to mention that a constitutional reform of 1986 established standards for the organisation of State courts. Indeed, as a result of this reform, article 116.III of the Constitution establishes a series of rules that seek to guarantee the independence and efficiency of State judicial powers. These rules refer to: job stability (State constitutions and laws have to establish the conditions for entry, training and tenure of the members of the Judiciary); the requisites to be appointed as State Magistrate (the same as those required to be a Justice of the Supreme Court, found in article 95 of the Constitution); life-tenure (Magistrates can only be removed for the causes and through the procedures fore-

---

[22] This happens thanks to a rule in Mexico's Constitution which allows what is known as 'concurrent jurisdiction': when only private interests are involved in a dispute that fall within the scope of federal law, plaintiffs can choose to bring their action before State courts (article 104.II of the Constitution).

seen in State constitutions and State laws on responsibility of public servants); economic stability (State Magistrates and judges' salaries cannot be diminished during their time in office). In general terms, the goal of the 1986 constitutional reform was to foster judicial autonomy and efficiency in the States of the Republic.[23]

The writ of *amparo* has had an interesting evolution in connection with the rules contained in article 116.III of the Constitution mentioned above, which can be summarised as follows: though the action of *amparo* in principle was intended to protect private individuals (or juristic persons) against unconstitutional governmental acts and resolutions, it has been used by judges who seek protection against State governors (and State legislatures) who have tried to remove them, in violation of article 116.III 'judicial guarantees'.

The first (and leading) case is the *amparo* in revision 2639/96, filed by Mr Fernando Arreola Vega. In 1986, Mr Arreola was appointed by the legislature of the State of Michoacán, upon the proposal of the governor, as Magistrate to the Superior Tribunal of that State, in principle, for a period of three years. At that time, article 72 of Michoacán's Constitution established that Magistrates could be re-appointed, in which case they would enjoy life tenure. In the case of Mr Arreola, he remained as Magistrate for 10 years, but he was never expressly re-appointed nor removed from that position by three consecutive State legislatures.

In 1996 a new governor sought to appoint 10 new Magistrates of Michoacán's Superior Tribunal, which implied the removal of the same number of Magistrates in office (including Mr Arreola). Yet, via a writ of *amparo*, Magistrate Arreola challenged his removal and the appointment of a new Magistrate in his place on two grounds:

a) The very fact that he had remained as Magistrate for 10 years (throughout the term of three consecutive State legislatures) could perfectly be understood as a tacit re-appointment, which in the light of article 72 of Michoacán's Constitution granted life tenure (protected by article 116.III of the federal Constitution).

b) In 1996 the State legislature had approved the appointment of new Magistrates without any sort of notification to Mr Arreola, nor with any kind of explanation concerning the legal basis and the motives

---

[23] The Second Transitory article of the Reform Decree, gave State legislatures one year to reform their constitutions and corresponding statute law, in order to adapt them to the new constitutional standards of article 116.III.

for the removal (against article 16 of the federal Constitution which says that all acts of authority must express their legal basis and their motives).

In its decision, the Supreme Court stated that the case should be decided by seeking to protect the value of judicial independence. In this way, the Court saw an irregular situation that had to be resolved in favour of Mr Arreola: first, if his original period as Magistrate had expired without the designation of a substitute, and if the time required by the State constitution for obtaining the right to life tenure had passed, then it had to be understood that he had been tacitly re-appointed, and that in this way he had acquired the privilege of life tenure. To understand this situation in a different way – the Supreme Court reasoned – would involve subjecting tenure to the discretion of the other powers of the State government, to the detriment of judicial independence, because through that mechanism the members of the Judiciary could permanently be maintained in a situation of uncertainty in connection with their job stability. Moreover, the Court said that the removal of the Magistrate did require an evaluation report explaining the legal basis and motives for not re-electing him.[24]

In other *amparo* cases whose facts were similar to the case of Mr Arreola, the Supreme Court has expanded and refined its doctrine on the judicial independence of State Magistrates. In this way, it has considered that Magistrates have the following constitutional rights:

a) To stay in their position for the entire time allowed by the State constitution;

b) To be re-appointed whenever they have shown through their performance in the relevant office that they do have the qualities that were recognised in them when they were originally appointed;

c) To life tenure; that is, the right not to be removed save for the reasons and procedures established by the Constitution and the corresponding State law on responsibility of public servants;

d) To continue in their functions while the new Magistrates are designated, and until they formally take office.[25]

[24] SCJ, *Semanario Judicial de la Federación y su Gaceta*, Novena Epoca, Plenary session, VII, April 1998, p 121, Thesis: P. XXX/98.
[25] Moreover, the Court has stated that these are not just constitutional rights of the Magistrates, but also constitute the guarantee for Mexico's society to have independent, professional and high-quality justice.

Finally, we have to refer to the capacity of Mexican courts to issue binding criteria. The term used in Mexico to refer to the idea of binding judicial decisions is *jurisprudencia*. Mexico's legal system has developed within the parameters of the so-called civil law tradition. In this way, statute law has been considered as the supreme source of law (being the expression of the 'general will' of the people, through their representatives in Congress); while judge-made law has been considered as having a secondary role, an idea closely related to the belief that judges should have a role limited to applying statute law. In tune with these ideas, the early years of Mexico's legal system did not develop a notion of precedent that resembled in any way the stare decisis principle typical of the common law tradition. In making their decisions, courts were supposed to stick strictly to the text of codified statute law; and codes were supposed to be coherent, complete and clear legal documents, capable of providing a solution to every possible dispute that could arise in society. When deciding cases, judges should not look at other (previous) judicial decisions, but at statute law passed by the legislature. Today, and after a process that took decades, binding decisions rendered in *amparo* proceedings are allowed at the federal level, as governed by the so-called Law on Amparo. Yet, they have several important limitations: a) only the Supreme Court and Collegiate Circuit Courts can issue binding rulings, but in both instances specific majorities are required to produce them; and b) the rulings thus produced are binding only on judges and not on all authorities.[26]

III. JUDICIAL POWER, CONTROL OF CONSTITUTIONALITY AND THE WRIT OF *AMPARO* IN MEXICO

1. The Origins of the Writ of *Amparo*

The idea of the need to have a mechanism to control the constitutionality of acts and resolutions of the different branches of government appeared early in Mexico's constitutional history. Basically, the country had two models at hand. One of them, which could be labelled as the 'Spanish' model, granted that power to the legislative branch of

---

[26] See JM Serna de la Garza, 'The Concept of *Jurisprudencia* in Mexican Law' (2009) 2 *Mexican Law Review.*

government.[27] The other model was the American one, which saw in courts the entities that should perform the function of being the 'Guardians' of the Constitution.

The federal Constitution of 1824 established a mixed system, that is, a sort of compromise between both models. On the one hand, articles 164 and 165 of that Constitution stated that only the National Congress would have the power to resolve questions concerning the meaning of the Constitution, and to pass legislation on the liability of those who violated the Constitution. On the other hand, article 137, section V, paragraph 6 granted the Supreme Court of Justice the power to hear cases involving a breach of the Constitution.[28] Yet, in actual practice the Spanish model prevailed: in 1826, in a case involving a challenge to a piece of State legislation that reduced the number of Justices in the Superior Tribunal of Oaxaca, the Supreme Court consulted Congress on the scope of its power, and Congress answered that the Court had no jurisdiction to hear claims against acts and resolutions of State legislatures.[29] Subsequently, the Federal Congress declared in a number of cases the unconstitutionality of different statutes passed by State legislatures.[30]

As explained by Fix Zamudio, after this initial experience with the 'Spanish' model, in the end the logic of the American model prevailed, with the creation and consolidation of the writ of *amparo*, an institution that was inspired by the American judicial review, particularly as explained by Alexis de Tocqueville in *La Démocratie en Amérique*.[31] Nevertheless, Spanish and French influence can also be traced in the evolution of this institution: the very term '*amparo*' comes from a procedural instrument that existed in Medieval Spain to protect persons from arbitrary detention. In addition, as will be explained in more detail

---

[27] Article 373 of the Cádiz Constitution established the right of every Spaniard to bring claims to the 'Cortes' (that is, Parliament) or to the King, seeking the fulfilment of the Constitution by all public agencies.

[28] Also under the American model, article 123 of the Constitution of 1824 stated that federal judicial power was vested in a Supreme Court, the circuit tribunals and District Judges.

[29] F Tena Ramírez, 'El Control de la Constitucionalidad bajo la vigencia de la Constitución de 1824' (1950) 46 *Revista de la Escuela Nacional de Jurisprudencia* 34–36.

[30] For a list of these cases see M Dublán and J M Lozano, *Legislación Mexicana*, vol II (Mexico, Imprenta del Comercio, 1876) 89–223.

[31] H Fix Zamudio, 'La Suprema Corte de Justicia y el Juicio de Amparo' in Poder Judicial de la Federación, *La Suprema Corte de Justicia y el Pensamiento Jurídico* (Mexico, Suprema Corte de Justicia de la Nación, 1985) 124–25.

below, one of the developments of the writ of *amparo* closely resembles the French 'cassation', which is used as a procedural device to ensure the 'correct' application of statute law by lower courts. The result of this mixture was the Mexican institution that par excellence has served as a mechanism for controlling the constitutionality of acts and resolutions of all public agencies: the so-called writ of *amparo*.

The writ of *amparo* is a complex institution that combines procedural instruments or remedies that have diverse functions, such as: 1. Protection of fundamental rights; 2. Testing allegedly unconstitutional statute law; 3. Contesting judicial decisions; 4. Petitioning against official administrative acts and resolutions; and 5. Protection of the social rights of peasants who are governed by the agrarian reform legal regime.[32] Historically, the writ of *amparo* has rested on three premises:

1. The defence of the Constitution is a task of the judicial power and not of the political branches of government;
2. Judicial intervention to protect the Constitution can only take place as a result of the petition of a person whose constitutional rights have been infringed;
3. The eventual declaration of unconstitutionality benefits only the party that obtained it in the concrete case concerned.[33]

The origins of these features can be found in the reasons given by one of the main creators of the Mexican *amparo*, Manuel Crescencio Rejón, who introduced this institution in the Constitution of the State of Yucatán of 31 March 1841. It is obvious that Rejón was well aware of the way in which judicial review worked under the United States Constitution, and the important role it played in that system. Following this experience, Rejón stated that it was important to strengthen judicial power in Yucatán, in order to avoid the omnipotence of the legislative branch of government.[34]

Yet, Rejón was also worried about the impact that such power vested in the judicial branch of government would have on the legislative branch. Thus, he argued that the power to invalidate legislation should be limited to particular cases. In this way, if judgments only benefited a

---

[32] H Fix Zamudio, 'A Brief Introduction to the Mexican Writ of *Amparo*' (1979) 9 *California Western International Law Journal* 316–17.

[33] F Tena Ramírez, *Derecho Constitucional Mexicano* (Mexico, Porrúa, 1978) 524.

[34] Suprema Corte de Justicia, *Homenaje a Manuel Crescencio Rejón* (Mexico, Suprema Corte de Justicia de la Nación, 1960) 63–65.

personal interest, the legislative power would be offended only in a tangential way: the statute would not be destroyed, but its moral force would be diminished, without suspending its material effect. For Rejón: 'Eventually, it [an unconstitutional statute] shall only die little by little by reiteration of judicial decisions'.[35]

Eventually, these features passed to the federal Constitution of 1857 (articles 101 and 102), mostly thanks to the influence of Mariano Otero who, from 1847 proposed the introduction of Rejón's *amparo* at the federal constitutional level. And from there, the same features were maintained in the Constitution of 1917, article 107 of which states that:

> The judgment shall always be such that it only shall be concerned with particular parties, limited to grant relief and protection in the special case related to the complaint, without making a general declaration with respect to the statute law or act that motivates the complaint.[36]

It is important to mention that this formula always had its critics. On the one hand, some have pointed out that the limited scope of *amparo* judgments formed part of an overall scheme that weakened the judicial power and strengthened instead the executive branch of government: judgments in *amparo* proceedings had no general effects. Besides, there were no other judicial review mechanisms that worked in practice and the Supreme Court was always cautious not to decide *amparo* cases against the president on politically sensitive issues.

On the other hand, critics have argued for decades that it is evident that the *amparo* 'inter partes' formula produces negative effects in terms of equality: a statute can be constitutional for some parties and unconstitutional for others, depending on their ability to obtain a favourable decision in an *amparo* proceeding. Besides, such ability is usually connected with economic capacity to hire expensive legal services.

This sort of criticism has led to a recent constitutional reform (10 June 2011), which has allowed, under specific circumstances, a wider scope of *amparo* judgments: if the Supreme Court declares that a 'general norm' (a statute, an administrative ruling) is unconstitutional on two consecutive occasions, it has to inform the authority that issued the norm of this circumstance. In turn, this authority shall have up to 90 days to 'solve' the problem of unconstitutionality. If this is not done,

---

[35] *ibid.*

[36] Article 107.II of the Mexican Constitution of 1917. See also Article 107.I: 'The *amparo* relief shall be granted only upon a petition of the aggrieved party'.

then the Supreme Court may issue a 'general declaration of unconstitutionality' of the contested norm (nullifying it with general effect), if at least eight out of the 11 Supreme Court Justices vote in that way.[37] Though still limited, this reform is aligned with the process of strengthening the Supreme Court in Mexico's constitutional system, a process that will be explained in section V of this chapter.

2. Evolution of the Writ of *Amparo*

There are two issues that have marked the evolution of Mexico's writ of *amparo*, which in turn have contributed to shape the country's judicial power. One relates to the inadmissibility of the writ of *amparo* in political matters and the other one has to do with the admissibility of the *amparo* to review judicial decisions of State Superior Courts (the so-called *amparo* as cassation).

A. Inadmissibility of the writ of amparo *in political-electoral matters.*

One of the most relevant legal debates that took place in the formative years of Mexico's court system (Stage 1 1824–82), had to do with the definition of the Supreme Court's power to review 'acts of authority'[38] issued by State and federal authorities whenever 'political questions' were involved. Basically, there were two positions in this debate. On the one hand, according to the so-called 'Thesis Iglesias' (also known as the 'incompetence of origin thesis'),[39] the Supreme Court could nullify an act of authority issued by a public authority that had not been properly and legally elected. For this perspective, these authorities were incompetent because they were illegitimate. Thus, the Court could nullify their acts.

On the other hand, the so-called 'Thesis Vallarta'[40] proposed that the Supreme Court had no power to review whether a public authority was

[37] Up to this moment, the Supreme Court has not used this power.

[38] 'Act of authority' is the technical concept used to refer to all those resolutions produced by Mexican public powers (including statutes, regulations, decrees, judgments, etc.), which can be challenged through the writ of *amparo*.

[39] After the name of a President of Mexico's Supreme Court (1873–76), José María Iglesias.

[40] After the name of another President of Mexico's Supreme Court (1877–82), Ignacio L Vallarta.

legitimately elected or not. According to this thesis, federal courts should limit themselves to examining whether or not the federal Constitution, the State constitution and the respective statute law granted competence (powers) to the relevant public agency to issue the acts of authority in question. For Vallarta, controversies raising the 'incompetence of origin' argument were political questions and not true legal disputes, and therefore the Supreme Court had to abstain from hearing them.

In the end, the 'Thesis Vallarta' prevailed in the Supreme Court's opinions of the late nineteenth century,[41] and for most part of the twentieth century. Indeed, this doctrine was functional for the political regime of dictator Porfirio Díaz (1877–1911), and was also consistently applied by courts for most part of the hegemonic party system's history.

This thesis was worded in a binding criterion of the Supreme Court of Mexico in the following terms:

> The Court has sustained the criterion that the judicial authority should not intervene to solve political questions that constitutionally are within the competence of other powers; in *amparo*, courts must not adjudicate on the illegality of the authority, but only on its competence; because if it is declared that an authority appointed as responsible was not properly an authority, the writ of *amparo* would be notoriously inadmissible. To state that article 16 of the Constitution pre-judges the issue of legitimacy of authorities, would lead to attacks on the sovereignty of States, without a constitutional basis, through the decisions of a power that, like the judicial power, lack the powers to do so, transforming itself into a referee on the existence of powers that must be independent from it.[42]

B. *Admissibility of the writ of* amparo *against State judicial decisions*

The other issue that has been widely debated throughout Mexico's constitutional history, refers to the so-called 'judicial *amparo*' or *amparo casación*, that is, the power of federal courts to review the decisions of the superior courts of Mexico's States, in matters that do not involve an issue referred to the federal Constitution, but to whether State law was

---

[41] See Vallarta's opinions as President of the Supreme Court in the cases of *León Guzmán* (23 August 1878) and *Salvador Dondé* (6 August 1881).

[42] Appendix to the *Semanario Judicial de la Federación (1917–1995)*, Suprema Corte de Justicia de la Nación, Fifth Epoch, Third Chamber, VI, p 199. Binding Thesis 243.

correctly applied by State courts in concrete cases. The Constitution of 1857 did not expressly refer to this power of federal courts. However, since the 1860s the pressure of litigants pushed federal courts to start making an interpretation of article 14 of the federal Constitution which allowed them to make that review. The justification was this: article 14 stated that 'No person shall be judged or sentenced, save according to statutes passed previously to the fact and *exactly applicable* to it, by a court that has been previously established by the law' (emphasis added). In the end, the Supreme Court interpreted this article in the sense that there was a constitutional right to the '*exact application* of statute law'. Therefore, if States' superior courts had not applied statute law 'exactly' when deciding disputes that were a matter of State law, litigants could seek the protection of that constitutional right through the writ of *amparo*, heard by federal courts.[43]

The 'judicial *amparo*' or '*amparo casación*' which under the Constitution of 1857 was a creation of the Supreme Court's case law, was expressly established in article 107 of the Constitution of 1917. Notably, this institution is at the centre of today's debate on judicial federalism in Mexico, which could be summarised by posing the following questions: 1) Does the *amparo casación* challenge the sovereignty of States? 2) Does the *amparo casación* challenge the principle of *res judicata*? 3) Does the *amparo casación* represent a 'distortion' of the writ of *amparo*? 4) Is the *amparo casación* a tool with which the citizens of the States can counteract the influence of powerful actors that operate at State level on State courts? In this chapter, I shall concentrate on the last question, since it gives an idea of the context in which the relationship between federal courts and State courts has developed throughout Mexico's constitutional history.[44]

In the debate on *amparo casación*, it has been argued that the institution is justified as the sole means of counteracting the influence that 'powerful men' and/or the governors usually exercise upon State courts. Specifically, in the project of reforms that Carranza put forward to the constituent assembly in 1916, he explained and justified the survival of the *amparo casación* based on the exposure of State justice systems to the

---

[43] The first '*amparo judicial*' was issued on 29 April 1869 in the case of *Miguel Vega v Superior Tribunal of the State of Sinaloa*, challenging article 8 of the Act on Amparo, which expressly prohibited *amparo* against judicial decisions.

[44] See JM Serna de la Garza, 'Notes on the Debate About the Amparo Casación in Mexico' (2004) 2 *Mexican Law Review* 131–45.

powerful influence of governors who 'clearly interfere in matters that are completely beyond their duties'; thus, 'it was necessary to have a remedy that leads them to resort to the federal judicial authority to repress such excesses'. Pursuant to the aforementioned project, the *amparo casación* should be preserved 'to be safe from judges' arbitrariness'.[45] As we can see from this quotation, within the *amparo casación* there is a safety-valve rationale, which allows 'external' review of State judicial procedures. In the end, the Constitution of 1917 established and consolidated the *amparo casación*, but the institution has always been seen by some as an improper evolution of the writ of *amparo*.

In sum, the *amparo casación* has been the safety-valve that local litigants have made use of to overthrow powerful local influence in State justice. It is an instrument for the citizens who, for any reason, have to appear before State courts to resolve a controversy related to them, their families or patrimony. Nevertheless, this development caused unexpected problems that affected the entire system of courts, as I shall explain in the following section.

IV. BACKLOG AS THE CONSEQUENCE OF THE *AMPARO CASACIÓN*: 'THE IMPOSSIBLE TASK OF THE COURT'

As a result of the development and consolidation of the *amparo casación*, the Supreme Court of Mexico became not only the guardian of the Constitution, but the guardian of the entire legal system, both at the federal and State levels. That is to say, it was in charge of checking the constitutionality of acts and resolutions of all public authorities in the land; but also was entrusted with the responsibility of checking that all federal and State courts apply federal and State statutes correctly.

As one can imagine, in a country with 31 States and one Federal District, whose population and urbanisation has consistently increased since the approval of the Constitution of 1917, the function of the Supreme Court as a tribunal of cassation soon overtook the Court's capacities. The number of cases that reached the Court through this kind of *amparo* was from the beginning very high, leading one commentator to define this function as the 'impossible task of the Court'.[46] Just

---

[45] Message by the First Head of the 1916 constituent convention, taken from F Tena Ramírez, *Leyes Fundamentales de México* (Mexico, Porrúa, 1995) 750 and 751.

[46] E Rabasa, *El Artículo 14* (Mexico, Porrúa, 1955) 103–4.

to give an idea of the numbers, by 1950 a total of 37,881 cases reached the Supreme Court through *amparo casación* proceedings.[47]

The initial response given to this problem was to increase the number of Justices of the Supreme Court and to organise them in separate and specialised chambers. In this way, in 1928 the Constitution was amended to increase the number of Justices from 11 to 16; besides this, the reform established that the Court would work either in plenary sessions (*en banc*) or in chambers (three). Each chamber would be formed of five Justices and would hear, respectively, *amparo casación* cases that arose from criminal, civil and administrative disputes.

Yet, the backlog problem continued, so in 1934 the number of Justices was increased to 21, with the creation of another chamber (specialising in labour matters). Later on, another reform (of 1951) created one more chamber (the 'auxiliary chamber') that helped the other chambers in connection with civil, criminal and fiscal matters,[48] thus the number of Justices reached a total of 26.

The reform of 1951 was particularly important, because it introduced another element to fight backlog: the creation of the Collegiate Circuit Courts (formed of three Magistrates), which shared with the Supreme Court and its chambers the competence to hear cases in *amparo casación*.[49] With the same aim, the reform of that year introduced the so-called 'dismissal for procedural inactivity', which meant that if in 180 days there were no motions made by the parties in an *amparo* case (in civil and administrative matters), the action had to be dismissed. The global result of this reform was that by 1965, 'only' 15,008 *amparo casación* cases reached the Supreme Court.

Subsequent reforms also had as their main goal the reduction of the number of cases that reached the Supreme Court, through a redistribution of the competences of that Court and the Collegiate Circuit Courts. For example, the reforms enacted on 25 October 1967 defined the amount involved in the dispute as a criterion for defining competence to hear the corresponding *amparo* suit (the Supreme Court would hear disputes in which the amount involved was superior to 100,000 Mexican pesos in civil matters and to 50,000 Mexican pesos in administrative

---

[47] Acuerdo del Pleno de la Suprema Corte de Justicia 9/1999, 3 August 1999.

[48] F Tena Ramírez, *Derecho Constitucional Mexicano* (1978), above n 33, 505–6.

[49] Five Collegiate Circuit Courts were created in 1951, based in the cities of Mexico, Puebla, Monterrey, Guadalajara and Veracruz.

matters).[50] Disputes in which the amount involved did not reach those sums, would be heard by Collegiate Circuit Courts.

Later on, and continuing this line of evolution dominated by the logic of 'alleviation' of the Supreme Court work-load, the reform of 1986 established that in principle *all* cases in *amparo casación* would be heard by the Collegiate Circuit Courts. This was seen by the framers of the reform as the culmination of a process of de-centralisation of federal justice and of bringing justice closer to the people.[51] Moreover, the reform of that year established the 'power of attraction' of the Supreme Court which basically means that at its discretion, the Court can attract and hear an *amparo casación* case that in principle should be heard by Collegiate Circuit Courts, when it considers that the case involves an issue of special national relevance.[52] Moreover, the reform of 1986 also granted to the Supreme Court the power to determine the number, division in circuits, territorial jurisdiction and specialisation of Collegiate Circuit Courts and of District Judges, as well as the power to issue 'General Orders' to allow a better and more efficient distribution of work among the chambers of the Supreme Court (before the reform, the distribution of tasks among the chambers required a legislative reform of the *Ley Orgánica del Poder Judicial de la Federación*).[53]

To close this section, we must note that one of the consequences of the line of evolution of the federal judicial power described above was its extraordinary expansion. If in 1951 there were five Collegiate Circuit Courts, six Unitary Circuit Courts and 46 District Judges, by 1990 there were 66 Collegiate Circuit Courts, 30 Unitary Circuit Courts and 148 District Judges. This, in turn, created an administrative problem of considerable dimensions: how would it be possible to guarantee order, discipline and quality in a structure as large as Mexico's federal judicial power? How could the Supreme Court be efficient in both deciding cases and administering this large administrative apparatus? This problem was addresses by the constitutional reform of 1994, which will

---

[50] H Fix Zamudio and JR Cossío, *El Poder Judicial en el ordenamiento mexicano* (Mexico, Fondo de Cultura Económica, 1996) 158.

[51] M Suárez Muñoz, 'La Evolución Constitucional de la Suprema Corte de Justicia de la Nación' in Instituto de Investigaciones Jurídicas, *Las Nuevas Bases Constitucionales y Legales del Sistema Judicial Mexicano, La Reforma Judicial 1986–1987* (Mexico, Porrúa, 1987) 338.

[52] This power of the Court can be exercised either ex officio, or upon the petition of the relevant Collegiate Circuit Court or of the Attorney General of the Republic.

[53] Article 94 of Mexico's Constitution.

discussed separately, in the following section, since it responded to an imperative which was different from the mere 'alleviation' of the Supreme Court's backlog.

V. TOWARDS A CONSTITUTIONAL COURT: THE REFORM OF 1994

The constitutional reform of 1994 restructured the federal judicial power in a number of ways. Its main goal was to strengthen the Supreme Court as a constitutional tribunal, specialising in the control of constitutionality, as a defender of the Constitution, for the sake of making the rule of law a reality in Mexico. The reform's central idea was that the Supreme Court should be devoted exclusively to the application and interpretation of the Constitution. Indeed, and after 18 years, there is enough evidence to say that this reform altered in an important way the balance of power between the Executive and the federal Judiciary.

The reform package was introduced by President Zedillo, in the context of great social unrest and complaints against the justice system.[54] In fact, the subject was one of the most important topics for all candidates in the presidential election of 1994. Political liberalisation of the previous two decades had opened up the way to increased demands for effective rights protection, which implied a redefinition of the role of courts within the system. Yet, apart from the pressure of public opinion, Fix Fierro, an expert on the subject, has suggested a number of reasons that fostered the ambitious judicial reforms of 1994: first, the calculation of a fraction of the hegemonic party political elite, that in the event of a loss of power, it would be better to have an independent Supreme Court rather that one subordinated to the incumbent Executive (the logic of 'insurance policy'). Secondly, Fix points to the very important process of change in economic policy that occurred in Mexico from 1982 (year of the debt crisis), that was deepened during the 1990s with the subscription of NAFTA with the US and Canada. This process implied an extensive programme of legislative change, mostly in those sectors that have

---

[54] The most radical and visible example of this was the uprising of the Zapatista movement in the southern State of Chiapas, in January of 1994. This social movement fostered a national discussion on the rights of indigenous people in Mexico that eventually led to the constitutional reform of 14 August 2001, which incorporated most of the standards of the ILO's Convention 169 on Indigenous and Tribal Peoples (Geneva, 27 June 1989) into article 2 of the federal Constitution.

to do with economic activity; but also required the strengthening of courts in their role as the 'guardians' of the legal system.[55] Eventually, by the end of 1994 the PRI government of President Zedillo managed to build a reform coalition with PAN legislators, whose programme as an opposition party had always proposed increased judicial independence. In essence, this reform can be summarised as follows:

A. The number of Justices of the Supreme Court was reduced from 26 to 11. The idea was to have a more compact entity, specialising in hearing disputes involving a constitutional matter. Yet, still the court retained the power to hear *amparo casación* cases through the 'power of attraction' described above. The five chambers were consolidated into two: the civil and criminal chamber; and the administrative and labour chamber. In addition, with this reform Justices would be appointed for a period of 15 years,[56] without possible re-appointment. They would be appointed by the president of the Republic (who proposed a three-name list for each vacancy) with ratification by two-thirds of the Senate (the purpose of this is to encourage the designation of non-partisan Justices). Yet, if the Senate did not decide in favour of one of the candidates within 30 days after the presidential proposal, the president would be able to pick up the name of the person to fill the vacancy. The same would happen if the Senate rejected in its entirety the three-name list proposed by the president on two consecutive occasions (article 96 of the Constitution). Moreover, they would be designated in a staggered way.

B. Justices were discharged from most administrative functions. Traditionally, the administration of the federal judicial power was performed by the Supreme Court Justices themselves, through the so-called 'Commission of Administration'. However, this changed in 1994, with the creation of the 'Council of the Federal Judiciary', which is an entity in charge of administering the formal federal judicial career of Circuit Magistrates and District Judges (designations, promotions, discipline, licences, training and continuing legal

---

[55] H Fix Fierro, 'La Reforma Judicial en México: ¿De Dónde Viene? ¿Hacia Dónde Va?' (2003), n 8 above, 268–77.

[56] The idea of the 15 years of tenure rule was to strike a balance between the benefits of long periods in office (in terms of judicial independence), and the need to recycle membership in order to introduce new perspectives into judicial decision-making. See *Exposición de Motivos* of the constitutional reform decree published in the Official Gazette of the Federation on 31 December 1994.

education).[57] The idea was to discharge the Justices of the Supreme Court from the burden of administrative work, so that they could concentrate on their substantive tasks, that is, on judicial decision-making, in the context of strengthening the Court as a tribunal specialising in the protection of the Constitution (and this was consistent with the reduction in the number of Justices referred to above). Today, the Council is formed of seven members. One of them is the Justice-President of the Supreme Court (who presides over the Council); three members are appointed by at least eight votes of the Supreme Court Justices themselves, from among the Circuit Magistrates and District Judges; two members are designated by the Senate and one by the president of the Republic (article 99 of the Constitution).[58]

C. The Supreme Court was strengthened as a constitutional tribunal, in connection with its jurisdiction to hear disputes of a constitutional nature between branches of the federal or State governments, and between the different levels of government of Mexico's federal system. This happened through two mechanisms:

a) The reform of the so-called 'constitutional controversies', established in article 105 of the Constitution. Originally, the Constitution of 1917 granted the Supreme Court the power to

> hear cases of controversies between two or more States, between the branches of government of one State on the constitutionality of their acts, and between the Federation and one or more States, as well as those in which the Federation is a party.

This clause had limited scope since it did not include, for example, the hypothesis of conflicts in which municipalities or the Federal District were involved.[59] Yet, the reform of 1994 broadened the scope of article 105, by including all sorts of conflicts

---

[57] H Fix Fierro, 'La Administración de la Suprema Corte de Justicia de la Nación' (1997) 95 *Revista de Administración Pública* 28–32.

[58] The idea of having three members designated from 'outside' of the judicial power is to avoid an inbreeding culture in the administration of this federal branch of government.

[59] Apart from this limited scope of article 105 of the Constitution, the unwritten rules of the hegemonic party system propitiated the resolution of disputes between public entities by political negotiation mediated by the president of the Republic, rather than by constitutional proceedings.

of competence that may arise between different branches of the federal government, and between the different levels of government of Mexico's federal system.

b) The introduction of a new constitutional procedure to challenge the unconstitutionality of statutes or treaties: the so-called 'action of unconstitutionality'. This is an abstract mechanism for controlling the constitutionality of statutes and treaties, since it does not arise from a concrete case of application of the challenged statute. In this way, the Supreme Court can hear cases that seek to have a statute or treaty declared null and void if brought by any one of the following: 1. at least 33 per cent of the members of the Chamber of Deputies in the case of federal statute law or statutes passed for the Federal District by the Congress of the Union;[60] 2. at least 33 per cent of the members of the Senate in the case of federal statute law, or statutes passed for the Federal District by the Congress of the Union or international treaties; 3. the Republic's Attorney General in the case of federal, State and Federal District statute law and international treaties; 4. at least 33 per cent of the members of the State legislatures in the case of State laws; 5. at least 33 per cent of the members of the Legislative Assembly of the Federal District in case of the assembly's statutes. Moreover, the corresponding action must be brought within 30 days of the publication of the challenged statute or treaty.

c) Originally, in 1994 article 105.II expressly established that the action of unconstitutionality could not be used to challenge electoral laws. However, in 1996 this article was amended, in order to allow this possibility, which eventually became a key element in the transformation of federal and State electoral legislation, in the context of Mexico's transition to democracy (see above Chapter 2). Moreover, article 105.II was amended once more in June of 2011, in order to allow the National Commission on Human Rights to bring the action of unconstitutionality against federal, State, Federal District statutes and international treaties that violate any of the human rights foreseen in Mexico's Constitution or international treaties on human rights signed by

---

[60] The Congress of the Union shares with the Legislative Assembly of the Federal District the power to pass legislation for the Federal District, each in different subject areas, defined in article 122 of the Constitution.

Mexico. The same power was granted to State and Federal District's commissions on human rights, to challenge State and Federal District statutes that violate human rights.

In both cases, a minimum of eight Justices must concur in a finding of unconstitutionality, to produce the effect of invalidity of the norm under challenge. This 'super-majority' rule is the result of seeking to strike a balance between the old tradition of Supreme Court decisions having only 'inter partes' effectin *amparo* (for considerations of separation of powers and deference to the legislative branch), and the perceived need to allow the Court to issue general declarations of unconstitutionality, with the effect of invalidation of the challenged norm, at least in some cases, in constitutional controversies and actions of unconstitutionality.

As we explained in Chapter 3, section VIII, the first notorious challenge to Executive power through a constitutional controversy occurred in 1999. Constitutional controversy 26/99 was brought by the Chamber of Deputies against the president's refusal to disclose information that was required to conduct an audit of a special fund created in 1995 to support banks that were in trouble as a consequence of the financial crisis that erupted in December of 1994. As we saw, the Executive was ordered to disclose the information.

For its part, the first action of unconstitutionality in which the Supreme Court decided against the Executive's party (PRI) was an action filed in 1998 by the PRD, against a reform to the State electoral code passed by the PRI dominated legislature and promulgated by the governor, both of the State of Quintana Roo. Calculating that they were on the brink of losing their absolute majority of the seats of the State congress in the next election, PRI politicians promoted a reform that sought to introduced into the electoral code the so-called 'governability clause', which gave additional seats as a 'premium' or 'award' to the political party that obtained the relative majority in the State legislature, up to the point of letting that party have the absolute majority of the legislature's seats. The plaintiff's most important argument was that the 'governability clause' was not recognised by the federal Constitution as a valid principle of representation to govern the composition of State legislatures (since article 116.II of the Constitution says that State legislatures shall be formed of legislators elected through the principles of plurality and proportional representation).

The Supreme Court decided, unanimously, in favour of the plaintiff. The decision was unprecedented for two reasons. First, because by declaring the unconstitutionality of a reform to the respective section of the State electoral code, it affected the fundamental interest of the PRI in keeping control of Quintana Roo's legislature; and secondly, because the Supreme Court inaugurated a kind of reasoning based on constitutional values rather than on the letter of the constitutional text. Indeed, the Court identified in the section of the Constitution that refers to the election of deputies to the federal Congress (article 54) the constitutional value of political pluralism, and used it as a parameter of control for assessing, and eventually declaring, the unconstitutionality of the 'governability clause' contained in a State electoral code.[61]

VI. THE COURT'S ARTICLE 97 INVESTIGATIVE POWER

Before the constitutional reform of 10 June 2011, article 97 of the Mexican Constitution established the so-called 'power of investigation' of the Supreme Court. This provision allowed the Supreme Court (at its own discretion or upon the petition of the federal Executive, or one of the Chambers of the federal Congress and of a State governor) to conduct an investigation under different hypotheses, which originally included the behaviour of judges, facts that might constitute a violation of fundamental rights, a violation of the citizens' right to vote, or any federal crime. After successive reforms, the Court's power of investigation was limited to facts that constitute 'serious violations of fundamental rights'.

Between 1917 and 1994 the Court conducted only one article 97 investigation.[62] Yet, between 1995 and 2010 the Court exercised this power five times.[63] I will refer to one of those cases (*Aguas Blancas* case,

---

[61] SCJ, Action of unconstitutionality 6/98, *President of the PRD v Legislature and Governor of the State of Quintana Roo*. Published in the Official Gazette of the Federation on 28 October 1998.

[62] In connection with the killing of a group of people as a consequence of a post-electoral conflict in the city of León, State of Guanajuato (1946). In this case, the Court determined that indeed there had been violation of fundamental rights, violation of the right to vote and the commission of federal crimes. However, the effect of this determination did not go beyond a mere declaration.

[63] The cases are: *Aguas Blancas* (1/1995); *Atenco* (3/2009); *Lydia Cacho* (2/2006); *Oaxaca* (1/2007); and *Guardería ABC* (1/2009).

1/1995), in order to illustrate how through this investigation power the Supreme Court started to play an increasingly relevant role in mediating very difficult and complicated conflicts in Mexico's recent history.

On 28 June 1995, a group of 17 peasants was massacred by personnel of the public security forces of the State of Guerrero, in a place called Aguas Blancas. The persons killed were all members of the Peasants' Organisation of the Southern Sierra (*Organización Campesina de la Sierra del Sur*) opposed to the PRI. The massacre ocurred when they were in their way to a political rally organised in the town of Atoyac. The police-men involved in the acts argued that the goal of the police operation was to dissolve an armed meeting, but later on it was known that the persons that had been attacked were indeed unarmed.

A set of social movements requested the Supreme Court to exercise its article 97 power of investigation. Yet, the Court was reluctant to do so. In the middle of discussions on who had legal standing to request an investigation, the federal Executive (controlled by the PRI) requested the Court's intervention on 4 March 1996. The Court decided to inter-vene by a 10-1 majority.

Interpreting the Executive's request as the withdrawal of political support, on 11 March 1996 the PRI governor of Guerrero requested from the State Congress an 'indefinite leave' (*licencia indefinida*) to facil-itate the investigation of the case by the Supreme Court.

In the end, the Supreme Court determined that the actions of State officials (including the State governor and other top officials) in the Aguas Blancas events constituted serious violations of the fundamental rights of the victims (freedom of expression, freedom of transit, due process rights). Moreover, it also established a criterion to determine what a 'serious violation of fundamental rights' is, in connection with its article 97 power of investigation: a 'serious violation' of fundamental rights was defined as one in which society is put in a state of material, social, political or legal insecurity, as a consequence of situations in which: a) the public authorities that have the duty to protect the popula-tion are the very ones that produce violent acts, on the pretext of estab-lishing social discipline; and b) public authorities do not act in cases of widespread disorder, or are negligent, indifferent or impotent to channel social relations in a pacific way.[64]

---

[64] SCJ, *Semanario Judicial de la Federación y su Gaceta*, Ninth Epoch, Plenary session, III, June 1996, p 459. Isolated Thesis LXXXVI/96.

In July 1997, 37 public servants that were involved in the Aguas Blancas events were sentenced to penalties that ranged from 26 years to eight months in prison.[65] However, neither the State governor nor top-level officials were investigated or convicted in connection with the killings. Eventually, the case was taken to the Inter-American Commission on Human Rights, which determined that the investigations conducted by the Mexican state to try and punish the people responsible for the massacre, had not been performed in the manner required by the standards established by the Inter-American Court of Human Rights.[66]

In spite of its more frequent use, the Supreme Court never felt comfortable with the power of investigation granted by article 97 of the Constitution. In the view of most of its members, it was not jurisdictional in nature and it was not compatible with the Court's design and functions as a constitutional tribunal. By the mid-2000s legislators of different parties proposed reforms intended to eliminate that power from the Constitution; in his annual report the President of the Supreme Court made public that he had manifested the federal Congress that a majority of the Court's Justices were in favour of eliminating the article 97 power of investigation.

This gave rise to a debate in favour of and against the proposal. For some, the investigation power broke with the principle of separation of powers; besides, the Court's resolutions were not judgments, but amounted only to a kind of report with no binding force. Moreover, critics of this power also argued that the institution had been created when Mexico had no other mechanisms to protect the Constitution, but since the 1990s the National Commission on Human Rights could perfectly well conduct investigations like those allowed by article 97 of the Constitution.

Others were in favour of preserving the Court's power of investigation, saying that it was an extraordinary mechanism for the protection of human rights, intended to work in cases of 'serious' violation of fundamental rights. In the context of Mexico, the authority of the Court

---

[65] *La Jornada*, 12 July 1997.

[66] The Commission recommended the Mexican state to complete the investigation in a serious, impartial and effective way against top governmental officials possibly involved in the massacre, and to establish a proper compensation to the relatives of the victims. See Inter-American Commission on Human Rights. *Report No 49/97*, 18 February 1997, paras 54–60.

could help to investigate cases in which no other entity would be willing or able to inquire.

In the end, the first posture prevailed: the constitutional reform of 10 June 2011 eliminated the Supreme Court's power of investigation. One only hopes that it is not missed in the future.

VII. CONCLUSION

We shall come back to examine the Court (particularly in connection with the constitutional controversies procedure) in Chapter 6 of this book, since it has played an important role in shaping the structure of relations among branches and levels of government of Mexico's constitutional system through its decisions. For the moment, I would only like to emphasise that today the Supreme Court has come out from its traditional political isolation. In fact, it can be argued that the reforms of 1994 have contributed to the judicialisation of the political process, as actors increasingly resort to the Court to resolve their differences. By changing appointment procedures of the federal Judiciary at all levels, that reform considerably transformed the incentive and opportunity structures of Justices and judges, in favour of increased judicial independence.[67]

Moreover, the Court's increased power within the constitutional system can be seen in its willingness to decide on highly contested economic and social issues (contrary to its tradition of self-restraint developed under the hegemonic party system). In this way, the Court has decided cases on: the capitalisation of interest on bank debt; the unconstitutionality of the luxury tax; the right of entrepreneurs to refuse membership in government-sponsored chambers of commerce; the federal government's right to audit the national university; the fining of the state-owned oil company for a spill on the Gulf of Mexico's coast; the denial of extradition to the United States of alleged criminals who could face the death penalty (this penalty is not constitutional in

---

[67] For the Executive, providing career incentives beyond the Supreme Court was a way both of subordinating the Judiciary to executive influence and of including the Judiciary within the sphere of state patronage and clientelist relations which characterised the hegemonic party system. See P Domingo, 'Judicial Independence: The Politics of the Supreme Court in Mexico' (2000) 32 *Journal of Latin American Studies* 725.

Mexico); the right of living individuals to sell their organs for transplants; and the de-criminalisation of abortion in cases of rape or severe foetal deformity.[68]

To conclude this chapter, we can say that in the 1990s economic liberalisation and political reform combined, in the context of a more complex and demanding society, to produce a process of institutional transition of the judicial power. According to some analysts, this transition has also been characterised by a greater intervention of legal rules and institutions in Mexico's social life. It seems that the law as such has started to transform itself into a true instrument for more technical and efficient regulation of social relations, and not a mere symbolic device for political use.[69] In this process, the Supreme Court of Justice has been called to play an increasingly relevant role, as the 'guardian' of the Constitution.

FURTHER READING

Cossío Díaz, JR, 'Perspectives on the Judicial Reform in Mexico' (2007) 7 *Mexican Law Review*.

Fix Fierro, Hector, 'Judicial Reform and the Supreme Court of Mexico: the Trajectory of Three Years' (1998) 6 *United States-Mexico Law Journal* 1.

Inclán Oseguera, S, 'Judicial Reform in Mexico: Political Insurance or the Search for Political Legitimacy?' (2009) 62 *Political Research Quarterly* 753.

Magaloni, B, 'Enforcing the Autocratic Political Order and the Role of Courts: The Case of Mexico' in Ginsburg, T and Moustafa, T (eds), *Rule by Law: The Politics of Courts in Authoritarian Regimes* (Cambridge, Cambridge University Press, 2008).

Ríos Figueroa J, 'Fragmentation of Power and the Emergence of an Effective Judiciary in Mexico, 1994–2002' (2007) 49 *Latin American Politics and Society* 31.

---

[68] This list of cases has been taken from JS Finkel, *Judicial Reform as Political Insurance, Argentina, Peru and Mexico in the 1990s* (Indiana, University of Notre Dame, 2008) 101–2.

[69] In fact, Fix Fierro argues that the reform of 1994 also opened the door for a gradual and on-going transformation of State courts (a sort of 'detonating' factor). Fix Fierro, 'La Reforma Judicial en México' (2003), above n 8, 266 and 277.

Sánchez, A, Magaloni, B and Magar, E, 'Legalist vs Interpretativists: The Supreme Court and the Democratic Transition in Mexico' in Helmke, G and Ríos-Figueroa, J (eds), *Courts in Latin America* (Cambridge, Cambridge University Press, 2011).

Shirk, DA, 'Justice Reform in Mexico: Change and Challenges in the Judicial Sector', Working Paper (San Diego CA, Mexico Institute, Woodrow Wilson International Center for Scholars and Trans-Border Institute, University of San Diego, 2010).

Vargas, JA, 'The Rebirth of the Supreme Court of Mexico: An Appraisal of President Zedillo's Judicial Reform of 1995' (1996) 11 *American University Journal of International Law and Policy* 295.

6

The Federal System

———◈———

Introduction – The Constitutional Formula for Allocating Legislative Competences – Fiscal Federalism – Mechanisms of Collaboration in Mexico's Federal System – Municipal Government – The Constitutional Status of the Federal District – Recent Developments in State Constitutionalism – Conclusion

I. INTRODUCTION

A S I HAVE already explained in the first chapter of this book, the issue on the federal form for the Mexican state was a matter of violent dispute during the nineteenth century. Nevertheless, in spite of the fact that in the end the groups that proclaimed the federal principle prevailed (approving the 1857 federal Constitution), living federalism was ineffective in the absence of a true constitutional government and rule of law both under the regime of Porfirio Díaz (1877–1911) and the hegemonic party system (1929–2000).

The improper use that Mexican presidents gave to the so-called procedure of 'disappearance of powers' foreseen in article 76.V of the Constitution is a good example to explain the terms on which federalism operated in the context of the hegemonic party system. According to this article, the Senate has the power to declare, whenever all the powers of a State have 'disappeared', that the time has come to appoint a provisional governor, who shall call elections in the relevant State. In addition, that article states that the appointment of the provisional governor shall be made by two-thirds of the members present of the Senate (during Congress recess, by the latter's Permanent Committee), after the proposal of a three-name list by the president of the Republic.

The origins of this article can be found in the reform of 1874 to the Constitution of 1857, and it was justified by the perceived necessity of having a constitutional solution to cases like this one: in 1872 the executive and legislative powers of the State of Yucatán were deposed by the federal Army, when both branches of State government decided to extend their mandate beyond the terms allowed by both the federal and the State constitutions. Yet, there was no constitutional mechanism to resolve a situation in which the powers of a State had 'disappeared'. Hence the rule of article 72.B.V of the 1857 Constitution was reformed in 1874, which passed with minor changes into article 76.V of the 1917 Constitution.

The most important issue concerning the interpretation of this article has to do with the scope of the Senate's role within the procedure described above: does it have the power to declare that the powers of a State have disappeared, at its own discretion? Or, given the case that the powers of a State have disappeared (for objective reasons), the Senate has the power to declare that under those circumstances, the moment has come to appoint a provisional governor who has to call an election?

The hegemonic party system favoured the first interpretation: the Senate could freely declare that the powers of a State had disappeared. In this way, controlling the Senate (and using as a pretext any internal conflict within the relevant State), the Executive was able to get rid of 'uncomfortable' governors on 62 occasions between 1917 and 1975.[1]

Yet, the way in which the procedure for 'disappearing' powers was used by Mexico's presidents was always a source of irritation and protest on behalf of the States. Eventually, this led Congress to pass a statute in 1978 that established objective standards and guidelines setting limits to the exercise of this power. Essentially, this statute made it clear that the Senate has the power to declare that a provisional governor should be appointed, but only under precise circumstances and for objective reasons: if the powers of a State breach the principles of the federal regime; if they abandon their functions, unless by reason of an Act of God; if they are physically unable to perform their functions; if they extend their terms in office beyond the time legally permitted; if they promote or adopt a form of government different from those foreseen in articles 40 and 115 of the Constitution (namely, democratic, republican and

---

[1] M González Oropeza, *La Intervención Federal en la Desaparición de Poderes*, 2nd edn (Mexico, UNAM, 1987) 155–233.

representative government and local government based on municipalities). Notably, since the approval of this statute, there has not been a single use of the mechanism of article 76.V of Mexico's Constitution. Today, Mexico's federal system faces the challenge of finding a new arrangement in the absence of a hegemonic party system. The president is not omnipotent any longer, though still heads a nation-wide public administration and, most importantly, controls most fiscal resources; for their part, governors have gained political strength (which cannot be said of State legislatures and judicial powers), but lack other resources to perform their existing functions or assume new ones. In addition, all these actors face the challenge of finding forms and mechanisms of collaboration and coordination to guarantee efficacy in the different policy areas.

It is important to notice that more intense interactions among the different levels of government have led to cooperation, but also to disputes on the identity of who has the constitutional power to do what. In this context, as we shall see in this chapter, the Supreme Court of Justice is playing an increasingly relevant role, as a referee that mediates in conflicts of competence through the judicial process. This is one of the new features of Mexico's federal system.

In this chapter, we shall examine some of the main features of Mexico's federal system, and their performance in the context of the democratic and multi-party system under construction. I shall study first the constitutional formula for allocating legislative competences and then I will contrast it with the formula for allocating taxation power (fiscal federalism). Later on I shall examine different mechanisms that have been designed to achieve some measure of collaboration and coordination between the components of Mexico's federal system. Afterwards I will refer to the constitutional configuration of the municipal government, which is the basis of the territorial division and political-administrative organisation of all Mexican States, with the exception of the Federal District (Mexico City) which has its own constitutional status (that will also be examined). Finally, I will make a brief reference to recent developments in State constitutionalism.

II. THE CONSTITUTIONAL FORMULA FOR ALLOCATING
LEGISLATIVE COMPETENCES

1. The Basic Formula: Article 124 of the Constitution

The basic organising principle for the division of competences in Mexico's federal system can be found in the residual clause established in article 124 of the Mexican Constitution of 1917. Partially inspired by the Tenth Amendment to the US Constitution, this article states that: 'It shall be understood that the powers not expressly attributed by this Constitution to the federal authorities, are reserved to the States'.

The similarity between this formulation and that of the Tenth Amendment to the US Constitution is apparent.[2] However, they are not identical and therefore their meanings and impact upon the allocation of powers are diverse. One of the differences has to do with the use that article 124 of the Mexican Constitution makes of the adverb 'expressly'.

Interestingly, the use of the word 'expressly' was a polemical issue in the debates that led to the Tenth Amendment. Section 2 of the Articles of Confederation stated that: 'Each State retains its sovereignty, freedom and independence, and every power, jurisdiction, and right, which is not by this Confederation expressly delegated to the United States in Congress assembled'. Eventually, the Tenth Amendment removed this word in 1791. In this way, it was understood that the federal government could exercise powers that were not expressly allocated to it by the Constitution.[3]

The antecedent of article 124 of the Mexican Constitution of 1917 was article 117 of the Mexican Constitution of 1857. The Mexican constituent assembly of 1856–57 borrowed part of the Tenth Amendment formulation, but decided to include the adverb 'expressly'. It was not a casual occurrence but rather a manifestation of intent. The intention was to create a more rigid system of division of competences between the federation and the States, in such a way as to make it perfectly possible to distinguish which defined set of competences belonged to the former, and which to the latter. As I have argued elsewhere, this seems

---

[2] The Tenth Amendment to the US Constitution reads: 'The powers not delegated to the United States by the Constitution, nor prohibited by it to the States, are reserved to the States respectively or to the people'.

[3] J Carpizo, *Estudios Constitucionales*, 2nd edn (Mexico, UNAM/LGEM, 1983).

to be linked with the perception that a flexible or ambiguous formula for allocating competences could lead to harsh conflicts and even to disintegration.[4]

Another difference between article 124 of the Mexican Constitution and the US Tenth Amendment lies in the reference that the latter makes to the 'prohibitions to the States'. Article 124 does not make that reference, but a systematic interpretation of the Mexican Constitution allows room for an identical reading of this article (in relation to the US Tenth Amendment). The Mexican Constitution itself establishes a series of prohibitions on the exercise of certain powers by the States. Some of those prohibitions have an absolute character, and are defined by article 117. In no way can these powers be exercised by the States.[5] Others are relative, which means that they could eventually be exercised by the States, but only with the authorisation of the federal Congress. These are listed in article 118.[6]

For its part, it must be mentioned that article 115 foresees a sphere of competences that belong to municipal governments. They have the competence to pass rulings related to the public services that fall under their exclusive jurisdiction, such as potable water, cemeteries, markets, parks, public security and tranport, among others; however, this competence has to be exercised according to the bases outlined by the legislature of the State to which they belong.[7]

The balance of power between the federation and the States can be measured by identifying the quantity and quality of the powers expressly allocated to the federation. Quantitatively, most of the subject areas expressly allocated to the federal Legislature are listed in article 73 of the Constitution. Notably, this is one of the longest articles in the

---

[4] JM Serna de la Garza, *El Sistema Federal Mexicano, un Análisis Jurídico* (Mexico, UNAM, 2008) 53–66.

[5] For example, they cannot enter into a treaty with a foreign government; they have no currency power; they cannot impose levies upon the transit of persons or merchandise through their territory; nor can they borrow money from foreign governments or institutions, amongst many other matters.

[6] For example, they cannot, without the authorisation of Congress, impose export and import taxes; or have a permanent army or a naval fleet.

[7] See article 115 of the Mexican Constitution. It must be pointed out that unlike the federal and local legislatures, the municipalities cannot pass 'enactments' (*leyes*). Yet, they are able to produce rulings that are known as '*bandos de policía y buen gobierno*', '*reglamentos*', '*circulares*' and '*disposiciones administrativas*'.

constitutional text.[8] Qualitatively, the matters that fall within the jurisdiction of the federal Congress include subjects as important as labour
relations, oil, mining, all commercial matters, electric and nuclear power,
and financial services, monetary regulation, anti-trust legislation, con-
sumer protection, telecommunications, nationality, immigration, postal
service, national waters, film industry, general communications, amongst
many others.

The Mexican version of the implicit powers clause can be found in
the last section of article 73 of the Mexican Constitution. It resembles
the US implicit powers clause. Yet, in Mexico this clause has not had the
relevance that it has had in US constitutional practice.[9]

An examination of the 'Temixco case' is relevant at this point, because
in the corresponding judgment the Supreme Court established a series
of fundamental guidelines concerning not only the way in which the
'new' Court (re-structured as a consequence of the 1994 constitutional
reform) understands the distribution of competences of Mexico's federal system, but also how it conceives its own powers to deliver constitutional justice.

The case derived from a procedure used to resolve a conflict of territorial limits between two municipalities of the State of Morelos
(Cuernavaca and Temixco). The Congress of this State issued Decree
No 92, recognising the municipality of Cuernavaca's jurisdiction over a
specified geographic zone of the State. Yet, the municipality of Temixco
considered that the decree violated its powers and jurisdiction granted
by the federal Constitution, and filed an action of constitutional controversy with the Supreme Court, alleging:

a) violation of due process rights as granted by article 14 of the
   Constitution (right to be heard, right to offer evidence in support of
   one's case); and

[8] Competences expressly delegated to the federal authorities can be found in
other articles: article 74 refers to the competences of the Chamber of Deputies;
article 76, to those of the Senate; article 89 refers to the powers of the president; and
articles 103–107 define which are the competences of the federal courts. Article 73
refers only to the competences of the federal legislative power.

[9] In Mexico, the expansion of federal competences has taken place through multiple reforms to article 73 and not through judicial interpretation based on the
implicit powers clause. Article 73 is the one that has undergone most reforms since
1917. Up to 9 February 2012, it is possible to count 201 decrees that have amended
the Constitution of 1917.

b) violation of the duty to express the legal foundation and motivation of all acts of authority, established in article 16 of the Constitution.

In turn, this case forced the Supreme Court to answer several questions:

a) Do the human rights foreseen in Chapter I of the Constitution (including articles 14 and 16) also protect public authorities?
b) Is judicial review exercised by the Court through the procedure of constitutional controversies[10] limited to cases of invasion of competences between levels of government or is the examination of any other kind of violation of the federal Constitution also permitted in this kind of proceeding?

The debate confronted a traditional and self-regulating vision concerning the role of the Court, with a perspective that considered that the Court had a new role to play in Mexico's constitutional system. In the end, the latter vision prevailed, as the majority of the Justices (8-2) opted for the invalidation of the challenged decree, on the basis of the following arguments:

a) The essential function of the Supreme Court in constitutional controversy procedures is to protect federalism and the supremacy of the Constitution;
b) Since 1994, the Court has been assigned the function of integrating the system of values contained in the Constitution, which sometimes manifest themselves with ambiguities, generic formulas, indeterminate content or even apparent contradictions;
c) Constitutional interpretation in constitutional controversies cannot be limited to technical and restrictive interpretations, because this would be contrary to the system of control of constitutionality and would result in inefficiency;
d) It was true that the challenged decision had a political character, but it also had juridical connotations and therefore could be examined by the Supreme Court;
e) Human rights create duties that have to be complied with by all authorities in their relations with individual persons and with other authorities;
f) Mexico's federal system is formed of several diverse 'partial legal orders', and arbitrary acts performed by public entities belonging to

---

[10] The action of constitutional controversy has been discussed above, in chapter 5.V.

any of them affect the harmony and provoke a disarrangement of the entire legal system. The Supreme Court of Justice is responsible for the integrity of the legal system through the procedure of constitutional controversy.[11]

Since then, the Court has manifested its intention of exercising its powers in a decisive way, displaying an expanded vision of its own powers. The polity got the message and the different levels of government started to use the procedure of constitutional controversy more frequently to defend their constitutional competences. In this way, in 1996 more than 50 constitutional controversies were filed with the Supreme Court; in 2003 more than 100, and in 2008 more than 150 (as was also the case in 2010 and 2011).[12] With this proceeding, Mexico's federal system has entered into a new dynamic, in which the Supreme Court performs a central role as a mediator of conflicts.

States and municipalities are by far the most common litigants in constitutional controversies. As reported by the statistics of the Supreme Court, between 1995 and 2009, 28 per cent of the controversies had to do with the allocation of public revenues; 17 per cent with procedures for the appointment or dismissal of public officials; a further category with the label of 'Others' (including municipal autonomy, the creation of new municipalities, the dissolution of municipal councils, social programmes management and impeachment procedures) amounts to 21 per cent of the total controversies filed in that period.[13]

2. Mexico's Notion of 'Concurrent' Powers

A number of policy areas are subject to a regime of 'concurrent powers'. However, and in spite of the name, the meaning of this concept in Mexico does not refer, as in the United States, to an area of competences delegated to the federation that can be 'occupied' by the States as long as the federation does not decide to step into it. This is not possible under the Mexican legal system, because of the rigidity of article 124

---

[11] Constitutional controversy 31/97, filed by the *Municipal Council of Temixco (State of Morelos) v Governor and Congress of Morelos*, judgment of 9 August 1999.

[12] Data taken from the web page of Mexico's Supreme Court of Justice (www2. scjn.gob.mx/alex/analisis.aspx).

[13] *ibid.*

concerning the distribution of competences between the federation and the States that was reviewed above.

By 'concurrent powers' we understand the possibility of sharing responsibilities among the different levels of government in the design and implementation of public policies on the same subject matter, according to a distribution of competences defined by the federal Legislature. In this way, there are some matters, like education, health, environmental protection and urban planning, on which the federal Congress can pass a statute law which distributes competences and responsibilities between the two (or three) levels of government.

For example, in the Act for the Protection of the Environment (passed by the federal Congress), there is a Chapter on 'Distribution of competences and coordination'. Within this Chapter, article 5 establishes the powers of the federation concerning the protection of the environment; article 7 sets the powers of the States on the same matter; and article 8 does the same with respect to municipal governments.

This is therefore a technique that allows the sharing of responsibilities in one subject area, between the three levels of government, but under the direction of the federation, since it is the federal Congress that defines what corresponds to each of the three levels.

This technique is similar to a technique used in other federal countries, such as Germany and Austria, in which the federal legislative power can pass what they call 'framework statutes'. However – and this is the difference with Mexico – in those countries the respective constitutions establish that when passing 'framework statutes', the federal parliament shall limit itself to establishing 'general bases', in order to allow a reasonable scope for State parliaments to develop their own legislation in the respective area, as required by local needs. In contrast, Mexico's federal Congress has no limits on its power to distribute competences between the three levels of government in passing statutes under the regime of 'concurrent powers'.

In connection with 'concurrent powers', it is relevant to examine some of the concepts of the Supreme Court in the constitutional controversy 29/2000, which was filed by the federal Executive against the Legislative Assembly and the Chief of government, both of the Federal District. The federal Executive's claim was that the Act on Education of the Federal District violated the constitutional allocation of powers established by the General Act on Education (education is a matter subject to the regime of 'concurrent powers').[14] Specifically, the plaintiff alleged that the Assembly had encroached on segments of education policy (ie the education of public teachers of basic education) that the General Act on Education defined as being of the exclusive competence of the federal government.

For its part, the defendants answered that the Act on Education did not violate the constitutional regime of 'concurrence', since it had been passed on the basis of article 122 of the Constitution, which empowers the Legislative Assembly of the Federal District to pass legislation on the 'social function of education in terms of section VIII of article 3' of the federal Constitution. Besides this, they alleged that the General Act on Education had been passed in July of 1993, that is, before the reforms of October 1993 which granted autonomy to the Federal District and its Legislative Assembly,[15] and for this reason the General Act had not taken into consideration the fact that since October 1993, the Assembly of the Federal District had powers to legislate on education. Furthermore, the defendants argued that this circumstance made the General Act on Education contrary to article 122 of the Constitution.

After an examination of both the General Act on Education and the Act on Education of the Federal District, in the light of the regime of 'concurrence', the Supreme Court decided that the Legislative Assembly had invaded the sphere of competence of the federal government. In addition, it defined the regime of 'concurrent powers' in the following way:

> Although article 124 of the Political Constitution of the United Mexican States establishes that 'It shall be understood that the powers not expressly attributed by this Constitution to the federal authorities, are reserved to the states', it is also true that the organ that reforms the Constitution determined, in diverse precepts, the possibility for the Congress of the Union to fix an allocation of competences called 'concurrent powers', among the Federation, the federative entities and municipalities and even the Federal District, in some matters such as: education, health, urban planning, public

[14] Article 3.VIII of the Constitution states that the federal Congress has the power to pass the statutes that are necessary to 'distribute the social function of education among the Federation, the States and municipalities'. For its part, article 73.XXV reiterates that Congress has the power to pass statutes with the purpose to 'distribute in a convenient way the function of education'.
[15] We will discuss the political-constitutional evolution of the Federal District in a later section of this chapter.

security, civil protection, sports. That is to say, in the Mexican legal system concurrent powers imply that federative entities, including the Federal District, the municipalities and the Federation, are able to act in respect with the same matter, but Congress shall have the power to determine the form and terms of participation of those entities through a general act.[16]

The term 'general act' (*ley general*) employed in the final sentence of the above quotation deserves a special reference, since it is closely related to the concept of 'concurrent powers' examined in this section. Indeed, in *McCain General v President of the Republic et al*, 'general acts' were defined as those pieces of legislation passed by the federal Congress that can validly have an impact on all the 'partial juridical orders' that integrate the Mexican state; these are acts of Congress in relation to which the '*pouvoir constituent*' has expressly waived its power to allocate competences to Mexican States, which in turn means that they are an exception to the principle established in article 124. In other words, 'general acts' are federal statutes that distribute competences among the different levels of government in specific policy areas, by delegation of the Constitution.

'Concurrent powers', in the terms explained above, mark a trend in the evolution of Mexico's federal system in the last decades, as an important number of subject-areas have been subjected to this kind of regime, such as: zoning and urban planning, education, health, civil protection, sports, tourism, the environment, cooperatives and fishing, among others. This kind of regime for organising competences has allowed some degree of de-centralisation, while allowing the federal Legislature to keep a good measure of control in those policy areas.

III. FISCAL FEDERALISM

In contrast with the general formula for the allocation of competences of Mexico's federal system, in the area of taxation the Constitution does not establish a clear cut delimitation of powers between the federation and the States. On the contrary, the regime adopted by the Constitution of 1857, which passed into the Constitution of 1917, has established

---

[16] SCJ, Constitutional controversy 29/2000. 15 November 2001, *Semanario Judicial de la Federación*, Ninth Epoch, Plenary session, XV, January 2002, p 1042.Thesis 142/2001.

what the Supreme Court and legal doctrine has called 'concurrence' of taxation powers at both levels of government.[17] The adoption of this regime responded to a deliberate purpose. Indeed, when the constituent assembly of 1857 discussed the issue, two options were considered: either to have a precise definition of which taxes could be imposed by the federation and which others by the States; or to avoid such precise definition, leaving open the possibility that both levels of government could create the taxes that were necessary in accordance with their expenditure forecasts established in their respective budgets. In the end, the second option was the one introduced into the Constitution of 1857, in its article 72.VII. (With a slightly different text, article 73.VII of the 1917 Constitution establishes the same formula, according to which the federal Congress has the power 'to create the taxes that are necessary to meet the requirements of the budget'.).[18]

The Mexican Supreme Court has interpreted this wording to mean that Congress has the power to create all those taxes that are necessary to finance all the items of the budget.[19] Moreover, both the Supreme Court and legal commentators have asserted that in Mexico there is 'concurrence' in the area of taxation. By that, they mean that some (not all) 'taxable bases' can be taxed on equal terms by the federal government and the States.[20] The federation can tax in respect of all imaginable matters, while the States can tax those matters that are not expressly allocated to the federation and those that are not prohibited to them. That is why Sergio de la Garza has asserted that in the area of taxation, the federation has 'unlimited concurrent powers' and the States have 'limited concurrent powers'.[21] The relevance of this interpretation can be observed in the fact that article 73.VII does not mention income tax

[17] However, the meaning of 'concurrence' in the area of taxation must not be confused with 'concurrent powers' described in the previous section.

[18] After examining Hamilton's opinions in *The Federalist*, Flores Zavala has suggested that the drafters of the Constitution of 1857 had in their minds the same reasons as the US founding fathers when defining the formula for the allocation of taxation power in Mexico's federalism. E Flores Zavala, *Elementos de Finanzas Públicas Mexicanas* (Mexico, Porrúa, 1963) 323.

[19] *ibid*, at 110.

[20] See the decision of the Supreme Court on the constitutionality of the federal Act that created the tax for the possession or use of automobiles (*Impuesto sobre la tenencia o uso de automóviles*), *Semanario Judicial de la Federación*, vol 44, First part, p 14, *Amparo* in revision 7056/63, *Trinidad Díaz González*, 1 August 1972, unanimity of 16 votes.

[21] SF de la Garza, *Derecho Financiero Mexicano* (Mexico, Porrúa, 1990) 220–30.

or value added tax as taxes that are collected by to the federation and, in spite of that, the federation taxes income of individuals and corporations, as well as value added to services and goods.

The practical result of the application of these criteria was multiple taxation or even 'fiscal chaos', which in turn produced conflicts between federal and State authorities in the very sensitive area of taxation and had a negative impact on the economy. To cope with this problematic situation, the Ministry of Finance organised three 'National Fiscal Conventions' in 1925, 1933 and 1947, in order to discuss and design a system for avoiding multiple taxation. In these conventions, a system of fiscal coordination was envisioned in order to delimit the taxable bases that related to each level of government, as well as to provide some uniformity.

In essence, the new system (which did not change the constitutional formula for allocating competences in the area of taxation), was (as it still is) based on the idea that the federation and the States would enter into agreements of coordination, by which the latter would give up their competence to create certain taxes in exchange for a share (called a 'participation') of federal tax revenues.

Needless to say, the emergence of this system of fiscal coordination has to be explained in the context of a hegemonic party system, which was able to subordinate State governors and thus design a system that has been rather centralised. As a result of this system of fiscal coordination, by the 1990s around 81 per cent of the tax revenues of the total public sector were concentrated by the federal government, while the States and the municipalities received only around 16 per cent and three per cent, respectively.[22] Today, in spite of the end of the hegemonic party system, this pattern of fiscal centralisation still seems to be in place.

Recent developments in Mexico's fiscal federalism are illustrated by disputes related to the legal nature of certain kinds of federal funds that are transferred to the States and by tensions on how federal funds are distributed within the States once they have been transferred by the federation. Behind these controversies there is usually a conflict between authorities identified with different political parties.

An example of this can be found in a series of disputes on the nature of different federal funds, which could be summarised as follows: apart

---

[22] *ibid*, at 97.

from federal 'participations', State and municipal governments also receive other federal funds called 'appropriations' (*aportaciones*), which are defined by article 25 of the Act on Fiscal Coordination as 'targeted', in the sense that they have to be used to achieve the specific objectives established for each type of appropriation as defined by statute.

Since the creation of this kind of fund, there was a debate on whether they could be freely used by States and municipalities, just as they do with 'participations', or not. According to one position, 'participations' and 'appropiations' were federal funds, and essentially shared the same nature. Thus, the latter, just as it happens with the former, could be freely spent by the corresponding state administrations. Yet, according to the opposite view, both kind of funds are different in nature and thus are subject to different kinds of legal regime. 'Appropiations' are federal resources that the federation allocates to States in support of specific activities; they are governed by a Chapter of the Act on Fiscal Coordination which is different from the one that refers to 'participations'. Therefore, 'appropriations' and 'participations are independent from each other. The implication being that the federation has the power both to check that States and municipalities use 'appropriations' for the specific purposes established by statute, and to impose sanctions on those entities and public servants that divert them to other objectives.

Delays in the transfer of funds from the federation to the States and from the latter to municipalities have also given rise to several legal battles. For example, in the constitutional controversy 5/2004, which involved the delay in the transfer of federal funds to a municipality, the Court stated that article 115 of the Constitution guarantees the punctual and effective transfer of federal resources to municipalities, through the States. For the Court, the constitutional power to approve municipal expenditure presupposes that municipalities have complete certainty as to the available resources. If the federation and the States do not make, or delay the transfer of funds that has been agreed, they deprive municipal government of the material and economic base to perform its constitutional duties. Therefore, delays in the transfer of those resources yielded the corresponding sums of interest which ought to be paid to municipal governments.[23]

---

[23] SCJ, *Semanario Judicial de la Federación*, Ninth Epoch, Plenary session, XIX, June 2004, p 883. Constitutional controversy 5/2004. *Municipal Council of Purépero (State of Michoacán)*, 8 June 2004. Thesis P./J. 46/2004.

Public revenues are still highly centralised in the hands of the federal government. Nevertheless, centralisation has been 'softened' to some extent, through the transfer of funds and the ability of States and municipalities to defend those funds through the action of constitutional controversy. Again, the Supreme Court has played a very relevant role in this field, mediating in an important number of conflicts.

Looking into the future, States and municipal governments may consider different options to increase their revenues. One alternative consists of finding taxes that can be created by State legislatures within the framework of the existing system of fiscal coordination.[24] This seems to be the case, for instance, with 'ecological taxes' on the emission of CO^2. Another alternative would consist of promoting a structural modification of the existing constitutional regime and laws on taxation. This could involve a precise definition of which taxes may be imposed by each level of government, and would require a decided increase in the capacity of States and municipalities to collect taxes.

IV. MECHANISMS OF COLLABORATION IN MEXICO'S FEDERAL SYSTEM

The hegemonic party system developed instruments and practices that guaranteed coordination and harmonisation among the different levels of government of Mexico's federal system. However, with the end of that party system those instruments and practices have disappeared, and as a consequence a series of constitutional mechanisms for achieving those goals that for years remained 'dormant' (so to speak) have grown in importance.

Indeed, there are a series of rules in the Mexican Constitution that allow the collaboration between the different levels of government of Mexico's federal system. For instance, one of those instruments refers to the possibility of having joint and coordinated planning and regulation of metropolitan zones that include two or more urban centres belonging to two or more States (article 115.VI of the Mexican Constitution). Thus, the federation, the States and the respective municipalities are able to

---

[24] Taxes that have not been given up or waived through the agreements of fiscal coordination referred to above.

work together, following the rules and principles established in the federal statute on that matter.[25]

Within the general framework of the rules established by article 115. VI mentioned above, article 122.G of the Constitution establishes more specific rules concerning the coordination of planning and execution of actions in the metropolitan zone of Mexico City, in the areas of urban planning; environmental protection; preservation and restoration of ecological balance; transport; potable water and drainage; collection, treatment and disposal of solid waste; and public security. In relation to these matters, the governments of the Federal District and the governments of the States and municipalities that surround Mexico City can enter into agreements for the creation of metropolitan commissions in which they shall cooperate in the policy areas referred to, according to the respective statutes.

On the basis of these rules, since the mid-1990s, the governments of the State of Mexico, the government of the Federal District (Mexico City), and the federal government, started to create a series of 'Metropolitan Commissions' for the joint and coordinated planning and execution of policies in different areas. Today, these commissions are:

a) Metropolitan Commission on Water and Drainage (27 June 1994).
b) Metropolitan Commission on Transport and Transit (27 June 1994).
c) Metropolitan Commission on Public Security and Justice (27 June 1994).
d) Metropolitan Commission on Human Settlements (23 June 1995).
e) Metropolitan Commission on the Environment (13 September 1996).
f) Metropolitan Commission on Civil Protection (6 March 2000).

Notably, these commissions have been created in a context in which the federal, Federal District and state of Mexico governments are in the hands of different political parties. In turn, this is evidence that parties are willing to cooperate in spite of their differences and disputes, when

[25] The federal statute on that matter is the so-called 'General Law on Human Settlements', which establishes general rules and guidelines on urban planning and urban regulation, which have to be followed by State legislatures when passing their own 'State Law on Urban Development' (these State statute laws are named in different ways in the different States). In addition, the municipal rulings on urban development and urban planning have to conform with both federal and State statutes on that matter.

they have access to governmental positions and are responsible for serving the public and making federalism work.

Other form of collaboration can be found in the form of agreements between a municipality and a State to allow the latter to be temporarily in charge of services or functions that belong to the exclusive competence of the former. In this way, the second paragraph of article 115.III of the Mexican Constitution states that when the municipal council considers it necessary, it shall enter into agreements with the State government it belongs to, to allow the latter, directly or through the relevant institution, to be temporarily in charge of services or functions that belong to the exclusive competence of the municipality. In this case the agreement can establish that the State government shall be fully in charge of the service or the function; or it can establish that the service or function shall be provided or performed in a coordinated manner by the State and the municipality. In the following section of this chapter (on municipal government) we shall examine some of the issues and controversies that have emerged in connection with this possibility of collaboration.

Finally, we shall simply mention some other forms of collaboration allowed by the Constitution, which have become increasingly important in the actual operation of Mexico's federal system: a) the possibility of inter-municipal coordination and of forming associations of municipalities; b) agreements between municipality and State, to allow the latter to administer taxes that in principle are within the competence of the former;[26] c) agreements between municipal and federal government to allow the former to be responsible for the administration of federal zones;[27] and d) agreements between federal government and States, by

[26] In Mexico's federal system, it is relatively common to find 'Agreements of Administrative Collaboration' between a State government and a municipal government, by which the latter transfers to the former the power to collect tax on real property (which is a tax that in principle falls within the exclusive competence of the municipal level of government). Typically, through these agreements the State government will be in charge of collecting the tax on real property that corresponds to the municipality; and the State government will be entitled to a portion of what it collects, having to transfer the rest to the municipal government.

[27] In actual practice this sort of agreement is signed by the federal government (though the Ministry of the Finance) and a State government, by which the latter, 'through a Municipality', becomes in charge of the operative functions of administration of federal taxes related to granting concessions, authorisations or extensions of concessions for the use of federal zones (ie beaches, which are under federal jurisdiction), or for the use of real property located in such federal zone.

which the latter become responsible for the exercise of functions, the execution and operation of public works and public services that are within the competence of the former.[28]

V. MUNICIPAL GOVERNMENT

During the revolutionary movement of 1910–17, the claim for having real democracy and political autonomy at the local level was always present. In fact, as part of his strategy to broaden the popular base of support for the revolution, the chief of the revolutionary forces, Venustiano Carranza, promulgated the 'Act on the Free Municipality' on 26 December 1914, which established a series of principles that would later appear in article 115 of the Constitution. This Act recognised that the dictatorial regime of General Díaz had subordinated municipalities and that the power of governors had been centralised and despotic; in particular, the Act was against the practice of the so-called 'political chiefs', who were persons appointed by governors as their personal representatives in the communities, who in fact displaced municipal authorities, and were agents of 'oppression', 'electoral fraud', 'dispossession of land' and 'extortion of taxpayers'. Moreover, according to the Act, a reinvigoration of municipal institutions would contribute to educating the people to perform democratic functions and would help to develop in the people an interest in public affairs and the need for a common effort for the defence of rights. For these reasons the Act established that: a) all States would adopt the municipal form of government as the basis of their territorial division and political organisation; b) Municipal Councils would be directly elected; and c) there would not be any intermediate authority between the governor of the State and municipal governments. These and other rules and principles appear today in article 115 of the Constitution.

In spite of these good intentions, the municipal form of local government could not escape from the centralising trends of Mexico's federal system after the revolution. Federal and State governments were able to control and subordinate municipal government, for the purposes

---

[28] It is common to find in actual practice 'Specific Agreements for the Assumption of Functions on Inspection and Surveillance of Forests', entered into by the federal government (through the federal Ministry on the Environment), and a State government, by which the federal government allows the State government to perform functions that in principle belong to the former.

of the hegemonic party system. In practice, this level of government did not develop the institutional weight and strength originally expected from it by the Constitution of 1917.[29]

This situation started to change in the 1980s as a result of an important constitutional reform on municipal government proposed by the federal Executive (President Miguel de la Madrid, 1982–88). According to the proposal, the centralised organisation of Mexico's formally federal system had reached its limits. Centralisation had been useful to accelerate the country's economic and social development, but by the 1980s it had become counterproductive. Under the reform proposal, the federal government could not be in charge of every public service and function, while municipal governments (the level of government closer to the population) had no institutional capacities to respond to local demands and needs. In turn, this meant a general lack of efficacy of Mexico's state as a whole.

The reform of 1983 (and another one of 1999 with the same spirit) sought to reverse this situation, establishing the basis for guaranteeing both increased financial resources and political autonomy for municipal governments; and establishing a list of public functions and services that would be of the exclusive competence of municipalities. For example, an important tax such as the tax on real property was defined as within the exclusive competence of municipalities. Moreover, a series of public functions and services were declared of exclusive municipal jurisdiction: potable water, public lighting, collection of wastes, public markets, cemeteries, streets, parks public security and transport, among others.

Recognising that many municipal governments simply lacked administrative capacity, a door was left open, allowing the possibility of collaboration between State and municipal governments (through agreements),[30] in cases in which the latter had no capability to control the functions and services that in principle fell to them to provide. Given the situation of institutional and administrative underdevelopment of most municipalities, this form of collaboration has not been uncommon in actual practice. In turn, this is at the root of one of the sources of conflict that has characterised the relationship between State and municipal governments in the last decade, as illustrated by the following case.

---

[29] Article 115 of the Constitution of 1917 referred (as it still does today) to the 'Free Municipality' as the basis of States' territorial division as well as of their political and administrative organisation.

[30] Article 115.III of the Constitution.

On 5 June 1996, the Council of the municipality of Xalapa, signed an agreement with the government of the State of Veracruz, by which the latter would be in charge of the service of public transport in the city of Xalapa (which is the capital city of Veracruz) and therefore, place of residence of the governor).[31] In 1998, with a recently elected government of a different political party from that of the governor, the Council of Xalapa decided to terminate the agreement, and requested from the governor the devolution of the service to the Council, including movable and immovable property, vehicles, financial resources and personnel with which the service of public transport had been performed since the signing of the agreement. The governor of Veracruz refused to comply with the request alleging, first, that the municipal council had signed an agreement which could not be terminated at the council's will. And secondly, that according to article 115.VII of the Constitution that was in force in those years, governors had the power to command public forces in the place where they resided and therefore, since the public service of transport was provided with the use of public force, the service was the responsibility of the governor and not of the municipal Council of Xalapa.

The Council of Xalapa filed an action of constitutional controversy to the Supreme Court of Justice, challenging the decision of the governor which, in the view of the Council, affected its constitutional sphere of competence. For its part, the Court decided in favour of the Council, saying that an agreement like the one signed between the municipal Council of Xalapa and the governor of Veracruz could not be indefinitely valid against a prerogative granted by the Constitution to municipal governments in its article 115.III. For the Court, the Council could recover its prerogative at any time, because an agreement cannot be above the Constitution. Therefore, the Court ordered that the State government had to devolve to the municipality of Xalapa the public function of transport, with all the implied resources, personnel and property.[32]

It is important to notice that as the case was being discussed in the Supreme Court, Congress was studying the proposal of a constitutional reform that addressed the same issue: devolution of public services and

---

[31] In those years, and since the reform of 1983, article 115.III stated that 'Public security and transit' were of the competence of municipal governments.

[32] SCJ, Constitutional controversy 25/98. *Municipal Council of Xalapa v Governor and State Legislature (State of Veracruz)*, 23 March 2000. Published in the Official Gazette of the Federation on 10 July 2000.

functions that had been transferred from a municipality to the relevant State government, through an agreement. The reform was passed before the Court's decision, and it established a series of standards for devolving public services and functions 'in an ordered way', according to a 'transfer programme' that should be drafted by the State government within a term of 90 days after the relevant request for devolution made by the municipal Council.[33] In its decision (rendered on 23 March 2000) the Supreme Court included the same standards, using the same language of that constitutional reform, seeking to organise devolution of public services from the State government of Veracruz to the municipal Council of Xalapa in an ordered manner.

Finally, cases like the one examined in this section have given rise to the approval of statutes by State legislatures, which have tried to organise devolution processes. Thus, today States like Veracruz, Chihuahua and Coahuila have statutes for the 'Transfer of Public Functions and Services from the State to Municipalities'.

VI. THE CONSTITUTIONAL STATUS OF THE FEDERAL DISTRICT

Originally, the Constitution of 1917 established that the Federal District (that is, Mexico City) would be governed by a governor freely appointed and removed by the president of the Republic; moreover, it preserved the municipal form of political organisation Mexico City had always had since the Constitution of 1824.

In 1928 General Obregón (running for the presidency for a second time) sponsored a reform to the legal regime of the Federal District, whose main point was the elimination of the municipal form of organisation. The reasons given by Obregón in his proposal were that in truth, municipalities had never really worked in the city. On the facts, it was the president of the Republic, through the governor, who provided most public services and functions, and the federal Congress was the main provider of rules and statutes for the Federal District. For Obregón, it was logical that this had happened, because of the need to have unified and homogenous public services and functions in Mexico City. Under those conditions – according to the proposal – municipal power had no reason to exist.

---

[33] The reform was enacted on 23 December 1999.

The reform proposal was approved and published on 20 August 1928. Municipalities disappeared and instead, new territorial demarcations called 'Delegations' were created, whose heads would be appointed by the 'Chief of the Federal District Department' (who in turn would be appointed by the president of the Republic). Notably, there were two main effects of this reform: the tightening of the president's political control on a nerve-centre such as Mexico City; and the significant reduction of political rights for the citizens of the Federal District who under the new rules would not be able to elect their local authorities.

Against this background, we can say now that the political-constitutional evolution of the Federal District in recent decades has been characterised by the progressive democratisation of the structure of government that was created in 1928; a democratisation that can be explained as a result of increased pressures coming from social and political movements, mediated and channelled by political parties opposing the hegemonic party system.

A key moment in this evolution was the constitutional reform of 10 August 1987, which created an elected body called the 'Assembly of Representatives' of the Federal District, which had the power to produce a number of norms that were relevant for the administration of the city's public functions and services (though most legislative power for the Federal District remained in the hands of the federal Congress). This was assessed by some as a 'timid' reform, yet, it opened the way for more ambitious and profound reforms, such as the ones that took place in 1990, 1993 and 1996, which created the current legal-constitutional structure of Mexico City's government:

A. The executive power is a 'Chief of government', directly elected by the citizens of the Federal District;
B. The legislative power is vested in a Legislative Assembly, with power to pass legislation on matters that are expressly indicated in article 122 of the Constitution;
C. The Magistrates of the Superior Tribunal of the Federal District are designated by the Legislative Assembly, upon the proposal of the Chief of government;
D. The Federal District is still divided into '*Delegaciones*', but those who head them are popularly and directly elected;
E. The Congress of the Union still has power to legislate on certain matters relating to the Federal District, with the exception of those

matters expressly allocated to the Legislative Assembly of the Federal District.

F. The federal Executive also has some powers in connection with the Federal District. For example: it can introduce bills in the federal Congress on matters related to the Federal District; it has a role to play in the definition of the Federal District public debt every year, which has to be authorised by the federal Congress.

Though still not to the extent implicated in the municipal form of organisation, these reforms to the structure of government of the Federal District have expanded the political rights of the citizens of Mexico City. Furthermore, they have made of the city's subsequent Chiefs of government political figures of great visibility, to the point that today those who occupy that office are usually considered as 'natural applicants' to run for Mexico's presidency.

Sometimes Mexico City's Chief of government and the federal Executive have had conflicts of national relevance. For example, on 5 March 2001, the Chief of government of the Federal District filed a constitutional controversy (5/2001) against a decree issued by the federal Executive that established four different time zones for the Republic and defined a new system of 'daylight saving time' (*horario de verano*). For the plaintiff, this was unconstitutional, essentially because according to article 73.XVIII of the Constitution, the power to define time zones lay with Congress and not with the Executive.[34] As a consequence of this, the challenged decree was also contrary to the principle of separation of powers established in article 49 of the Constitution. Finally, the Chief of government of the Federal District argued that the decree was contrary to article 89.I of the Constitution, which established the power of the Executive to issue administrative rulings required for the implementation of statutes passed by Congress. However, according to the plaintiff in the present case the rulings were unconnected with any piece of legislation approved by Congress. In the end, the Supreme Court agreed with both arguments of the plaintiff and ruled unanimously against the Executive, declaring the invalidity of the decree with respect to the territory of the Federal District only.[35]

[34] According to article 73.XVIII Congress has the power to pass legislation on 'weights and measures'. In the plaintiff's argument, time zones are 'measures of time' and therefore fall within the scope of Congress's power.

[35] Not all the Supreme Court judgments in constitutional controversies have general effect. Under certain circumstances they might have only inter partes effect. The

VII. RECENT DEVELOPMENTS IN STATE CONSTITUTIONALISM

To conclude this chapter, I would like to say a brief word on what could be rightly called a new trend in Mexico's constitutionalism, which also was made possible by the breakdown of the hegemonic party system. This trend has to do with the revival of state constitutionalism, which basically has been characterised by: a) the emergence of systems for guaranteeing the supremacy of the State constitution; and b) the establishment of human rights catalogues into State constitutions.

Under the hegemonic party system, State constitutionalism was subordinated to national constitutionalism. In other words, constitutional change in the States occurred as a consequence, as a reflex reaction, to changes in the federal Constitution. In contrast, under a multi-party and competitive system, new room for manoeuver has been created, allowing State political actors to shape their State constitution in original and creative ways, trying to solve and respond to local needs and demands.

This trend was inaugurated by the State of Veracruz in 2000, whose congress reformed its Constitution in order to include a Chapter on Human Rights that anticipates rights not included in the federal Constitution and a clause that incorporates at the State level rights established in international treaties signed by Mexico. In addition, the reform also created procedural mechanisms for the protection of the State constitution: a) the procedure for the protection of human rights (analogous to the federal *amparo*); b) an action of constitutional controversy (to resolve disputes of competences between State branches of government, between the latter and municipal governments, or between municipal governments); c) an action of unconstitutionality (as an abstract mechanism of constitutional review at the State level); and d) an action against legislative omissions (that seeks to force the State congress to pass a piece of legislation whose omission thus far affects mandates of the Constitution of Veracruz).

The reform was challenged through an action of constitutional controversy filed by several municipalities of Veracruz (controlled by a political party different from that of the governor and of the majority of the State Congress). Yet, the Supreme Court decided that to the

case analysed here falls within this second category. See SCJ, Constitutional controversy 5/2001, *Chief of Government of the Federal District v Federal Executive*, Federal Official Gazette, judgment of 19 September 2001.

extent that the Constitution of Veracruz established human rights that were different from those foreseen in the federal Constitution; and considering that the new mechanisms of constitutional review were intended to guarantee only the rights foreseen in the State constitution, it did not breach the federal Constitution.[36]

This decision encouraged other States to follow the same path. However, after a period of intense debate, and relevant efforts of institutional design and normative creativity, the new trend lost momentum, mainly because of the influence exercised by an older trend that has characterised Mexico's legal and justice system: the all absorbing federal writ of *amparo*, by which State courts' decisions derived from the new procedures, started to be reviewed by federal courts. Why should plaintiffs resort to State judicial review procedures, if the decisions rendered at this level could be later reviewed by federal courts through the writ of *amparo*?

Finally, it is important to note that as Mexico's legal community was discussing these issues, a series of developments changed radically the terms and coordinates of the debate. I am referring to: a) the influence of a series of judgments of the Inter-American Court of Human Rights and specifically its doctrine of 'control of conventionality'; and b) the constitutional reform of 10 June 2011 on human rights and the understanding of Mexico's Supreme Court of Justice of all the implications of the country's incorporation into the Inter-American system on human rights. We will examine these developments in the following chapter. Yet, for the moment and in the light of judicial federalism, these developments have meant that all courts in the land, federal and from the States, have the power to 'disapply' statutes they deem contrary to human rights established in the Constitution or in international treaties signed by Mexico. This is an important step away from the traditional 'centralised' system of judicial review (control of constitutionality), towards a 'diffuse' system of constitutional justice.

VIII. CONCLUSION

In spite of the formal resemblance between Mexico's and the US federal system, the way in which Mexico federalism has functioned and evolved

---

[36] SCJ, Constitutional controversy 16/2000, *Semanario Judicial de la Federación y su Gaceta*, Ninth Epoch, Plenary session, XVI, August 2002, p 903. Published in the Official Gazette of the Federation on 21 June 2002. Thesis: P.XXXIII/2002.

differs importantly from the US experience. The crucial factor to explain this difference has been the weakness of constitutionalism in Mexico. True, we have always had a Constitution, but the Constitution has not been a living document, respected, obeyed and followed by all, and mainly, by the people in government.

Between 1877 and 1911 the Constitution of 1857 was in force, but this was the time of a one-man dictatorship which occupied the presidency for more than 30 years, a general, Porfirio Díaz. Later on, the Constitution of 1917 was in place yet the regime that emerged from the late 1920s was not precisely a democratic one, but one based on a dominant (hegemonic) party that controlled most political processes (mainly electoral results) through non-democratic mechanisms. In turn, this situation had an impact on the institutional design and way of functioning of Mexico's federal system. What happened in this evolution was that a culture of centralisation was introduced into the constitutional design and practices of Mexico's federalism, which meant a predominance of the federal government over State governments, and a subordination of the latter to the former.

This trend had different manifestations. One example is the weight and number of subject-areas that are of the exclusive competence of the federal government. Another one had to do with the high degree of centralisation of public revenues.

Nevertheless, the breakdown of the hegemonic party system and the strengthening of the Supreme Court have produced a new dynamic in Mexico's federal system. State governors are not subordinates of the federal Executive any longer; federal, State and municipal governments are controlled by political personnel with different political affiliations. All of them are able to protect their sphere of competence through different mechanisms of constitutional justice. Thus, as stated by Guillén, the fabric of national political negotiation has extended beyond the party leadership, beyond the leadership in both houses of the federal Congress, and beyond the previously all-powerful federal Executive, to encompass the governors and their organisation, the so-called National Conference of Governors (CONAGO).[37]

---

[37] T Guillén López, 'Federalism and the Reform of Political Power' in A Selee and J Peschard (eds), *Mexico's Democratic Challenges, Politics, Government and Society* (Stanford CA, Stanford University Press/Washington, DC, Woodrow Wilson Center Press, 2010) 195.

In this context, the different levels of government are forced (and also willing) to cooperate, disregarding their political and ideological differences, developing a new pattern of inter-governmental politics. This cooperation is taking place through the mechanisms that for that purpose were already contained in the Constitution, which remained 'dormant' for decades. Today, the creation of new instruments for coordination, for sharing responsibilities and harmonisation is an important part of the agenda of Mexico's federal system.

FURTHER READING

Remes, A, 'Democratization and Dispersion of Power: New Scenarios in Mexican Federalism' (2006) 22 *Mexican Studies/Estudios Mexicanos* 175.

Serna de la Garza, JM, 'Constitutional Federalism in Latin America' (2000) 30 *California Western International Law Journal* 277.

Serna de la Garza, JM, *El Sistema Federal Mexicano, Un análisis jurídico* (Mexico, UNAM, 2008).

Serna de la Garza, JM, 'Mechanisms of Cooperation in Mexico's Federal System' in de Villiers, B (ed), *Crossing the Line: Dealing with Cross-Border Communities*, Occasional Papers (Johannesburg, Republic of South Africa, Konrad Adenauer Stiftung, 2009).

Ward, PM and Rodríguez, VE, 'New Federalism, Intra-Governmental Relations and Co-Governance in Mexico' (1999) 31 *Journal of Latin American Studies* 673.

Ward, Peter et al, *New Federalism and State Government in Mexico: Bringing the States Back In* (Austin TX, University of Texas Press, 1999).

7

The Protection of Human Rights

Introduction – Domestic and International Pressures and the Shift Towards a New Human Rights Policy in Mexico – Changes in the Supreme Court's Interpretation of Human Rights – Constitutional Reform Relative to the Criminal Justice System – The Emergence of a New Paradigm on Human Rights – Freedom of Religion and the Separation of State and Church – Conclusion

I. INTRODUCTION

THE CONSTITUTION OF 1917 contains a declaration of individual and social rights. Individual rights directly connect with the tradition of political liberalism of the Constitution of 1857, which already included a long and detailed list of first-generation human rights; social rights were incorporated into the constitutional text as a consequence of the 1917 constituent assembly's intention to put revolutionary demands at the highest possible normative level. Originally, social rights included the right to education (article 3); the right to land (article 27) and rights of workers in the context of labour relationships (article 123). Later on other social rights were added, like the right to housing and the right to the protection of health. More recently, third-generation human rights have been also added to the Constitution, such as the right to a healthy environment and the right to access to culture.

In spite of the well-developed and detailed catalogue of civil, political, economic, social and cultural rights, Mexico has had trouble to make them truly effective. The reasons for this have been explored by several scholars in connection with Latin America, referring either to constitutionalism in general or to human rights in particular. For instance, Rosenn has argued that the causes for what he assesses as the 'failure' of constitutionalism in Latin America, are: the absence of real revolutionary change; inexperience with self-government; the imported flavour of Latin American constitutions; the difficulties in establishing the rule of law; difficulties in developing procedural institutions to check abuses of executive power; failures of economic integration; the persistence of militarism and lack of widespread economic pay-off.[1] For his part, Schor has identified cultural causes that explain the weakness of effective constitutionalism in Latin America: in his view, what is needed is an attitudinal shift so that the citizens and elites become wedded to the rules of the constitutional and democratic political game. Citizens have to be willing to support the constitution against inroads by elected leaders, says Schor.[2]

Referring specifically to Mexico and specifically to human rights problems, Jorge Madrazo (a former president of the National Commission for Human Rights (CNDH)) has also put the stress on cultural causes: the national culture regarding human rights is incipient and fragile.[3] Anaya has pointed out that the procedural mechanisms available to protect and enforce human rights in practice are inadequate.[4]

Apart from cultural and procedural-legal factors, the political context is also important to understand the situation of human rights in Mexico. From a historical perspective, the hegemonic party system was not a harsh military dictatorship whose rule was based on widespread repression of political opponents and cancellation of human rights of Mexican citizens. It was an authoritarian system which used selective repression against the groups and actors that refused to enter into the regime's mechanisms of political control and co-optation, and limited significantly the efficiency of political rights.[5] Sometimes, repression was particularly intense, as in the late 1960s and early 1970s 'dirty

[1] K Rosenn, 'The Success of Constitutionalism in the US and its failure in Latin America: An Explanation' (1990) 22 *University of Miami Inter-American Law Review* 2.

[2] 'A constituency for a constitution is more difficult to construct than is a constituency for elected leaders' M Schor, 'Constitutionalism Through the Looking Glass of Latin America' (2006) 41 *Texas International Law Journal* 5.

[3] J Madrazo, 'Challenges and prospects of Mexico's non-jurisdictional human rights protection system' (1995) 32 *Voices of Mexico* 17.

[4] A Anaya Muñoz, 'Transnational and Domestic Processes in the Definition of Human Rights Policies in Mexico' (2009) 31 *Human Rights Quarterly* 36.

[5] See chapter 2 of this book.

war'.[6] Individual rights were protected by courts to the extent that they did not contradict the logic of political control of the regime; while social rights were applied in a way that was functional to the hegemonic party system: agrarian reform was 'administered' in a piecemeal way in order to maintain the regime's political base in the countryside, and labour rules were used and manipulated by the trade union leadership in conjunction with labour authorities, in order to maintain the discipline and political loyalty of the industrial labour force.

Moreover, and on another front, ill practices, vices and corruption in the criminal justice system were tolerated as long as its different operators responded positively to the needs of political control of the hegemonic party system. As a result, disrespect for human rights was particularly intense in the field of the criminal justice system. Torture, intimidation, coercion and all forms of mistreatment have been and still are perpetrated against persons detained in the course of a criminal investigation.[7]

Nevertheless, and in spite of this negative scenario of human rights effectiveness in Mexico, it is possible to point out a series of developments and dynamics, that have tended to change the situation in a more positive way. To the extent that they have a constitutional dimension, these developments shall be addressed in this chapter.

In this way, first I shall refer to the context in which a series of changes took place during the 1990s that eventually led to the creation of the National Commission for Human Rights (1991), and to Mexico's acceptance of the contentious jurisdiction of the Inter-American Court of Human Rights (1998). Secondly, I shall argue that increased efficacy of human rights contributed to the breakdown of the hegemonic party system, which in turn opened up the space for increased independence of the Supreme Court. This, in turn, has had an impact on the interpretation of human rights contained in the Constitution, as the Court started to play a more active role in the protection of human rights.

---

[6] The 'dirty war' was conducted by the federal government, without having much concern for human rights, against *guerilla* and social movements that emerged in different parts of the country in those years. A number of trials against Mexico in the context of the Inter-American system for human rights refer to violations committed by Mexico's government in that period.

[7] Lawyers Committee for Human Rights, *Legalized Injustice, Mexican Criminal Procedure and Human Rights* (New York, Lawyers Committee for Human Rights and Miguel Agustín Pro Juárez Human Rights Center, 2001) 1.

Thirdly, I shall examine the constitutional reform of 2008 which has involved the introduction of a new paradigm into the criminal justice system, but whose implementation and practical consequences remain for the moment uncertain. Finally, I shall examine the challenges, problems, debates, doubts and opportunities derived from the constitutional reform on human rights passed in June of 2011; this reform, combined with the effects that several judgments of the Inter-American Court of Human Rights have had on Mexico's judicial and human rights communities, constitute a new paradigm that will frame strategies and practices for the protection and enforcement of human rights in the coming years.

II. DOMESTIC AND INTERNATIONAL PRESSURES AND THE SHIFT TOWARDS A NEW HUMAN RIGHTS POLICY IN MEXICO

After decades of having no explicit and nation-wide policy on human rights, during the 1990s Mexican governments started to take a series of steps intended to change this situation. Two manifestations of this policy shift were the creation of the National Commission on Human Rights (CNDH) and Mexico's acceptance of the contentious jurisdiction of the Inter-American Court of Human Rights.

The CNDH was created by presidential decree of 5 June 1990, as an entity within the Ministry of the Interior that would be in charge of designing and implementing a national policy for the protection and promotion of human rights in Mexico. Jorge Carpizo, the first president of the CNDH and one of the most important legal minds behind the creation of this entity, has stated that the main reason for the creation of the agency was the alarming increase in human rights violations committed mostly by public prosecutors and federal police forces who were in charge of investigations and prosecutions of drug-related crimes. A series of human rights violations cases shocked Mexico's society in those years and were well known all around the world, forcing the government to take measures, like the creation of the CNDH, in order to stop this kind of action.[8]

After one year of initially positive results, the president of the Republic decided to propose a constitutional reform that was intended to grant to

---

[8] J Carpizo, 'La Reforma Constitucional de 1999 a los organismos protectores de los Derechos Humanos' (2000) 3 *Cuestiones Constitucionales* 28–29.

the CNDH autonomy from the federal government.[9] In his view, this would increase the credibility of the institution before domestic and international audiences.[10] On 13 September 1999, another reform to article 102 of the Constitution sought to strengthen the CNDH's autonomy, eliminating the participation of the Executive in the process of designating the CNDH's president;[11] and establishing the duty of State legislatures to create similar entities at the State level.

For their part, Keck and Sikkink have argued that the creation of the CNDH can be explained in terms of increasing international pressure on Mexico's successive governments which, in spite of having actively participated in the elaboration of international instruments on human rights, in actual practice were responsible (by action or omission) for serious violations on human rights. In this way, according to these authors the combined action of transnational advocacy networks and international organisations that involved multiple, national and domestic actors, was able to produce a 'boomerang effect' that in turn led to the creation of the CNDH.[12]

Moreover, as reported by Anaya, during the administrations of Presidents Zedillo (1994–2000) and Fox (2000–06), the Mexican government's approach to human rights shifted significantly. The reasons for this have to do with pressure generated by a transnational advocacy network, and domestic political factors, particularly those related to the political preferences of the Fox government and the role of key decision-makers. According to this author, the new approach involved Mexico's opening itself to international monitoring and assistance, the ratification of important international instruments, the promotion of constitutional and legal reforms, changes in government institutions

[9] The president of the CNDH would be appointed by the president of the Republic with the approval of the Senate.

[10] The reform was approved and enacted on 28 January 1992.

[11] Since 1999, the latter is appointed by the Senate alone, by a two-thirds majority of the members present.

[12] With the 'boomerang effect' domestic actors seek support of international actors to put pressure on a State that violates human rights, with the goal of producing a series of changes favourable to the cause of human rights. Keck and Sikkink also suggest that the creation of the CNDH could be linked to a strategy of Mexico's government which sought to prevent opposition by human rights advocacy groups against commercial association between Mexico, the US and Canada, in the context of NAFTA (which entered into force in 1994). M Keck and K Sikkink, *Activists Beyond Borders: Advocacy Networks in International Politics* (Ithaca NY, Cornell University Press, 1998) 108–16.

and the elaboration of a National Human Rights Programme that took into account the conclusions and recommendations of the National Diagnostic on Human Rights in Mexico drafted by the United Nations High Commissioner for Human Rights.[13]

On the other hand, Mexico's recognition of the contentious jurisdiction of the Inter-American Court of Human Rights (IACtHR) on 24 February 1999 has meant the incursion of a new dynamic for the interpretation application and efficacy of human rights. It is a new dynamic compared with the previous way of thinking in terms of entirely domestic parameters and procedures. Under the new scheme, in the first place, human rights contained in the Constitution co-exist with human rights established in different international sources.[14]

Secondly, we must recall that Mexico's ratification of the American Convention on Human Rights is particularly relevant, since by doing so the Mexican state (that is, all of the country's public entities) has accepted the international obligation of respecting rights and freedoms of the Convention, and the duty of adapting domestic law to the terms of the Convention, adopting the legislative measures and measures of any other character that are necessary to make those rights and freedoms effective.[15] In the framework of the Inter-American system for the protection of human rights, today Mexican courts are required not only to apply human rights contained in the Inter-American Convention on Human Rights, but also to take into account its interpretation by the Inter-American Court of Human Rights.[16]

Beyond constitutional and legal reforms, looking into the facts we could say that after an initial big push, the CNDH has so far had a limited impact on the significant reduction of human rights violations in Mexico. According to Human Rights Watch, this is due to the CNDH's own policies and practices: it has not fully complied with its duties and has not maximised the use of its considerable resources; it has not com-

---

[13] See Anaya Muñoz, 'Transnational and Domestic Processes in the Definition of Human Rights Policies in Mexico' (2009), n 4 above, 37–38.

[14] As reported by Jorge Carpizo, Mexico has signed practically all international instruments on human rights. See J Carpizo, 'México: Poder Ejecutivo y Derechos Humanos, 1975–2010' in J Carpizo et al, *Evolución de la Organización Político-Constitucional de México, 1975–2010* (Mexico, UNAM, 2012) 30.

[15] Article 2 of the American Convention on Human Rights.

[16] We shall come back to this when we discuss the doctrine of 'control of conventionality' developed by the Inter-American Court of Human Rights, in section V of this chapter.

pelled State agencies to repair the human rights abuses and violations it has documented; it has not promoted the necessary reforms to prevent violations; it has not opposed statutes, policies, practices that are contrary to human rights international standards; and it has not always entered into constructive relations with key actors that advocate in favour of human rights in Mexico.[17]

As for State commissions for the protection of human rights, a recent report has stated that with some exceptions, they have not been able to become effective counterweights to impede abuses by different local authorities and violations of human rights. According to this study, more than half of the 32 commissions are headed by persons who are close to the incumbent State government, particularly to the governor. In many cases, the personnel that occupy positions in State entities in charge of protecting human rights have political connections and loyalties with respect to those State agencies they are supposed to check. Thus – concludes the report – most of them have not succeeded in modifying of practices of State public entities that violate human rights.[18]

For its part, Human Rights Watch has found that in spite of the fact that State commissions do have the power to investigate, frequently they do not take the basic measures required to investigate complaints, they do not initiate investigations even when there is evidence of abuses, or they put an end to investigations in a premature way; and finally, they do not take the measures to assure that their recommendations are implemented in practice.[19]

Today, much has to be done in the human rights front. There is serious concern on the effects that the 'war on drugs' launched by President Calderón are having on this matter, particularly in connection with how the military are affecting the civilian population in operations against organised crime. In this field, as we will see later, the Inter-American system has already had an impact. Moreover, this concern explains another recent reform to the Constitution (of 10 June 2011) that we will examine in some detail in the final section of this chapter, which has sought to

---

[17] Human Rights Watch, *La Comisión Nacional de los Derechos Humanos de México Una evaluación crítica*, vol 20, no 1 (B), February 2008, at 2: (www.hrw.org/sites/default/files/reports/mexico0208sp_1.pdf).
[18] Comisiones estatales de derechos humanos, Ombudsman de Papel, Section 'Enfoque' No 920, *Diario Reforma*, 11 December 2011, at 4–6.
[19] Human Rights Watch, *Ni Seguridad, Ni Derechos, Ejecuciones, desapariciones y tortura en la 'guerra contra el narcotráfico' en México* (México, HRW, 2011) 15.

form the basis of a stronger national policy for the protection of human rights in Mexico. However, the results of that reform and the impact in the real world, still remain to be seen and are, for the moment, uncertain.

III. CHANGES IN THE SUPREME COURT'S INTERPRETATION OF HUMAN RIGHTS

The hegemonic party system took care of modelling a judicial power that was functional to its needs, operation and maintenance. The Supreme Court's appointments procedure and the high level of turnover of Supreme Court Justices described in Chapter 5, section II were factors that contributed to creating a weak court that rarely opposed the Executive in cases in which they had a particular political interest. Few exceptions to this general rule can be found in this period.

The constitutional reform of 1994 opened up the expectation of increased Supreme Court independence and of a more active role in the protection of human rights. Nevertheless, between that year and 2007 we can find little evidence of a shift in the Court's attitude and role as a guardian of constitutional rights. In spite of this, there were a couple of exceptions like the one related to the so-called 'exclusion clause' of collective agreements between trade unions and employers. Again, this case has to be examined in the context of the government's intervention policy into the internal affairs of trade unions, as it happened during the administration of President Alemán (1946–52), who embarked on the country on a project of accelerated industrialisation through import-substitution that the Second World War had introduced. Particularly important during his regime was the elimination of radical trade union leaders who opposed the restructuring of the labour market that Alemán's project considered necessary. The typical strategy was the imposition of trade union leaders with the help of coercion and through the manipulation the union's internal rules. In that period, the government developed thus a set of strategies to divide trade union leaderships, co-opt them and make them cooperate with the administration's economic goals. This strategy can be seen as one of the instruments for regulating peasant and industrial workers' organisations and the demands they posed to the political and economic system.[20]

---

[20] L Medina, 'Civilismo y Modernización del Autoritarismo' in *Historia de la Revolución Mexicana, 1940-1952*, vol 20, ch 4: 'El Charrismo Sindical' (Mexico, El Colegio de Mexico, 1979) 151–75.

Moreover, these strategies and practices were mounted in a specific legal framework. One of the key pieces of this framework was the so-called 'exclusion clause' foreseen in articles 395 and 413 of the Federal Labour Act, according to which in collective agreements between a company and its workers (represented by the trade union), the two parties can establish a clause by which the company agrees to employ only workers that belong to the relevant trade union; and also accepts to terminate the labour relationship with respect to those workers that decide to quit the trade union or those who are expelled from the trade union.

Originally, the 'exclusion clause' had the goal of strengthening trade unions vis-à-vis employers. It was supposed to foster unity of trade union organisations.[21] However, in the context of Mexico's hegemonic party system, this clause soon transformed into an efficient instrument to maintain strict control of the rank-and-file by trade union leaderships.

Notably, courts played an important role in giving constitutional legitimacy to the 'exclusion clause'. Here we find an example of how, in key aspects of the hegemonic party formation since the 1930s, the interpretation of human rights by courts was functional to the formation and reproduction of the system. It is no coincidence that precisely in the years of emergence and consolidation of the hegemonic party system, the Supreme Court decided cases in the following terms:

A. The employer does not have the duty to verify the legality of the trade union's decision to exclude a worker because to do so would imply an intervention into the internal affairs of the workers' organisation, which is contrary to the law.[22]

B. In the application of the exclusion clause, the employer only has to check: a) the authenticity of the document by which he is informed in connection with the application of the clause by the relevant trade union; b) the existence of the clause in the collective agreement; and c) that the excluded workers do belong to the trade union that applies the clause. Once these three requirements are met, the employer has the duty, without any liability, to dismiss the employees as requested

---

[21] M de la Cueva, *El Nuevo Derecho Mexicano del Trabajo* (Mexico, Porrúa, 1993).

[22] SCJ, Appendix of the *Semanario Judicial de la Federación, 1917–1995*, Fifth Epoch, Fourth Chamber of the Supreme Court, vol V, First Part, Thesis 55, p 37.

by the union, and has no right to intervene in the internal procedures of the workers' organisation.[23]

C. The loss of work by virtue of the application of the exclusion clause is the consequence neither of an act of public authority, nor of an imperative mandate of statute law, but is the result of the express and free will of the persons grouped in a trade union, who, with the purpose of strengthening their organisation, agree upon the clause with the employer. Therefore, the articles of the Federal Labour Act that establish the possibility of including the exclusion clause in a collective agreement, cannot be considered unconstitutional.[24]

In 2001 the Supreme Court changed its criteria, stating that the exclusion clause in collective agreements between employers and employees was unconstitutional. According to the Court, there was no express text in the Constitution allowing or prohibiting the exclusion clause. Therefore, the solution to the case filed by a group of workers of the sugar company 'El Potrero SA' who had resigned as members of the trade union and for that reason had been dismissed after the petition of the union (based on the exclusion clause), had to be based on a systemic interpretation of the sections of the Constitution that refer to freedom of association, freedom to work, freedom to form unions, as well as on the analysis of the previous decisions of the Court and academic doctrine on the matter.

For the Court, there was no indication that the framers of the Constitution had the intention of making the freedom to form unions an exception to freedom of association. Neither could it be found that the framers of the Constitution had intended that the 'exclusion clause' represented a general interest of workers and their unions that should prevail over the individual interests of particular workers guaranteed by freedom of association. According to the Court, in connection with individual constitutional rights, exceptions can only be admitted if they are expressly mentioned in the Constitution. Therefore, the 'exclusion clause' was contrary to the Constitution.

---

[23] SCJ, *Semanario Judicial de la Federación*, Fifth Epoch, Fourth Chamber of the Supreme Court, vol LXV, p 3257. Direct *amparo* 1535/40. *Compañía de Servicios Públicos de Nogales, SA*, 6 September 1940.

[24] SCJ, *Semanario Judicial de la Federación*, Fifth Epoch, Fourth Chamber of the Supreme Court, vol LXXIII, p 5829. Direct *amparo* in a labour dispute 3975/42. *Lozada Delfino et al*, 7 September 1942.

Furthermore, the 'exclusion clause' also violated the freedom to work, because it did not coincide with the limits established by article 5 of the Constitution;[25] and it also violated the article on the freedom of association, which since the decision in the Chambers of Commerce case, included the right to belong, not to belong, and to resign as a member of any association.[26]

It is evident that the new interpretation by the Court represents a serious blow to the system of control created in the trade union movement of the hegemonic party system. Moreover, it might also have implications in labour relationships, since employers will be able to employ workers without the intervention of the trade union and agree upon different working conditions with different sets of workers within the same company.[27]

This decision was an exception. As argued by Abad, between 1994 and 2007 the Supreme Court remained distant from constructing a better identity in the field of the protection of human rights.[28] The reasons for this —Abad argues — seem to be connected to the very nature of institutional change, which depends not only on the modification of formal rules (this to an important extent occurred with the reform of 1994), but on the alteration of the informal norms that guide and orientate individuals in making decisions. Institutional change, in addition, occurs in an incremental manner and is influenced by the wider social and political context. In this way, it has taken time for the Court to put at the very top of its institutional objectives the protection of human rights, and to orientate its formal and informal organisational norms to the achievement of those objectives. Moreover, the Court has been cautious in the definition of its new role, in the context of a political system

---

[25] Article 5 of the Constitution establishes the following limits to the freedom to work: the activity performed has to be 'licit', and it must neither affect the rights of third-parties nor offend the 'rights of society'.

[26] SCJ, *Semanario Judicial de la Federación*, Ninth Epoch, Plenary session, XIII, May 2001, pp 443–44. Theses: 2a. LIX/2001 and 2a. LVIII/2001. Direct *amparo* in revision 1124/2000. *Abel Hernández Rivera et al*, 17 April 2001.

[27] Nevertheless, the decision in this case did not nullify the rules of the Federal Labour Act that allow 'exclusion clauses', due to the 'inter partes' effect of *amparo* decisions.

[28] A Abad Suárez Avila, 'The Mexican Supreme Court as a Protector of Human Rights' (2011) IV *Mexican Law Review* 244–45. In contrast, in the same period the Supreme Court transformed itself into an important arbiter of conflicts between political actors, mostly through the renewed constitutional controversy proceeding.

that is just taking shape, after decades of the hegemonic party system. Finally, it has taken time for social and political actors to become familiar with the new Court's role, with the different judicial proceedings that exist today and the possibilities they open for the protection and the redefinition of human rights.[29]

Yet, it seems that in 2007 the Supreme Court started to modify its attitude, playing a more active role in the protection of human rights, fuelled by factors such as the significant increase in the budget of the federal judicial power,[30] the appointment of new Justices to the Supreme Court who have brought 'fresh air' to the Court's deliberations and decisions,[31] and Mexico's immersion in the Inter-American system for the protection of human rights.[32]

Evidence of the changing attitude of the Supreme Court can be seen in a series of cases it has recently decided that involve sexual and reproductive rights. In this way, it declared the constitutionality of: a) a reform to the criminal code of Mexico City which de-criminalised the termination of pregnancy within the first 12 weeks;[33] b) the right of transgender persons to modify their officially-recognised sex without having to register their original sex in the corresponding birth certificate;[34] and c) gay marriage and adoption by gay couples, as approved by Mexico City's legislature.[35]

Yet, perhaps one of the most important examples that shows the increased relevance and visibility of the Supreme Court, as well as its ability to resist pressure in polemic cases that polarise public opinion can be seen in the so-called *Acteal* case (Direct *Amparos* 9/2008, 16/2008, 10/2008, 8/2008 and 33/2008).

On 22 December 1997 an armed group killed 45 individuals of the 'Tzotzil' indigenous community in a place called Acteal, located in the

---

[29]   *ibid*, at 245–47.

[30]   Every year since 2006 the budget authorised by Congress for the federal judicial power has increased. Between 2006 and 2012, the increase amounted to 82 per cent. *Excélsior*, 29 May 2012.

[31]   Between 2003 and 2009 six new Justices have been appointed to the Supreme Court.

[32]   Mexico accepted the contentious jurisdiction of the Inter-American Court of Human Rights, on 16 December 1998, and the acceptance was published in the Official Gazette of the Federation on 28 February 1999.

[33]   SCJ, Action of unconstitutionality 146/2007.

[34]   SCJ, *Amparo* in revision 6/2008.

[35]   SCJ, Action of unconstitutionality 2/2010.

southern State of Chiapas. Since 1994, this State was under particular
social and political strain, as the result of the uprising of the Zapatista
movement, an insurgent movement which challenged the national and
State 'establishment' as being responsible of centuries of indigenous
peoples' misery. The official version was that the killings had been the
result of a fight between different Indian communities. Yet, according
to some journalistic reports, the assassinations had been perpetrated by
paramilitary groups that had been formed with the tolerance (if not
with the support) of federal and State authorities.

In the middle of a national and international outcry against the massacre, around 100 persons were captured (most of them members of
different indigenous communities of Chiapas) and were put on trial,
accused of having perpetrated the killings. Eventually, in 2007 close to
40 persons were sentenced to between 25 and 40 years' imprisonment.
They challenged their sentences through the writ of *amparo*, whereupon
the First Chamber of the Supreme Court exercised its power of attraction.[36] After an examination of the case, the First Chamber concluded
that fundamental due process rights of the accused had been violated
during the criminal trial,[37] ordering the immediate liberation of 20 of
the accused and the retrial of another six persons.[38]

Mexico's public opinion divided along two extremes: on the one
hand, some saw the Court's decision as a measure that guaranteed impunity to the perpetrators of the massacre; on the other hand, there were
those who assigned a greater value to constitutional due process rights,
and considered that this case had to be seen as a lesson for the future by
the different authorities of the criminal justice system: their powers
have to be exercised in the frame allowed by the Constitution.

The greatest losers in this scenario have been the victims of the crime
and their relatives. Up to this day, there has been no ultimate sanction
against the perpetrators of the massacre, and there has been no proper

[36] The Supreme Court power of attraction was explained above, in chapter 5.IV.
It basically means that at its discretion, the Court can attract and hear an *amparo
casación* case that in principle corresponds to Collegiate Circuit Courts, when it considers that the case involves an issue of special national relevance.
[37] These irregularities included disappearance of evidence, tampering with the
scene of the crime, and fabricated testimonies, among others.
[38] In three other cases the First Chamber decided the same way, and for the same
reasons. Thus, up to 2012 a total of 36 persons accused and sentenced in connection
with the *Acteal* massacre had been released.

reparation of the damage and harm suffered by the victims. The case has been brought to the arena of the Inter-American system for the protection of human rights. The Mexican state is being accused of supporting the organisation of paramilitary groups and of failing to provide protection to the people that were killed in the *Acteal* case, as well as of denying justice to the victims and their relatives. The complaint was admitted by the Inter-American Commission on Human Rights in November 2010 and the case is still pending in that instance.[39]

In spite of some positive developments, it seems that the new role and approach of the Court in connection to human rights should not be exaggerated. Still the Court has a list of pending tasks in connection with the construction of a constitutional doctrine that gives new meaning and substance to fundamental rights. As Magaloni has suggested, it is possible that the consolidation of the Supreme Court as a protector of human rights will have to come from two fronts: a change in the 'judicial philosophy' that guides the idea of what is the 'proper' method of constitutional interpretation when resolving cases, and the 'strategic' vision in the Court's use of its 'power of attraction'.[40] In connection with these two topics, Magaloni has argued that the legalistic and formalistic method of interpreting and applying the Constitution that prevails with most Mexican judges (I would add, with most of the legal profession) is linked to a tradition that was fostered by the hegemonic party system that sought to subordinate and limit judges in their ability to frame issues in terms that are more favourable to human rights.[41] Moreover, Magaloni also suggests that the Court's 'power of attraction' can be viewed as a functional equivalent of the American writ of *certiorari*, which could be used to select cases and thus develop the content of human rights in a casuistic way.[42]

---

[39]   Mr Ernesto Zedillo (President of Mexico between 1994 and 2000) was sued in a civil action that seeks damages of US$50 million, brought in December of 2011 before a court in Connecticut by some of the victims. However, the Mexican government has requested diplomatic immunity in his favour as the head of state that he was at the time in which the *Acteal* events occurred. Up to this moment, the decision is in the hands of the US State Department.

[40]   The Supreme Court's 'power of attraction' was explained in chapter 5.IV.

[41]   AL Magaloni Kerpel, '¿Por qué la Suprema Corte no ha sido un instrumento para la defensa de Derechos Fundamentales?' in E Ferrer and A Zaldívar (eds), *La Ciencia del Derecho Procesal Constitucional, Estudios en Homenaje a Héctor Fix Zamudio en sus Cincuenta años como investigador del Derecho*, vol II (Mexico, UNAM, 2008) 279–84.

[42]   ibid.

From this opinion, it is possible to infer that a shift by the Court in the area of human rights protection will take time, since it requires fundamental changes at the level of legal education. Yet, probably a major push may come from the international front: the impact of the Inter-American System may induce Mexico's Supreme Court to take more decided steps to play a more active and firm role in this field.[43]

IV. CONSTITUTIONAL REFORM RELATIVE TO THE CRIMINAL JUSTICE SYSTEM

One of the areas in which the difference between 'law on the books' and 'living law' is more striking is the criminal justice system. In this field, according to Reed, there is a clear disconnection between the provisions of the Constitution and the alternative reality that exists in practice.[44]

By the mid-2000s, and particularly during the first year of the administration of President Calderón, there was a deep concern for what was perceived as a serious public security crisis, characterised by an escalation of violence, as well as widespread impunity, corruption, and lack of expertise and technical capacity of personnel in the criminal justice system. According to Carbonell and Ochoa, in those years 85 per cent of the victims of crime did not report them; 99 per cent of criminals went unpunished; 92 per cent of the hearings in criminal trials took place before court clerks and assistants but without the presence of a judge; 80 per cent of Mexicans thought that criminal judges could be bribed; 60 per cent of detention orders were not executed; 40 per cent of prisoners had not received a guilty verdict; and 80 per cent of prisoners had never spoken with the judge who sentenced them.[45]

Against this scenario, since 2006 legislators of different political parties and the Executive introduced a series of bills, seeking to reform the criminal justice system. In the end, after months of discussions, an ambitious constitutional reform was passed and promulgated on

[43] We will come back to this in section V of this chapter.
[44] G Reed Horton, 'Cartels in the Courtroom: Criminal Justice Reform and its Role in the Mexican Drug War' (2011) III *Mexican Law Review* 240.
[45] M Carbonell and E Ochoa Reza, '¿Necesitamos reformar nuestro sistema de justicia penal? Algunos indicadores empíricos y teóricos' (2007) LVII, 248 *Revista de la Facultad de Derecho de México* 189.

18 June 2008, the main elements of which included: 1) changes to criminal procedure through the introduction of new oral, adversarial procedures, alternative sentencing and alternative dispute resolution mechanisms; 2) a greater emphasis on the rights of the accused (ie, the presumption of innocence, due process and adequate legal defence); 3) modifications to police agencies and their role in criminal investigations; and 4) tougher measures for fighting organised crime.[46]

According to the new rules introduced by the 2008 constitutional reform, every single hearing within a criminal trial shall take place in the presence of a judge, who cannot delegate the taking and weighing of evidence to any other court official. Only those pieces of evidence that are brought to the court in a public hearing shall be taken into account; the presentation of arguments and of evidence shall take place in a public hearing, orally, and in an adversarial procedure; the public prosecutor has the burden of proving that the accused is guilty (innocence of the latter shall be presumed); judges are not allowed to discuss anything related to the criminal trial with one of the parties alone, without the presence of the other; the criminal trial can end in an anticipated manner, through mechanisms such as plea-bargaining and alternative dispute resolution as defined by the relevant statute law; any evidence obtained in violation of human rights shall not be valid in the trial.

The reform also contains the recognition of a series of rights of the accused, such as: the presumption of innocence; the right to give evidence or to remain silent; the right to know the reasons for his detention; prohibition of holding a detainee incommunicado, intimidation and torture in detention; any confession rendered without the presence of a defence lawyer shall not be valid as evidence; and the right to a defence (if the accused cannot or decides not to appoint a defence lawyer, the judge shall designate a public defence lawyer).

Moreover, the reform has established a list of rights of the victim: the right to play an active role in the criminal trial, in support of the public prosecutor's work; the right to claim damages (the public prosecutor has to claim damages on the victim's behalf); the public prosecutor has the duty to guarantee the protection of victims and witnesses during the trial; victims have the right to challenge omissions by prosecutors

---

[46] DA Shirk, 'Criminal Justice Reform in Mexico: An Overview' (2011) III *Mexican Law Review* 203.

that take place during criminal investigations and a decisionnot to file charges, or to withdraw the charges that were filed.

All these rules and principles of the new criminal justice system form part of the constitutional text today, and both the federal and State criminal justice authorities and procedures have the duty to conform to them. In fact, the reform decree established a period of eight years in which to adapt State and federal legal systems to the new roles. That is to say, by 2016, the new model will have to be in place across the country. The practical result of all this effort remains to be seen.

In addition, it is important to note that the reform of 2008 also established a set of special provisions that severely limit due process rights of suspects connected with organised crime. Critics have pointed out that this in fact means the creation of two different and parallel criminal justice systems. One for 'normal' criminals, inspired by the liberal principles of criminal law; and another one for organised crime, in which the rights of the accused are significantly reduced. In turn, this dualism has been justified by the context of the 'war' against organised crime (particularly the drug cartels), the increase in the power of these criminal groups and the need to make it easier for law enforcement agencies to prosecute criminals that belong to those groups and to undermine their economic power. Examples of this dualism include measures like the so-called '*arraigo*': the accused can be subject by the judge to a special restriction of his freedom of movement for up to 80 days, which is a kind of pre-trial detention that takes place not before a judge, but before officials from the office of the Attorney-General, who have the power to perform a series of judicial acts and evaluate evidence and present the means of proof before the person is charged. In 1999 *arraigo* in State codes of criminal procedure was declared unconstitutional by the Supreme Court. Yet, the reforms of 2008 made it possible at the federal level and in connection with organised crime prosecutions.

V. THE EMERGENCE OF A NEW PARADIGM ON HUMAN RIGHTS

Current debates on human rights in Mexico are dominated by one idea: the emergence of a new paradigm, that is to say, the formation of new coordinates and parameters for the interpretation and application of human rights in this country. In turn, the pillars of the new paradigm are: the doctrine of 'control of conventionality' developed by the

Inter-American Court of Human Rights (IACtHR) and its reception in Mexico; and the constitutional reform on human rights of 10 June 2011. The judicial doctrine of 'control of conventionality' appeared for the first time in the IACtHR's judgment in *Almonacid-Arellano v Chile*:

> 124. The Court is aware that domestic judges and courts are bound to respect the rule of law, and therefore, they are bound to apply the provisions in force within the legal system. But when a State has ratified an international treaty such as the American Convention, its judges, as part of the State, are also bound by such Convention. This forces them to see that all the effects of the provisions embodied in the Convention are not adversely affected by the enforcement of laws which are contrary to its purpose and that have not had any legal effects since their inception. In other words, the Judiciary must exercise a sort of 'conventionality control' between the domestic legal provisions which are applied to specific cases and the American Convention on Human Rights. To perform this task, the Judiciary has to take into account not only the treaty, but also the interpretation thereof made by the Inter-American Court, which is the ultimate interpreter of the American Convention.[47]

Later on, the doctrine was reframed in other decisions. One of them was issued in the *Radilla v Mexico* case:

> 339. With regard to judicial practices, this Tribunal has established, in its jurisprudence, that it is aware that the domestic judges and tribunals are subject to the rule of law and that, therefore, they are compelled to apply the regulations in force within the legal system. But once a State has ratified an international treaty such as the American Convention, its judges, as part of the State's apparatus, are also submitted to it, which compels them to make sure that the provisions of the Convention are not affected by the application of laws contrary to its object and purpose, and that they do not lack legal effects from their creation. In other words, the Judiciary shall exercise a 'control of conventionality' ex officio between domestic regulations and the American Convention, evidently within the framework of its respective competences and the corresponding procedural regulations. Within this task, the Judiciary shall take into consideration not only the treaty but also the interpretation the Inter-American Court, final interpreter of the American Convention, has made of it.[48]

---

[47] Inter-American Court of Human Rights, *Almonacid-Arellano et al v Chile*, Judgment of 26 September 2006.

[48] Inter-American Court of Human Rights, *Radilla Pacheco v United Mexican States*, Judgment of 23 November 2009.

Equally important in the definition of the new coordinates is the Supreme Court's resolution of the case '*Varios* 912/2010' (Several 912/2010), in which it discussed the proper terms in which the Court itself should comply with the judgment of the IACtHR in the case of the 'enforced disappearance' of Mr Rosendo Radilla mentioned above, which took place in the State of Guerrero (Mexico) in 1974, in the context of the 'dirty war'. In its judgment of 23 November 2009, the IACtHR condemned the Mexican state for a series of breaches of the American Convention on Human Rights, in connection with the disappearance of Mr Radilla, as well as the denial of due process and access to justice for him and his family. In this case, the Mexican state was ordered to provide compensation to the family, and to investigate, prosecute, and punish the persons responsible for Mr Radilla's forced disappearance, as well as to reform the military and criminal codes in order to make them compatible with international laws and standards.

It is important to elaborate a little bit more on this last component of the judgment, because the way it was 'received' and processed by the Supreme Court of Justice gives a good idea of the new winds that are blowing in Mexico, concerning the judicial protection of human rights. Mexico's article 13 of the Constitution states on its face that when a member of the military commits a common crime (that is, a crime that does not fall within the scope of 'crimes against military discipline' – such as disobeying the orders of superiors, mutiny, rebellion, treason, and the like – that by definition can only be committed by members of the armed forces), the perpetrator should be judged by ordinary civilian courts.

The Code of Military Justice establishes a definition of 'crimes and faults against military discipline', which extend the jurisdiction of military courts beyond the original and textual constitutional scope. Indeed, article 57.II of that Code includes as crimes against military discipline all the crimes committed by members of the military 'in active service or in connection with acts of service'. This rule has allowed military courts to assume jurisdiction over nearly all crimes committed by active-duty soldiers. In turn, this has lead to impunity by soldiers that commit common crimes against the civilian population: military courts have tended to cover up and protect soldiers involved in these kind of situations, because they lack true independence and impartiality.[49]

---

[49] This has been stated in the Report of the Inter-American Commission on Human Rights in *Ana, Beatríz, and Celia González Pérez v Mexico*, Case 11.565, Report

In a series of cases (like in *Radilla*) the IACtHR has found that Mexico's military courts lack impartiality, and has ordered that cases of human rights violations perpetrated by soldiers should be excluded from military courts. In particular, it has ordered Mexican authorities to reform article 57.II of the Code of Military Justice, provoking two effects in Mexico. First, President Felipe Calderón introduced a bill into Mexico's federal Congress, proposing a reform to that Code. Nevertheless, the bill excludes from military courts' jurisdiction only three crimes: rape, torture and forced disappearance. In these cases, soldiers would be tried by ordinary courts. Yet, in all other cases in which soldiers commit ordinary crimes when 'on active service or in connection with acts of service', they would still be tried by military courts. Obviously, on the one hand, the president is trying to comply with the IACtHR's judgments but, on the other hand, he is making a concession to the military, in the context of a 'war on drugs' decided by his administration, which has been based on military actions rather than on intelligence investigations, selective use of force and decided fight against money laundering.

The other effect of the IACtHR judgments in cases like *Radilla* can be seen in the shift in the interpretation of the Supreme Court of article 13 of the Constitution. Formerly, the Court considered that article 57.II of the Code of Military Justice was constitutional. But in July 2011, and in clear adoption of the IACtHR criteria on the issue, it stated that military jurisdiction should be limited to crimes and misdemeanours committed by soldiers against military discipline only, and could not be extended to members of the military that commit 'ordinary' crimes when in service.

In its new interpretation of article 13 of the Constitution, the Supreme Court said that when military courts hear cases in which members of the military committed violations of human rights of civilians, they exercise their jurisdiction not only in connection with the accused, but for the victim (who is a civilian), who has the right to participate in the criminal trial not only seeking the reparation of damages, but also for exercising his right to truth and justice. Civilians who are victims of crimes committed by the military have the right to have their cases heard and resolved by the competent non-military court. In this reasoning, the

No 53/01, paras 80–82 (2000). In this case, three indigenous women from the Mexican State of Chiapas were raped and tortured by a group of soldiers in 1994, with the goal of forcing them to confess that they were members of a *guerrilla* army.

importance of the victims of a crime extends beyond the sphere of military justice, because values which are relevant to ordinary justice are implicated. In sum: for the Supreme Court, article 57.II of the Code of Military Justice is contrary to article 13 of the federal Constitution (interpreted in the light of articles 2 and 8.1 of the American Convention on Human Rights), because it does not guarantee to civilians or their relatives who are victims of human rights violations perpetrated by the military, the possibility of submitting to the jurisdiction of an ordinary court.[50] Finally, the Court also indicated that in future cases, judges will have the duty to follow these new criteria. This means that if a case is brought before them they will not be able to dismiss it, alleging lack of jurisdiction, as they used to do in the past.

Moreover, in *Varios* 912/2010 the Supreme Court stated something that went far beyond the terms of the *Radilla* judgment: as a consequence of the 2011 constitutional reform on human rights, the rights contained in the Constitution should be interpreted in accordance with international treaties in the way that best protects the person (principle *pro persona*); and that all Mexico's judges, both federal and from the States, have the duty to verify that statutes they apply are in accordance with the Constitution and international treaties on human rights (and their interpretation by the IACtHR). For the Supreme Court, all judges shall be able to decide on the non-application in a concrete case of the norms that they consider are contrary to the Constitution and to international treaties on human rights.

These new rules go against traditional and historic criteria that had governed the powers and competence of courts in Mexico. Historically, and after a series of cases decided by the Supreme Court, federal courts have monopolised the power to declare that a statute or any other norm is unconstitutional, and to determine its invalidity in the concrete case. This, in spite of the text of article 133 of the Constitution, which on its face appears to allow all judges to declare the unconstitutionality of norms.[51] Yet, in *Varios* 912/2010 the Court opens the gate for all judges

---

[50] SCJ, *Varios* 912/2010, paras 40–43.

[51] Article 133 of the Constitution states that: 'This Constitution, the laws of Congress that come from it, and all the treaties that are in accord with it, that have been concluded and that are to be concluded by the President of the Republic with the approval of the Senate will be the Supreme Law of all the Union. *The judges of every State will follow this Constitution and these laws and treaties in considering dispositions to the contrary that are contained in the constitutions of laws of the States*' (emphasis added).

to declare the non-application of unconstitutional (and 'unconventional') norms in concrete cases. It is for this reason that we talk about the emergence of a new paradigm in the interpretation and application of human rights in Mexico.

To complete the picture, we have to say that the reform of 10 June 2011 modified 11 articles of the Constitution, and was explicitly intended to strengthen the protection of human rights, and to promote a culture that is adequate to achieve that purpose. With this reform: 1. Human rights contained in the international treaties signed by Mexico were raised to a constitutional status; 2. Courts must guarantee individuals the most favourable interpretation of human rights law (principle *pro persona*); 3. Respect for human rights is defined as the purpose of education policies in Mexico; 4. All public authorities have the duty to promote, respect, protect and guarantee human rights; 5. Recommendations of the national and State commissions on human rights were strengthened;[52] 6. State constitutions and statutes shall foresee rules to guarantee full autonomy of State ombudsmen as well as procedures that include public consultation and transparency in the designation of ombudsmen; 7. The national ombudsman was granted the power to file actions of unconstitutionality to challenge statutes and norms which are contrary not only to the Constitution, but to human rights contained in international treaties signed by Mexico.

Finally, we have to say that the restriction of military jurisdiction and more in general the constitutional reform on human rights of 2011, has to be understood in the context of the security policy pursued by the administration of President Calderón, which has relied heavily on the participation of the armed forces. This strategy has provoked an increase in human rights violations by members of the armed forces. The regime's moves to limit military jurisdiction and to strengthen human rights have been intended to counteract the perception (and reality) of lack of civilian control of those forces.

---

[52] All public servants have the obligation to comply with recommendations. If they do not do so, they have the duty of explaining the motives and legal basis of their refusal to comply, and make them public. The Senate and State legislatures have the power to call public servants that refuse to comply with said recommendations, after the request of the national or State commissions on human rights.

VI. FREEDOM OF RELIGION AND THE SEPARATION OF STATE AND CHURCH

In Chapter 1 of this book I explained the process that led to the inclusion of the principle of State-Church separation in the Constitution; and I also mentioned that as the result of the historic confrontation between the State and the Catholic Church a series of restrictions and prohibitions on religious institutions were imposed.[53] Indeed, that confrontation had an impact on the scope of freedom of religion recognised in article 24: on the one hand, originally the Constitution of 1917 recognised that freedom with respect to all individuals, but on the other hand it ordered that the right to practise public acts of worship would be restricted to the temples, and that the state would have the power to inspect them.[54]

In addition, article 130 of the Constitution contained a series of rules that rather than establishing the separation of State and Church, established the supremacy of the former over the latter:

A. The federal powers would be able to exercise the supervision required by law in matters relating to religious worship and outward ecclesiastical forms. Other authorities would act as auxiliaries of the federation.

B. Congress could not enact laws establishing or prohibiting any religion.

C. Marriage was considered a civil contract. This and other acts of a civil nature concerning persons would be within the exclusive competence of civil officials and authorities, in the manner prescribed by law, and would have the force and validity defined by law.

D. The law would not recognise any personality in religious groups called churches.

E. The legislatures of the States would have the power to determine the maximum number of ministers of religious denominations necessary for local needs.

F. To practise the ministry of any denomination in the United Mexican States it was necessary to be a Mexican by birth.

G. Ministers of the different religious denominations were not allowed, in a public or private meeting constituting an assembly, or in acts of

---

[53] See chapter 1.V of this book.
[54] Article 24 of the Constitution.

worship or religious propaganda, to criticise the fundamental laws of the country or the authorities of the government, specifically or generally. They would not have an active or passive vote, or the right to form associations for religious purposes.

H. Periodical publications of a religious character, whether they were such because of their agenda, title, or merely because of their general tendencies, would not be able to comment on national political matters or public information on acts of the authorities of the country or of private persons directly related to the functioning of public institutions.

I. The formation of any kind of political group the name of which contained any word or indication whatever that it was related to any religious denomination, was strictly prohibited (this is the reason why no party in Mexico can be named 'Christian-Democrat'[55]). In addition, meetings of a political character could not be held in places of worship.

Furthermore, article 3 of the Constitution originally established that public education as well as primary, secondary and higher education provided by private schools, had to be secular. In addition, no religious corporation, or any religious minister, was allowed to establish or administer schools of primary education.

Nevertheless, the enforcement of these rules led to resistance on behalf of the Catholic Church hierarchy and, since January 1926, to open rebellion. This in turn provoked a military confrontation that in Mexico's history is known as the Cristero War, which ended in 1929 thanks to an agreement between the government and the Church: the text of articles 3, 24 and 130 of the Constitution would remain unchanged, but its rules would not be strictly enforced by the government (particularly with respect to the participation of the Catholic Church in the field of education). It could even be argued that this 'entente' contributed to the stability of the hegemonic party system formed in the 1930s and consolidated in the following decades.

In 1992 some of the constitutional rules contained in articles 3 and 130 were modified. Basically, the legal personality of all churches was recognised and therefore their legal capacity to own property (though still with some restrictions). Moreover, priests were allowed to vote (but

---

[55] Though the PAN clearly shares the vision of Christian-Democrats of other countries.

not to be elected to public office). Fundamentally, with the reform of 1992 the duty of private schools to provide secular education was eliminated, as well as the prohibition on religious corporations and ministers of cult participating in the creation or administration of primary schools.

There were political reasons that led to those reforms: the election of 1988 was highly disputed, and ended up with accusations of electoral fraud and the shadow of illegitimacy for the winner (Carlos Salinas). Under this situation, and once in office, the Executive searched for strategies to counterbalance his original political weakness: it seems that the president of the Republic decided to make a concession to a key political actor, such as the Catholic Church, capable of providing an important source of political support. The constitutional reform of 1992 meant a positive response to some of the Church's historical demands.

As explained by Blancarte, the reform of 1992 has permitted religious associations to adopt a different kind of relationship with the state. Before that reform, the lack of legal recognition limited them enormously and left them vulnerable to the discretionary power of public authorities.[56] In contrast, today they can act in politics without fear and with few limits, and can fully display their considerable social influence to advance their agenda (particularly the Catholic Church). This can be specifically seen in the conflict on abortion, which can be summarised in the following way.

In May of 2007, the legislature of the Federal District (Mexico City) with a majority of seats controlled by the leftist PRD, approved a reform to the local criminal code (and the local statute on health), in order to de-criminalise the voluntary termination of pregnancy within the period of 12 weeks after conception. Yet, the reform was challenged through two actions of unconstitutionality (146/2007 and 147/2007) by the federal Attorney General[57] and by the president of the Commission on Human Rights (Mexico's federal ombudsman), alleging that it was contrary to the right to life of the product of conception granted by the

---

[56] R Blancarte, 'Churches, Believers, and Democracy' in Selee and Peschard (eds), *Mexico's Democratic Challenges, Politics, Government and Society* (Stanford CA, Stanford University Press/Washington, DC, Woodrow Wilson Center Press, 2010) 293.

[57] The Attorney General formed part of the PAN government of President Felipe Calderón. The PAN is the political party more closely identified with the interests of the Catholic Church in Mexico.

Mexican Constitution, as well as by a series of international instruments ratified by Mexico, such as the Convention on the Rights of the Child, the International Covenant on Civil and Political Rights, and the American Convention on Human Rights. Moreover, they argued that the reform violated the right to protection of the gestation process foreseen in articles 4 and 123 of the Constitution; and the right to equality, procreation, and paternity foreseen articles 1 and 4 of the Constitution. Finally, they alleged that the reform constituted an invasion of the sphere of competences of the federation, which has the power to pass legislation on health under a regime of 'concurrent powers',[58] according to articles 4 and 73.XVI of the Constitution.

In contrast with these arguments, a majority of the eight Justices of the Supreme Court decided that:

a) The right to life is not expressly stated in the Constitution (a surprising argument that is evidence of a culture of constitutional interpretation strictly based on text).

b) No international instrument ratified by Mexico recognises the right to life as an absolute right; nor do any of them determine the specific moment at which the duty to protect that right starts; what they do is to establish a set of guarantees to prohibit the arbitrary deprivation of life and rules to prohibit the death penalty.

c) Article 4.1 of the American Convention cannot be understood as if it established the right to life of the product of conception from the moment of conception itself. This article states that

> 1. Every person has the right to have his life respected. This right shall be protected by law and, in general, from the moment of conception. No one shall be arbitrarily deprived of his life.

For the majority of the Court, the term 'in general' was introduced in that article, in order to propitiate the ratification of the American Convention both by the States that wanted to protect life from conception and by the States who did not want to grant protection from that moment.

d) Besides, the majority pointed out that when Mexico ratified the American Convention in 1981, it formulated an interpretative declaration precisely on the issue under discussion, in the following terms:

---

[58] An explanation of 'concurrent powers' as a formula to distribute competences in Mexico's federal system can be found in chapter 6.II.2 of this book.

a) Concerning paragraph 1 of Article 4, [Mexico] considers that the expression 'in general', used in that paragraph, does not constitute the obligation to adopt or maintain in force legislation that protects life 'from the moment of conception', because this matter belongs to the domain reserved to the States.[59]

e) There is no mandate in the Constitution or in any international instrument ratified by Mexico establishing the obligation of the federal or State legislatures to criminalise abortion. Moreover, the existence of fundamental rights does not imply the duty to criminalise conduct that affects them. Thus, even if it was accepted that life was constitutionally protected, this would not mean that legislatures have the duty to impose a criminal sanction in connection with conduct that affects life. The democratic legislator can de-criminalise those acts that, according to its judgement, no longer deserve public sanctions.

f) The right to life can be regulated by the relevant legislature, in conformity with its competences and powers: the Legislative Assembly of the Federal District has the power to pass and reform its criminal code; and under the regime of 'concurrent powers' in the field of health, that Assembly has the power to regulate medical attention of women during pregnancy, as well as to define measures of 'family planning'.

g) Therefore, the challenged act was not contrary to the Constitution.

The Catholic Church's hierarchy reacted immediately against this decision. When the judgment was made public, the bells of Mexico City's Cathedral and of other churches in the land tolled in mourning for the children who in their view would be killed as a consequence of this decision.[60] In constitutional terms, the most important reaction of the Catholic Church was the organisation of a campaign throughout the entire country, promoting reforms to State constitutions establishing the principle that life shall be protected from the moment of conception. In a tour de force that showed the Church's political muscle, between 2008 and 2011, 18 out of the 31 States of Mexico reformed

---

[59] On 26 September 2011 President Felipe Calderón (of the PAN) sent to the Senate a proposal to repeal the Interpretative Declaration concerning article 4.1 of the American Convention on Human Rights. As of June 2012, it has not been approved.

[60] The PAN federal Minister of Health declared that terminations of pregnancy would not be practised in federal hospitals located in Mexico City.

their constitutions to this effect (with the support of PAN-PRI legislative coalitions).

Another episode of this struggle took place in May 2010 when the PAN governor of the State of Jalisco filed a constitutional controversy (54/2009) challenging a federal Official Norm on Health (number 046) which established the obligation of State health authorities to offer the so-called 'morning after pill' (as an emergency contraceptive method) to every woman who has been a victim of rape. Among other arguments, the governor stated that the federal authority was not competent to produce norms related to the care of victims of crimes of the jurisdiction of States, such as the crime of rape. In his view, the care of victims in crimes like rape was part of the law enforcement functions of the 'Public Ministry' (prosecutor), which in turn was of the exclusive jurisdiction of the State of Jalisco. Moreover, the governor argued that an administrative ruling such as the challenged Official Norm was interfering in a field of regulation that according to the Constitution belonged to the legislative power. Finally, he argued that the Official Norm was unconstitutional because it ran against the recently reformed Constitution of Jalisco, which established the protection of life since the moment of conception.

The Supreme Court decided (10-1) against the plaintiff, arguing that according to the federal Constitution, the care of victims of crimes in the States was not of the only and exclusive competence of the state Public Ministry. When the Constitution establishes the Public Ministry's duty to provide care for the victims of crime (article 20.B. III and V), it does not grant a monopoly in the provision of that function, but allows other authorities to intervene. Besides, this is reinforced by the fact that the Public Ministry does not have the capacity, knowledge, and specialisation to treat victims of rape from a medical point of view.

Furthermore, the Court reasoned that the medical treatment of victims implied that this kind of case entered into the field of the constitutional regime of 'concurrence' that governs the subject-matter of 'health'. After an analysis of this regime, the Court concluded that the federation was allowed to issue 'technical norms' common to general health in Mexico and applicable in all States, to assure uniformity in principles, criteria, policies and strategies in that policy area. Finally, the Court stated that the 'morning after pill' could not be considered as contrary to the reformed Constitution of Jalisco, since technically speaking that treatment was not 'abortive' but 'contraceptive'.

VII. CONCLUSION

Historically, Mexico has had difficulty in protecting and enforcing human rights contained in its Constitution and in making them truly effective. In spite of this, there are a series of relatively recent developments that have started to change this situation. On the one hand, the breakdown of the hegemonic party system has cleared the stage for increased independence of the Supreme Court, which has had an impact on the interpretation of human rights contained in the Constitution. On the other hand, Mexico's acceptance of the contentious jurisdiction of the Inter-American Court of Human Rights in 1998 (entering into force on 24 February 1999), and the impact of the latter's judgments, have subjected all Mexican authorities to external scrutiny, and this has started to produce changes in perceptions of and behaviour of domestic actors.

Furthermore, the relatively recent reform of 2007 mandating both federal and State governments to guarantee transparency and access to public information, has the potential (if effectively implemented) to significantly reduce the traditional secrecy of public administration, which has been the source of corruption and lack of accountability in many governmental agencies.[61]

Though these developments show positive signs, we cannot be over-optimistic: the record of Mexico in the field of human rights is poor, particularly in the fields of the criminal justice system and the efficacy of social rights. In this context, the Supreme Court of Justice, the entities in charge of the protection of human rights and society at large still have a long way to go.

FURTHER READING

Carbonell, M, *Los Derechos Fundamentales en México* (Mexico, CNDH, 2004).
Carbonell, M and Salazar, P (eds), *La Reforma Constitucional de Derechos Humanos: Un Nuevo Paradigma* (Mexico, UNAM, 2011).

[61] Fox and Haight report that Mexico's experience on transparency is unusual because it involved creating a special agency dedicated to encouraging citizens' information access, including the right to easily appeal if agencies deny their requests. See Fox, Jonathan and Haight, Libby, 'Transparency Reforms: Theory and Practice' in Selee and Peschard (eds), *Mexico's Democratic Challenges, Politics, Government and Society* (2010), n 56 above, 137.

Donde Matute, J, 'The Duty to Prosecute Human Rights Violations before the Supreme Court of Justice of Mexico' (2009) 124 *Boletín Mexicano de Derecho Comparado* 173.

Lawyers Committee for Human Rights, *Legalized injustice; Mexican criminal procedure and Human Rights* (New York, Lawyers Committee for Human Rights, 2001).

Madrazo, A and Vela, E, 'The Mexican Supreme Court's (Sexual) Revolution?' (2011) 89 *Texas Law Review* 1863.

Metz, A, 'Mexican Church-State Relations under President Carlos Salinas de Gortari' (1992) 34 *Journal of Church and State* 111.

Metz, A, 'Protestantism in Mexico: Contemporary Contextual Developments' (1994) 36 *Journal of Church and State* 77.

8

The Constitution and the National Economy

Introduction – The Constitutional Regime of Property Rights in Mexico – Public Property – Planning – Agrarian Reform and Social Property – Expropriation of the Oil Industry – The Electric Power Sector – Conclusion

I. INTRODUCTION

Property rights define the model of economic and political organisation of a polity. From the economic point of view, they define the rules for the appropriation of goods and distribution of resources available for productive use, and therefore determine the conditions for the functioning of the market. From the political point of view, property rights define who has control of resources in a given society and to what extent, and thus determine the capacity of different actors to influence and lead society as a whole. The legal regime of property determines to an important extent the balance of forces that is in the foundations of every state.

There are a series of elements that have to be explained in order to understand the current constitutional and legal regime of property rights in Mexico. First, Mexico was a colony of Spain for more than 300 years, which left a legacy of a social and economic structure typical of colonial situations (eg very unequal distribution of wealth). Secondly, the independent state inaugurated in 1821 was born as a poor state, in many senses: a weak fiscal state, with few capacities to build up an economic base to support its structures and functions; a state with no property, since all available wealth was already in the hands of large landowners or of the Catholic Church; weak in terms of the lack of institutional and administrative capacities to procure order and lead society to achieve goals of public interest; poor in terms of education and democratic culture.

By the end of the nineteenth century, order and governability had been achieved through the consolidation of a military dictatorship that lasted for more than 30 years. Yet, the country's situation from the point of view of economic and social development was rather fragile and unfair. Specifically, the regime of property rights established under the Constitution of 1857, based on the principles of economic liberalism, in practice produced a situation in which more than 87 per cent of the land was in the hands of less than one per cent of the population. Moreover, a public policy of very generous concessions, permits and authorisations of Díaz's successive governments had led to a situation in which the enormous mineral wealth of the country was controlled by a few foreign companies. In turn, this had created the pattern of exploitation and production of agricultural and mineral products typical of the so-called 'enclaves': oriented towards exports, but with few positive effects in the country's domestic economy and society.

Widespread poverty and extreme inequality, as well as a reaction against the mechanisms of social, political and military control established to guarantee the maintenance and reproduction of the existing order led to civil war, that is, the Mexican revolution of 1910, from which many social and political demands emerged, that were later incorporated into the Constitution of 1917. In turn, this Constitution established a new regime concerning property rights, defining a new balance of forces between public power and private owners, both national and foreign.

In this chapter, I shall explain the constitutional regime of property rights, which has been the basis for the creation of a public sector that has been in charge of: the agrarian reform programme (cancelled in 1993); planning Mexico's economic development; and the formation of an important group of public enterprises intended to foster Mexico's industrialisation (eg in the oil and electric power sectors). Furthermore, I shall explain how some of the constitutional rules and principles that allowed the creation of that public sector, have entered into conflict with the recent trends towards the design and implementation of more market-oriented economic policies.

II. THE CONSTITUTIONAL REGIME OF PROPERTY RIGHTS IN MEXICO

The starting point to understand the scope and limits of property rights in Mexico can be found in the concept of 'original property' in article 27 of the Constitution, which is a contribution of the constituent assembly of 1917 and, paradoxically, seems to have its antecedents in a legal tradition identified with colonial times, in the following sense: in the same way as the Spanish King had the character of 'Lord' in connection with the territories of his colonies, the Constitution of 1917 determined that the nation would be considered as 'original' owner of all the lands and waters located in Mexican territory.

Interestingly, the Supreme Court of Justice has adopted this interpretation, recognising that when Mexico ceased to be a colony of Spain, it assumed all the property rights that corresponded to the Spanish Kings and, therefore, all that patrimony passed to the nation as a whole, and not to its parts (that is, the States).[1] This interpretation was produced in connection with constitutional controversy number 2/1932, derived from the following facts: on 9 January 1932, archeologist Antonio Caso discovered Tomb No 7 of Monte Albán (an archeological site in the State of Oaxaca in South Mexico). This is one of the richest tombs ever found in Mexico, in terms of jewels and other precious objects. The archeological expedition had been financed by the federal government: the Ministry for Education. Being informed about the discovery, the Minister of Education declared that the treasure should be transported immediately to Mexico City, not only for the sake of its preservation but also because all archeological zones in the territory of Mexico were under federal jurisdiction.

The governor of Oaxaca opposed this decision, and using extraordinary powers to legislate (granted by the State legislature since December 1931), he passed a statute on Oaxaca's archeological zones, to make it clear that everything found in archeological sites located within the territory of Oaxaca, belonged to the State of Oaxaca.

In turn, the federal government filed an action of constitutional controversy to the Supreme Court, seeking a declaration of unconstitutionality of the Oaxaca statute. The plaintiff's main argument was based

---

[1] SCJ, Constitutional controversy 2/1932 *Federation v State of Oaxaca, Semanario Judicial de la Federación*, XXXVI, p 1074, 15 October 1932.

on the implicit powers clause: it was true that in 1932 the Constitution did not explicitly grant the matter of archeological zones to the federal Legislature. However – the federal government argued – the federal Congress had also implicit powers, that is, it could pass legislation that was necessary to make its explicit powers effective (Congress had the explicit power to legislate on the creation of institutions of culture for all the inhabitants of the Republic).

The Supreme Court concurred with this argument, and stated that the power of the federation to regulate archeological zones was an implicit power, which was necessary to make effective the explicit power of the federation to establish institutions for the promotion of culture. Since archeological sites were closely related to the general culture of Mexicans all over the territory, the federal government was the body entitled to regulate them.[2]

But getting back to the notion of 'original property of the Nation', we must note that one of its most important consequences is that it defines the derivative character of the diverse forms of appropriation of goods that are allowed under Mexico's legal system, which are: public property, private property and social property.

On the one hand, and in connection with private property, its derivative character can be seen in the last sentence of the first paragraph of article 27 of the Constitution, according to which the 'Nation has the right to transfer the domain of lands and waters which are of its original property, to individuals, thus constituting it private property'.

On the other hand, the derivative character of the different forms of property that exist in Mexico explains also the pre-eminence of the public interest over private property, in terms of the second paragraph of article 27 of the Constitution: the nation has at all times the right to impose on private property the modalities dictated by the public interest.

The genesis of the concept of 'original property' and the regime derived from it is directly connected with the intention of the constituent assembly of 1917 to establish the basis of an agrarian reform programme, which it was hoped would put an end to a regime that had favoured the concentration of land ownership. In this way, a group of legislators within the constituent assembly, led by Pastor Rouaix, consid-

---

[2] The next year, in 1933, the constitutional amendment came: article 73 of the Constitution was reformed to establish explicitly that archeological sites were a matter of federal law.

ered that land reform should not be based on expropriation powers of the Executive alone (which were already recognised by the Constitution of 1857 and were justified for 'causes of public utility'). Instead, land reform should be based on the rights of the nation on all the land.[3] Eventually, this notion was incorporated in the first paragraph of article 27 of the Constitution, under the form of the 'original property' of the nation we mentioned earlier. This conception altered in a profound way the constitutional and legal regime established under the Constitution of 1857, which considered property as a fundamental right that admitted few restrictions.

Instead, private property was considered as a right with a relative value, which was derived from a right that enjoyed superiority: the rights of the nation. Therefore, private property was subjected to the possibility of being strongly regulated by the state, through the establishment of 'modalities' dictated by public interest.

These modalities have implied the establishment of several limits to the exercise of property rights, such as these:

A. Not all available assets can be appropriated. There is a category of assets defined as being of the 'direct domain' and 'property of the Nation' (that we shall examine later in this chapter), that cannot be subject to the regime of private property.
B. Private property in rural areas has precise limits, established by article 27.IV and 27.XV of the Constitution.
C. There are also limits on the legal capacity of foreigners to own real property in certain portions of Mexico's territory.[4]
D. There are some limits on the capacity of certain kinds of persons to own real property. For example, religious associations can only acquire, possess or administer the property that is strictly needed to achieve their goals, with the requirements and limits established by an act of Congress (article 27.II of the Constitution).
E. The use of private property by owners can be limited by different statutes of administrative law, as would be the case with laws on urban planning and zoning, protection of the environment, historical monuments and archeological zones, among others.

[3] P Rouaix, *Génesis de los Artículos 27 y 123 de la Constitución Política de 1917* (Mexico, Comisión Federal de Electricidad, 1978) 125–45.
[4] Foreigners cannot own real property within a zone of 100 km along the borders and of 50 km along the county's coasts. See article 27.I of the Constitution.

F. Private property can be expropriated for causes of 'public utility' and 'through compensation'.

For its part, article 27 of the Constitution defines a category of assets that in principle can be owned and exploited by private owners, but which are subject to a particularly strong regulatory regime by the state. These are the so-called 'natural elements disposed for appropriation', but which are subject to a particularly strict regulatory regime: for example, wild animals, wild flora (including forests and rainforests), soil, waters that do not qualify as national waters in terms of article 27 paragraph 5, and air.

On the basis of this constitutional provision, for instance, the federal government can create national parks to protect wild animals and flora. However, since matters related to environmental protection and 'human settlements' are subject to a regime of 'concurrent powers',[5] a series of disputes has arisen in order to define what is the proper sphere of competence and powers that federal, State and municipal governments have in this area. That was the case, for example, with the 'Tulum National Park', created by the federal government in the early 1980s in the southern State of Quintana Roo (in the Yucatán peninsula) to protect specific endangered species of turtles and mangroves. On 5 June 2007, the council of the municipality of Solidaridad (located in Quintana Roo), passed an amendment to its Programme of Urban Development, intending to exercise its zoning powers in parts of that national park.[6] It seems that the intention of the municipal council was to legalise the situation of businesses that had settled (illegally) in parts of the park, and to fulfil a series of promises made by the government of the State of Quintana Roo to sell portions of land located in the park to private owners.[7] Yet, the federal government filed a constitutional controversy (72/2008), alleging that the municipal council had exceeded its competences in trying to regulate a zone that was under the exclusive jurisdiction of the federation.

---

[5] On 'concurrence' as a formula for the distribution of competences among the levels of government of Mexico's federal system, see above chapter 6.II.

[6] Article 115.V.a) and d) of the Constitution grant municipal councils the power to pass rulings on zoning, urban development and use of land applicable in their territory.

[7] Article by Julia Carabias, 'Avances frenados en Tulum', *Reforma*, 12 November 2011.

A majority of 10 Supreme Court Justices decided in favour of the plaintiff, reasoning that an analysis of articles 27 and 73.XIX-G of the Constitution led to the conclusion that the national park was a 'national asset subject to the regime of public domain of the federation', and that municipal councils could not exercise their zoning and use of land powers in relation to that kind of asset. Moreover, the Court noted that the Constitution allows the possibility that the federation, the States and municipal governments perform coordinated activities in connection with 'national assets' such as national parks (for example, through 'agreements of coordination'). Nevertheless, the Court also made it clear that in the case under examination, coordination always would have to take place within the terms defined by the federation, since those assets fall within the exclusive jurisdiction of the federal government and thus the latter has a power of direction in this area.[8]

In sum, the Constitution of 1917 established a regime that had as its background the model of an interventionist and regulatory state, which clashed with a conception of ownership typical of political liberalism found in the Constitution of 1857. In spite of that, the latter concept did not completely disappear. Private property is still considered as a fundamental right which can be defended against acts of authority that are unconstitutional, through the writ of *amparo*. Moreover, articles 14 and 16 of the Constitution establish due process rights, which are requirements that have to be complied with by all authorities that seek to affect, regulate or limit private property in some way.[9]

Interestingly, and in connection with private property, the Supreme Court has recently changed its interpretation and understanding of the Executive's expropriation power under article 27 of the Constitution. For years, the Court's criterion was that the exercise of that power was not controlled by article 14, paragraph 2 of the Constitution, which establishes a person's right to be heard before he is deprived of his property by any authority. This was so because article 27 of the Constitution did not explicitly say that the expropriation power was limited by article 14. Moreover, the Supreme Court was of the opinion that

[8] SCJ, Constitutional controversy 72/2008. The judgment was published in the Official Gazette of the Federation on 18 June 2011.
[9] Apart from the constitutional dimension of property rights, they also have a private law dimension, governed by the federal and State civil codes, with reference to the acquisition and transfer of said rights in the relationships between private owners.

the due process rule found in article 14 was intended to limit courts only, and not administrative authorities. In addition, the Court also considered that article 14 contained protection of individual rights, but article 27 contained social rights that were superior to the rights of individuals. Finally, the Supreme Court used to put forward a pragmatic consideration: the expropriation power implied the necessity to execute an action urgently in order to satisfy a public need: due process requirements would involve delays, and make expropriation pointless.

This criterion, which was reiterated by the Court in a series of decisions between 1939 and 1942, was rejected in 2006. In this year, the Second Chamber of the Supreme Court said that:

A. A systemic interpretation of articles 14 and 27 led to the conclusion that the Constitution had not established the expropriation power of the latter article as an exception of the due process rights in the former.
B. Social rights do not prevail automatically, and in every possible case, over individual rights. There is no absolute and abstract solution in their hierarchy applicable in all cases.
C. The Act on Expropriation allows alternative measures to occupy property immediately in urgent cases.
D. There should be a logical relationship, a correspondence between the extremity of the act of expropriation and the intensity of the protection against possible arbitrary actions that affect private property.

Therefore, the Court was of the opinion that the expropriation power is subject to the rules of article 14, and the owner has the constitutional right to be heard to contradict the authority that claims that there is a reason of 'public utility' justifying expropriation.[10]

This change of criteria is congruent with the general policy environment that has consolidated in Mexico since the mid-1980s, prone to support market-oriented policies and to reduce state intervention in the economy. Moreover, it can rightly be seen as an example of the line of expansive interpretations of human rights provisions by the Court, made possible by the breakdown of the hegemonic party system.[11] As a consequence of this new criterion, the Act on Expropriation was amended

[10] SCJ, *Expediente Varios* 2/2006-55, Modification of a Binding Criteria, *Semanario Judicial de la Federación y su Gaceta*, Ninth Epoch, Second Chamber, XXIV, December 2006, p 526.
[11] See above, chapter 7.III.

on 5 June 2009, in order to introduce a due process proceeding: before the expropriation of private property can be decreed by the Executive, there must be a 'Declaration of Public Utility', which must be served on the affected private owner, and can be challenged by him or her.

III. PUBLIC PROPERTY

As I mentioned above, not all kinds of assets can be owned by private owners. In fact, the Constitution expressly states that certain kinds of assets that correspond to the 'direct domain' and to the 'property of the Nation' cannot be owned by persons other than the state. In this way, all minerals, including hydrocarbons, belong to the 'direct domain' of the nation; while most water resources (both surface water and groundwater), are considered as 'property of the Nation'.[12] In connection with all these resources, the nation (that is, the federation) has exclusive rights of use and exploitation. Yet, with regard to some of these resources the Constitution itself allows the possibility of granting concessions allowing their use and exploitation by private owners (individuals or corporations).[13]

Originally, the Constitution allowed these concessions in all areas. However, throughout the twentieth century, article 27 of the Constitution was reformed on several occasions in order to remove the possibility of granting concessions for the exploitation of certain natural resources. In turn, this was the basis for the creation of the so-called 'para-state' sector of the economy, formed of a group of public enterprises that have played a very important role in the country's industrial development. In this way, in 1940 the Constitution was amended to prohibit concessions in the area of oil and its by-products. Later on, in 1960, concessions were forbidden in the area of 'production and distribution of the public service of electric power'. Finally, in 1975 concessions were forbidden in connection with exploitation and use of radioactive minerals. The targets of these prohibitions were the publicly-owned oil and electric energy enterprises,

---

[12] The water resources that have the characteristics defined in paragraph 5 of article 27 of the Constitution are considered as 'national waters' which are of the exclusive property of the nation. Waters that do not share those characteristics can be appropriated by private owners.

[13] Paragraph 10 of article 28 of the Constitution states that the state, according to the corresponding statutes, shall be able to grant concessions over public services or for the exploitation or use of public property of the federation, with the exceptions established by law.

which were the basis of a strategy of economic development in which the state played a crucial role, between the 1930s and the early 1980s.

Furthermore, in 1983, the Constitution was reformed in order to introduce a concept that has to be explained in more detail in this section, because it has to do with the constitutional regime of property rights, state regulation of the economy, and public participation in the industrial sector. I am referring to the concept of 'strategic areas', foreseen in articles 25 and 28 of the Constitution.

To explain it in short, the Constitution states that certain economic activities correspond exclusively to the state, including the ownership and control of the public enterprises established for the performance of those activities, which include: mail; telegraphs; oil and all other hydrocarbons; basic petrochemicals; radioactive minerals; the generation of nuclear power; electric power, 'as well as other activities that are expressly determined by statutes approved by the Congress of the Union'.

The antecedents of and reasons for the constitutional reform that incorporated these concepts into the Constitution are linked to the economic and political context in which that reform was passed, characterised by: a) one of the deepest economic crises lived by Mexico in the twentieth century, accompanied by a political debate on the liability of the state for the production of the crisis (bankruptcy in public finances, an enormous increase in public indebtedness, high levels of inflation, lack of economic growth); b) a harsh confrontation between the public and the private sectors, as a consequence of a decision taken by the president of the Republic in September of 1982 in the middle of the crisis: the expropriation of all private banks; c) a particularly unfavourable international situation (drastic decrease in the price of oil in international markets); and d) the end of a presidential administration and the inauguration of new government on 1 December 1982.

After an examination of these factors, it is possible to say that the constitutional reform of 1983 sought to reconstruct the pact between the public and the private sectors (which had been the basis of Mexico's strategy of economic growth since the 1940s), to recover legitimacy and achieve a consensus around the incoming presidential policies to control and overcome the economic crisis.[14]

---

[14] Diego Valadés notes that, in parallel with the reforms to the constitutional articles that referred to economic regulation, other reforms that also entered into force in 1983 had the objective of decreasing the levels of corruption in the government and thus giving the private sector a positive signal on the transaction costs of

The opinion of the committee of the Chamber of Deputies that studied the reform proposal illustrates two of the ideas that justified it: the need to overcome the trauma of the expropriation of private banks, and the need to create a new legitimising consensus among domestic production sectors. In fact, these goals appear behind the 3rd paragraph of article 25 of the Constitution: 'The public, social and private sectors shall concur with social responsibility to achieve national development'.

The discourse found in the justification of the constitutional reform, starts with recognition of the relevance of the state in achieving economic and social development for the country, for integrating the nation and for breaking down the structures of the colonial order. For these reasons, the reform incorporated into article 25 the notion that the state is responsible for leading the nation's development and article 26 specified that the instrument to perform that role would be planning.[15]

Nevertheless, the reform of 3 February 1983 was highly debated and questioned by different political actors and for different reasons. On the one hand, it was attacked for being too state-oriented, since it established the state's leadership in fostering development. On the other hand, it was accused of favouring the business community, since implied in the concept of 'strategic areas' was the idea that the state would leave the 'non-strategic areas' in the hands of private sector.

In addition, with the constitutional reform under examination, the last paragraph of article 25 stated that: 'The law shall promote and protect economic activities performed by private persons and shall create the conditions with which the development of the private sector shall contribute to national economic development'. And paragraph 4 of article 28 of the Constitution stated that to incorporate a new economic activity into the category of 'strategic areas' an act of Congress would be required (the message was: this sort of incorporation will never again happen through a presidential decree of expropriation, as happened with the expropriation of private banks in 1982).

doing business with the government and increasing its prestige. In this way, new constitutional bases were established for improving accountability of public servants (articles 108–114) and for establishing as a general rule mandatory public tender in government procurement procedures (article 134). See D Valadés, 'La Función Constitucional de la Regulación Económica' (2006) 3 *Economíaunam* (e-journal).

[15] Planning existed before this reform. However, it was in 1983 that the function and responsibility of planning was put into the Constitution, and the entire scheme for planning was rationalised through a series of reforms to existing statutes and new statutes.

Finally, the reform of 1983 defined the so called 'priority areas' of national economic development (telecommunications and railways). This implied that these activities would be considered of special national interest, and that the state would have the duty to promote them, either alone or in association with the private or the social sectors of the economy (article 25, paragraph 5; and paragraph 4 of article 28 of the Constitution).[16]

In summary, the constitutional reform of 1983 established the basis of a 'mixed economy', drawing a line between what would adhere to the private and the public sector, and allowing the possibility of association between them. Moreover, it also established the constitutional duty of the state to support the private sector. The intention was to guarantee legal certainty and security, reducing the Executive's capacity to impact discretionarily upon private property, sending a clear message that decisions like the expropriation of private banks through a presidential decree would never happen again in the future.

IV. PLANNING

The reform of 1983 also established a series of rules on planning at the constitutional level. As part of organising governmental action, planning had existed in Mexico at least since the '*Plan Sexenal*' of 1933, prepared by President Lázaro Cárdenas. Since then, other presidential administrations have prepared their own plans, establishing the different sets of objectives and priorities of the incumbent federal government. In all those cases planning was a process internal to the federal public administration, with little input from civil society: the plan was an instrument of government, intended to guide the action of the federal public administration in the different fields.

In contrast, the reform of 1983 established the so-called 'System of Democratic Planning', granting the federal government powers to make a plan intended to foster national development, and establishing a mechanism of social participation intended to give legitimacy to the measures adopted by the federal government, following its plan. Planning is the instrument through which the federal government exercises its 'leadership'[17] in Mexico's process of economic development.

[16] The so-called 'social sector' is formed of cooperatives and farmers who produce under a collective scheme of land ownership.

[17] The Constitution uses the term '*Rectoría*' (Article 25).

According to article 26 of the Constitution, in the formulation of the plan, the federal government has to take into account the 'hopes and demands of society' through the mechanisms defined in the relevant statute law.[18]

Under these rules, the plan has an important political meaning. On the one hand, it was justified in terms of the need to channel a growing political organisation and participation of Mexico's civil society. In his reform proposal, President de la Madrid recognised that the legitimacy of the regime was increasingly related to the perception of society in connection with the government's capacity to lead national development. Thus, as established by the reform of 1983, planning supposed the injection of legitimacy to governmental actions that would be guided by the Plan, in turn, designed on the basis of social demands.

Obviously, planning was intended to be a mechanism for legitimising the political regime, distinct from and parallel to traditional mechanisms of the hegemonic party system. It was also intended to neutralise accusations by the private sector on authoritarian tendencies of the government. Yet, in the last instance it was a move intended to strengthen the president, as the whole process of planning was organised around him. The design of the plan, the 'consultation' of civil society, the execution of the plan, was (as it still is today) a process that takes place within and through the federal public administration, though with connections with civil society. With this, the president of the Republic has become the 'great mediator', as the centre of this formidable instrument to negotiate with social groups the elaboration of the federal government's plan every six years.[19] Thus, the 'System of Democratic Planning' can be seen as a mechanism to strengthen and legitimise the presidency itself, considering in addition, that Congress has little role to play: the Law on Planning states that the president shall refer the plan to Congress for its 'examination and opinion'. In turn, Congress can make 'observations' to the plan, to its execution and evaluation, but these observations have no binding effect at all on the Executive.

---

[18] This statute is the Law on Planning, the current version of which was passed on 6 January 1983.

[19] M González Oropeza, 'Planeación y División de Poderes' in *La Constitución Mexicana: Rectoría del Estado y Economía Mixta* (Mexico, UNAM-Porrúa, 1985).

V. AGRARIAN REFORM AND SOCIAL PROPERTY

Having started against another re-election of General Porfirio Díaz and as a claim for democracy in 1910, the Mexican revolution soon transformed into a broad social movement that demanded land reform. The factors that led to this violent social explosion incubated over the second half of the nineteenth century, and were the consequence of a set of statutes, policies and practices that favoured the dispossession of peasant communities of their land. The result was a pattern of high concentration of land ownership in the hands of very few families. Millions of poor and landless peasants lived in conditions of serfdom, and formed a mass of cheap labour available to work for the owners of the large and powerful '*haciendas*'.

Under these conditions, it is not surprising that when Francisco I Madero called the Mexican people to rebel against the regime of General Díaz on 20 November 1910, on the grounds that the presidential election of that year had been illegal and manipulated, thousands responded positively by taking up arms. Yet, the claim for democracy was taken over by the demand for social justice, mostly under the form of land redistribution. Eventually, this demand was directed at the constitutional text in 1917, specifically its article 27.

Until 1992, article 27 of the Constitution contained a series of rules concerning the agrarian reform programme, whose main objectives were the expropriation of large land properties (known as '*latifundios*'), their division and distribution to landless peasants. The agrarian reform programme was based on two kinds of action: the action of restitution, which could be filed by those peasants who had a claim to title of land of which they had been dispossessed; and the action of endowment ('*dotación*') for those who had no title to any land at all. Notably, both actions corresponded not to individuals, but to groups of peasants. Therefore, those who were benefited by the agrarian reform programme were communities of peasants that as such were endowed with portions of land. This is the origin of the communal kind of property that is known as '*ejido*', under which around half of rural land in Mexico is organised today. Through this programme, around 100 million hectares were distributed to more than two million peasants.

Until 1992, the *ejido* form of property (which is also known as 'social property'), was characterised by a series of limitations and prohibitions, such as:

a) Limitations on the right of selling the land, that is, *ejido* lands could not be sold. In other words, *ejido* land was out of the market in an absolute manner.

b) Prohibition of changing the *ejido* regime into the regime of private property.

c) Prohibition of associations between private investors and *ejido* communities, for the exploitation of *ejido* land.

The reasons for these limitations and prohibitions had to do with the aim of protecting traditionally weak peasants communities against voracious private owners and agricultural companies, and in that way preventing the repetition of the nineteenth century experience that had led to dispossession and unjust concentration of land ownership.

Moreover, it is important to mention that the agrarian reform programme was connected with the construction of mechanisms of clientelistic control of peasant organisations, which were incorporated into the hegemonic party as part of the strategy of consolidating social bases of support for the authoritarian political system. As we said before, a piecemeal administration of the agrarian reform programme allowed Mexican presidents to form a political alliance with peasant organisations: the Executive would use its broad powers on the subject-matter and in return peasants' organisations would deliver political support to the president and the 'official' political party. This pact allowed the incorporation of most peasant organisations into the hegemonic PRI.[20]

This regime changed entirely in 1992 with the constitutional reforms that cancelled the agrarian reform programme and changed the legal regime of *ejidos*. The reasons behind this reform were the need to bring capital and investment to Mexico's agrarian sector, and the intention to bring legal security in connection with land ownership. These were seen as necessary measures to counterbalance the stagnation of Mexico's agricultural sector, which would help to increase the sector's productivity in order to keep pace with the growth of the population.[21] Specifically, the reform allowed the assembly of '*ejidatarios*' (*ejido* owners) to decide on the change

---

[20] See above, chapter 4.III.1

[21] Mexico started to import increasingly significant amounts of grain, including the traditional corn (*maíz*), from the late 1960s. Between 1950 and 1970 Mexico's population almost doubled, growing from 25.7 to 48.2 million people. The yearly rate of growth in that period was 3 per cent.

from the *ejido* regime to private property on certain portions of their land. The idea was to open the possibility of bringing parts of *ejido* land back to the market, and allow the possibility of setting it up as collateral for obtaining credit. Moreover, the prohibitions on stock companies acquiring rural land were eliminated, but new rules were established intended to prevent the formation of 'covered' large estates that surpassed the extension limits established by the Constitution. Furthermore, the reform established rules that allowed the formation of associations between private investors and *ejido* communities. Finally, the action of endowment ('*dotación*'), through which peasants communities had the constitutional right to apply for land, was eliminated.

In spite of the intentions of this reform, the expected effects in terms of increasing productivity of Mexico's countryside have not been produced. Today, the country's rural sector faces difficult moments. This situation has deep and structural causes that cannot be solved by constitutional and legal reforms alone.

VI. EXPROPRIATION OF THE OIL INDUSTRY

Article 27 of the Constitution of 1917 declared that all the mineral wealth of the country was under the 'direct domain' of the nation.[22] This reversed the previous legislation which vested ownership of underground oil in the surface landholder. In spite of this, the application of Article 27 was softened under foreign pressure: President Carranza allowed oil companies to proceed as if there had been no change in the law.[23] These rules applied to oil and all other hydrocarbons until 1938, the year in which the oil industry, in the hands of a group of foreign companies (American, British and Dutch), was expropriated by President Lázaro Cárdenas.

The Mexican oil expropriation was the result of the escalation of a conflict between oil workers and foreign oil companies. The former pushed for better working conditions, and the latter resisted, alleging a lack of resources to meet the workers' demands. After a series of strikes President Cárdenas offered his mediation, though he was clearly playing in favour of workers. The oil companies filed suits with the Federal Board of Conciliation and Arbitration (a federal court with jurisdiction

[22] Para 4 of art 27 of the Constitution of 1917.
[23] AW Macmahon and WR Dittmar, 'The Mexican Oil Industry Since Expropriation' (1942) 57 *Political Science Quarterly* 28, 50.

to hear labour disputes), seeking a declaration of illegality of the strikes. Yet, the labour board decided for the workers. In turn, the oil companies challenged the board's decision, filing an action of *amparo* with the Supreme Court, which confirmed the decision, according to which the companies had to pay around 26 million pesos for lost salaries to the workers. The companies refused to comply with the Supreme Court's order, threatening to paralyse oil production and take away their capital from the country.

Facing this situation, President Cárdenas decided to expropriate all oil reserves and facilities of oil foreign companies operating in Mexico. The decree of 18 March 1938 was justified on the basis of the power of expropriation for causes of public utility foreseen in article 27 of the Constitution. It mentioned the companies' refusal to comply with a constitutionally-based award of the Federal Board of Conciliation and Arbitration, and explained the negative effects of this refusal in the field of labour relations. Moreover, the decree referred to all the consequences for Mexico's economy that would result if the oil industry were paralysed.

Interestingly, as reported by Macmahon and Dittmar, the legality of the presidential decree of expropriation was challenged in the Supreme Court, which decided in favour of the Executive:

> Basing its opinion in part on the law of capture, the court drew an analogy between the peregrinating nature of oil in its reservoir underground and that of wild animals. The owner of a concession had the right to discover and to produce oil but, because he acquired ownership only of the oil that he produced and had no ownership of what was still underground, his right to produce was of no value. A concession was construed as mere tenancy at will, terminable at any time by the government.[24]

In tune with the oil expropriation, on 9 November 1940, article 27 of the Constitution was amended in order to prohibit concessions in the oil industry. From that moment onwards, the entire oil industry would be in the hands of the federal government, through a public enterprise specifically set up of for that purpose: Petroleos Mexicanos (PEMEX). In turn, this prohibition was reinforced on 20 January 1960, with another amendment to article 27, which prohibited not only concessions, but

---

[24] Macmahon and Dittmar, *ibid*, 34. This was relevant for the calculation of the indemnity: should the value of the oil underground be included or excluded in that calculation?

also 'contracts' with the expropriated oil industry. This reform was passed because through different sorts of 'contracts', national and foreign private companies still were able to participate in some segments of the oil industry, which was against the spirit of the reform of 1940 mentioned above.

The expropriation of the oil industry can be seen as a piece (a fundamental one) of the strategy of economic development based on increased state intervention in the economy, which in fact was pursued by Mexican governments until the early 1980s. However, for a series of reasons that we will not discuss here, that strategy entered into a period of decay from the early 1970s, eventually collapsing in the following decade, as the debt and financial crises of 1982 showed. In the face of this situation, the administration of President Miguel de la Madrid (1982–88) introduced a series of economic reforms that meant a change in the strategy of development, closely following the recommendations of international financial agencies: structural adjustment; privatisation of public enterprises; devaluation of the currency; and the reduction of the public sector apparatus.

Subsequent presidential administrations only deepened the reforms initiated by President de la Madrid. However, the new strategy conflicted with a series of constitutional principles that referred to the nation's control of the country's mineral wealth, which were the basis of the previous strategy. In turn, this conflict has taken the form of a series of ideological and political confrontations on the criteria for administering Mexico's natural resources, which have led to a series of legal and judicial battles.[25] Two examples illustrate this: one relates to the so-called 'multiple services contracts' designed by the administration of President Fox (2000–06), intended to allow the participation of private investors in some segments of the oil industry. The other one has to do with the debates on the legislative reforms by President Calderón, which sought to introduce a series of important changes in Mexico's oil industry.

Multiple services contracts are agreements entered into by PEMEX and private companies specialising in exploration and extraction of natural gas. Since the Fox administration, they have been justified in terms of: (a). the urgent need to expand the production of natural gas; (b). PEMEX's lack of capital and technology to expand that production

---

[25] This has also happened in connection with the electric power industry as we shall see below.

in the short term; and (c). the convenience of sending a clear message to private investors (domestic and foreign) that Mexico had embarked on a decided process of structural change of its economy.

In spite of the debates and serious doubts as to their constitutionality, the administration of President Calderón (2006–12) continued signing this kind of contract, until the Congress of the Union challenged them through a constitutional controversy. Yet, the Supreme Court dismissed the action (15 April 2011) without examining the merits of the claim, alleging that Congress had no 'legitimate interest' to file the action, since the signature of those contracts by PEMEX did not affect its sphere of competence.

The conflict between the new strategy of economic development and the constitutional principles regarding the nation's control of the country's mineral wealth (specifically oil and all other hydrocarbons) could be better seen in the debates around the proposal to reform Mexico's oil industry introduced by President Calderón into the Senate on 8 April 2008. The proposal was justified in terms of Mexico's lack of capital and technology to expand oil production. Thus – the Executive argued – it was urgent to modify the legal framework of the oil industry, in order to allow the participation of private investors in segments of that industrial activity.

For example, the president proposed to amend articles 2 and 3 of the Oil Act,[26] stating that specific segments of the oil industry would be considered as the 'strategic areas' of that industry (in terms of articles 25 and 28 of the Constitution), which would be of the exclusive competence of the federal government, through PEMEX. The implication was that all those activities that were not included in the concept of 'strategic areas' of the oil industry, could be performed by private investors. In the debate, opponents of the reform proposal pointed out that this was unconstitutional, because the concept of 'strategic areas' in connection with the oil industry, referred to the entire industry, and not to certain portions of it. Going against articles 25 and 28, the Executive's proposal was arbitrarily making a division between 'strategic areas' and 'non-strategic areas' as fractions of the oil industry.

Furthermore, the Executive's proposal expressly allowed the participation of private investors in transportation, deposit and distribution of gas, products derived from oil refining and basic petro-chemicals. For

---

[26] *Ley Reglamentaria del artículo 27 constitucional en el Ramo del Petróleo.*

their part, critics of the reform proposal stated that these activities were all segments of the oil industry which could not be put in the hands of private investors without violating the text and spirit of the Constitution. Thus, and unable to achieve the required legislative consensus, the amendment of the legal framework of the oil industry proposed by President Calderón, did not pass in Congress.

In the future, three factors may push in favour of a fundamental revision of Mexico's constitutional regime on petroleum. First, Mexico's public sector relies heavily on revenue that comes directly from PEMEX.[27] Secondly, Mexico is the third most important supplier of oil to the US market after Canada and Saudi Arabia; thirdly, oil and gas production is declining. Considering these factors, some will argue that the only way to increase production is by opening of the sector to private investment. Yet, it is clear that any move in that direction will require constitutional reform, which in the context of a multi-party system will need the formation of a broad political consensus on its necessity and convenience. This will not be an easy task, since on one hand, some argue that PEMEX has the potential of doing the job alone, if only the public corporation were allowed to re-invest in exploration, exploitation and refining part of the revenue it generates.[28] On the other hand, and beyond ideology, powerful vested interests that profit from the current situation extracting different sorts of 'rents' out of PEMEX will surely oppose any reform. As argued by Elizondo, constitutional reform in Mexico's oil sector is not likely to come until a massive crisis becomes an imminent possibility, PEMEX faces a major accident or, in the context of declining production, the trade unions pick an unpopular fight against a popular and capable reform-minded leader.[29]

---

[27] According to the federal government's *Programa Económico 2011* (Economic Programme 2011), oil revenues provided by PEMEX amount to almost 33 per cent of the federal budget.

[28] This option would involve a fundamental tax reform in Mexico, in order to compensate for the loss of public revenues that come from PEMEX.

[29] These vested interests include the trade unions, managers, contractors (businessmen in the transport, construction, machinery and other sectors connected with the oil industry) and powerful local politicians (typically based in the regions in which PEMEX has infrastructure and workers). See C Elizondo, 'Stuck in the Mud: The Politics of Constitutional Reform in the Oil Sector in Mexico', *Documento de Trabajo*, No 235 (Mexico, CIDE, 2012).

VII. THE ELECTRIC POWER SECTOR

As I said above,[30] article 27, paragraph 6 of the Constitution was reformed in 1960 in order to state that the generation, conduction, transformation, distribution and provision of electric power as a public service, belongs exclusively to the nation, explicitly prohibiting concessions to private companies in the provision of that service. The reform was justified for three reasons: the relevance of the electric power industrial sector for the social and economic development of Mexico; the collective use and exploitation of natural resources for the production and consumption of electric power for the benefit of the Mexican people; and the idea that electric power generation should not be subordinated to the logic of the market, not only for political or ethical reasons, but also for technical and operative imperatives.[31] In the political context, it was a move to neutralise voices that on the left criticised the government of President López Mateos (1958–64), and was intended to show that the government still was in the line of the Mexican revolution (in 1960 the government was celebrating the first 50 years of the Mexican revolution initiated in 1910); furthermore, the reform was also intended to give the government a clear advantage in negotiations with the business sector (as it would be the only provider of electric power in the land).[32]

Since the financial crisis of 1994, investments in Mexico's electric power sector were significantly decreased. A series of rigidities produced by the legal framework of the industry (which is mostly dominated by a public enterprise, the Federal Commission of Electricity, or CFE in its acronym in Spanish), and also by the power and influence that the trade union of the CFE workers has had on the electric power industry, produced high costs by international standards. In turn, for decades the political and economic impacts of these costs were softened by subsidies that meant a significant financial drain for the federal government.[33]

---

[30] See section III of this chapter.
[31] Chamber of Senators, *Diario de los Debates*, 28 October 1960.
[32] See D Valadés, 'La Función Constitucional de la Regulación Económica', (2006) 3 *Economíaunam* (e-journal).
[33] C Hernández, *La Reforma Cautiva, Inversión, trabajo y empresa en el sector eléctrico mexicano* (Mexico, CIDAC, 2007) 23–25.

In this context, the administrations of Presidents Zedillo (1994–2000) and Fox (2000–06) took the decision of opening the electric power sector to the participation of private investors. President Zedillo submitted to Congress his 'Proposal of Structural Change in the Electric Power industry in Mexico' on 2 February 1999. The core of the proposal was to declare that the generation of power through nuclear plants and the control of the national network for the transmission of electric power would be considered as a 'strategic area' under the exclusive control of the state. Yet, the rest of the activities related to the electric power industry would be considered as 'priority activities', in which the public, private and social sectors would be able to participate. The reasons given to justify the reform were that the federal government did not have enough resources to expand the electric power infrastructure and therefore would not be able to satisfy future demand for electric power; in addition, the proposal stated that technological development had modified the technical conditions for generating electric power, and this was changing the forms and opportunities for participation and competition in the power industry; finally, it was argued that the exclusivity of the state in the industrial sector had transformed itself into an obstacle for the modernisation and expansion of the industry.[34] Nevertheless, in the context of the presidential campaign and elections of 1999–2000, Congress froze the proposal and no constitutional or legal reform was passed (Zedillo's proposal apparently collided with the constitutional rule referred to above).

For his part, and more modestly, President Fox (2000–06) tried to partially open the electric power sector through an amendment to the Regulations to the Act on the Public Service of Electric Power. His goal was to increase the amount of electric power that could be sold by private companies to the CFE, and to simplify the administrative procedures for doing so. Here we have to recall that the constitutional prohibition mentioned above does not cover electric power that is not destined for the public at large. Therefore, the production of power by private companies for self-consumption; the importation of power for self-consumption; and the installation of transmission lines for private use are allowed through a system of permits granted by the Commission for the Regulation of Energy (and these sort of activities are what Fox proposal intended to expand).

---

[34] The proposal can be seen at: www.cec.org/Storage/40/3215_Breceda-s_FR. PDF.

The federal Congress successfully challenged the reform to the Regulations on the Federal Act on the Public Service of Electric Energy issued by the President, for alleged invasion of the Congress' sphere of competence. In the view of Congress, the reform to the Regulations violated the principle of separation of powers because it invaded an area that was reserved to be governed by statute only, in connection with the rules on self-supply of electric power.[35]

The constitutional battle has gone on. For some, in spite of the Court's decision, the government has continued granting permits that allow private entities the production of electric power outside the standards allowed by the Constitution and the relevant statute. That is why in 2003 some legislators denounced this practice to the Superior Audit of the Federation (SAF). In turn, the SAF drafted a report and started investigations to determine possible liabilities of the public servants involved. For its part, the Executive brought an action of constitutional controversy against the SAF, challenging the constitutionality of the SAF's power to make such investigation.[36] In the end, the Supreme Court decided 6-5 in favour of the Executive, reasoning that: a) the granting of the permits was not connected with the financial management of the federal government, and therefore was not in the scope of powers of the SAF; and b) the SAF had violated the constitutional principle of 'annuity', by examining permits granted in years that were previous to the Annual Account under examination.

As in the case of the oil sector discussed in the previous section of this chapter, it seems that the creation of an electric market in Mexico, allowing private investment in the generation, transmission, distribution and sale of electric power in Mexico, will require a constitutional reform and therefore a broad political coalition in its favour.

VIII. CONCLUSION

Since the 1930s, Mexican political and economic elites reached an agreement to design and implement a strategy of economic development based on import-substitution industrialisation, protectionism and heavy

---

[35] The judgment of the constitutional controversy 22/2001 was published in the Federal Official Gazette on 3 June 2002.

[36] The judgment of the constitutional controversy 61/2004 was published in the Federal Official Gazette on 2 February 2007.

intervention of the state in the economy. This pact gave stability to the hegemonic party system, at least until the early 1980s, a decade in which the strategy started to breakdown. In addition, this strategy of economic development was legitimised by several principles that were already in the original version of the Constitution of 1917, which was later amended on a number of occasions in order to strengthen the constitutional basis of those policies (ie planning, nationalisation of key industrial activities).

Things started to change in the 1980s. International and domestic factors forced a change in the strategy of economic development. The new strategy involved export-orientation of the economy; trade liberalisation; reduction of the public sector; and deregulation. Yet, most of these policies conflicted with well entrenched principles found in the Constitution.

Since the 1990s, Mexico's constitutional evolution and debates that refer to the economy, the market and property have to be interpreted in terms of the collision between the constitutional conceptions of the previous strategy of economic development, and the legal and normative requirements of the new one. This collision, as we have seen in this chapter, has led to a series of conflicts in different legal battlefields that involve constitutional and legal reform, Executive decisions and decrees, and judgments of the Supreme Court of Justice. Beyond these struggles, it is notable how political conflicts and disputes for the appropriation of economic surplus, are to an important extent translated into legal terms, and find a legal solution through the judicial process and constitutional discourse.

FURTHER READING

Azuela, A, 'Property in the Post-post-revolution: Notes on the Crisis of the Constitutional Idea of Property in Contemporary Mexico' (2011) 89 *Texas Law Review* 1915.

Camil, J, 'Mexico in Contemplation of NAFTA: Is the Government Abdicating the Rectoría del Estado?' (1993) 15 *Loyola LA International and Comparative Law Journal* 761.

Cossío Díaz, JR, 'Constitutional Framework for Water Regulation in Mexico' (1995) 35 *Natural Resources Journal* 489.

Cuadra, H, 'El Modelo Normativo de la Rectoría Económica del Estado 1917–1987' (1988) 10 *Alegatos* 10.

Díaz y Díaz, M, 'El Aprovechamiento de los Recursos Naturales, Hacia un nuevo discurso patrimonial' (2000) 24 *Revista de Investigaciones Jurídicas* 130.

González, JJ, 'The Scope and limitations of the Principle of National Property of Hydrocarbons in Mexico' in McHarg, A, Barton, B, Bradbrook, A and Godden, L (eds), *Property and the Law in Energy and Natural Resources* (Oxford, Oxford University Press, 2010).

Kelly, JJ, 'Article 27 and Mexican Land Reform: The Legacy of Zapata's Dream' (1994) 25 *Columbia Human Rights Law Review* 541.

Ruiz Massieu, JF, 'La Rectoría del Estado y las Nuevas Bases Constitucionales del Derecho Administrativo Mexicano' in Instituto de Investigaciones Jurídicas, *La Constitución Mexicana: Rectoría del Estado y Economía Mixta* (Mexico, UNAM-Porrúa, 1985).

Serna de la Garza, JM, 'El régimen constitucional de la propiedad en México' in Serna de la Garza, JM (ed), *Derecho Comparado Asia-México* (Mexico, UNAM, 2007).

Xopa Roldán, J, *Constitución y Mercado* (Mexico, Porrúa, 2004).

Concluding Thoughts: Democratic Transition and Constitutional Change in Mexico

RANSITIONS TO DEMOCRACY in Latin America have been closely related to processes of constitutional reform. As shown by the experiences of countries like Argentina, Brazil, Chile, Perú and Uruguay, the transition from authoritarian regimes to democracy has entailed the creation of a new constitutional design or institutional arrangement. In these and other countries of the region, the negotiations and pacts that led to progressive political liberalisation and democratisation were followed by a phase of constitutional re-definition, either through a new constitution or through a fundamental reform of the existing one.

Using the distinction between political liberalisation and democratisation proposed by some scholars,[1] it is possible to say that Mexico embarked upon a process of political liberalisation in the 1970s, which transformed itself into democratisation by the end of the 1980s and certainly during the 1990s. In its first stages, this process involved the transformation of the electoral system, which required a series of constitutional reforms (in 1977, 1990, 1994 and 1996). Electoral reform was the priority, as a pre-condition to having access to the public agencies and bodies from which reforms in other areas of the constitutional system could be promoted and achieved.

Since the mid-1990s, without electoral issues having lost their relevance in Mexico's political debate, political actors have started to show an increasing interest in discussing the possible re-definition of

---

[1] O'Donnell, Guillermo, P Schmitter and L Whitehead (eds), *Transitions from Authoritarian Rule* (Baltimore, MD and London, Johns Hopkins University Press, 1988).

the constitutional system in respect of the separation of powers, the rules that govern the relations and interactions between the different branches of the federal government and the rules on federalism and inter-governmental relations. In this way, for example, in January of 1996 the leaders of the different political parties and the representatives of the 'official' party designed an agenda of constitutional reforms intended to change the profile of the political regime.

Moreover, on 29 March 2007 the federal Congress passed a statute known as the Law for the Reform of the State, which established a method for organising public hearings and consultations; for initiating negotiations and promoting the construction of agreements, whose aim was to produce a broad national consensus on constitutional reform in the following areas: rules on the regime of the state and Government; democracy and the electoral system; federalism; the courts system; and social rights. However, the only two matters in which there was actually reform were the electoral system[2] and to some extent the courts system.[3] Today, it is possible to say that in the opinion of most of the political party and public opinion leaders, as well as political analysts and scholars, the so-called 'Reform of the State' required to complete Mexico's transition to democracy is still pending.

For many years, with its programme of social reform the Constitution of 1917 was a source of legitimacy of the political system that emerged after the revolution of 1910; but it also was the normative framework that allowed the construction of the hegemonic party system and a political regime clearly weighted in favour of the federal Executive. It certainly guaranteed political stability and governmental efficacy for decades, yet today this seems not to be the case. The new party system that exists today, as well as the emergence of a more complex, heterogeneous, demanding and organised civil society, have created a new system of political relations, a new correlation of forces, that has demanded a new constitutional structure required to consolidate Mexico's democratic transition.

A good deal of constitutional change has already occurred. As we have seen throughout this book, in the last four decades Mexico's political and constitutional evolution has been marked by the transition from:

---

[2] Published on 13 November 2007. Mentioned above, in section IV of chapter 2.
[3] Particularly in the criminal justice system. The reform was enacted on 18 June 2008. See above, section IV of chapter 7.

A. A hegemonic party system, to a multiparty system.
B. Non-competitive elections, to competitive elections and the possibility of rotation in government.
C. A presidential system in which the Executive was clearly predominant, to a presidential system with more balanced relations among the different branches of government.
D. A Congress of one political colour, dominated by the Executive, to a plural Congress that negotiates with the president.
E. A courts system that was functional in the hegemonic party system, to a courts system that is searching for a new functionality in the plural democracy under construction.
F. A federal system dominated by a logic of centralisation, to a federal system in which State governments are increasingly a real locus of power vis-à-vis the federal government.
G. A declaration of fundamental rights subordinated to the logic of control by the hegemonic party system, to a declaration of rights whose efficacy is increasingly assured by national and international courts.

Finally, and beyond the constitutional reforms that have already been passed and those that are still pending, bridging the gap between the formal Constitution and what could be regarded as the living constitution presents Mexican politics and society with one of its great contemporary challenges.

Index